Internet UK

IVAN POPE

PRENTICE HALL

New York   London   Toronto   Sydney   Tokyo   Singapore

First published 1995 by
Prentice Hall International (UK) Limited
Campus 400, Maylands Avenue
Hemel Hempstead
Hertfordshire, HP2 7EZ
A division of
Simon & Schuster International Group

Printed and bound in Great Britain by
Redwood Books, Trowbridge, Wiltshire

Library of Congress Cataloguing-in-publication Data

Pope, Ivan.
    Internet UK/Ivan Pope.
        p.   cm.
    Includes index.
    ISBN 0-13-190950-9
    1. Internet (Computer networks)   2. Computer networks – Great
    Britain.   I. Title.
TK5105.875.I57P66   1994   94-31395
004.6'7–dc20   CIP

British Library Cataloguing in Publication Data

A catalogue record for this book is available from the British Library

ISBN 0-13-190950-9

2   3   4   5   99   98   97   96   95

Contents

1 Overview 1

Only connect! 2
Why use the Internet? 3
Net developments in the UK 7
How Internet will change our lives 12
Who has access? 14
Problems: hackers, pornography 16
Parliment and the Internet 17
Public interest: CommUnity 20
Guide to the UK 21

2 Using the Internet 23

A client/server relationship 24
Types of access 24
IP software 27
Who connects? 39
Conferencing plus 40
Internet provision for individuals and small companies 41
Educational sector 42
Choosing a provider 43
UK Internet providers' list 43

3 Tools, resources and services 59

UK flavour Internet 60
General network information 60
Tools of the trade 64
Mailing lists 70
Usenet News 84
Anonymous FTP 91
Telnet 97
Hytelnet 103
Gopher 104

Contents

Veronica   120
WAIS (Wide Area Information Service)   121
WWW: World Wide Web   124
IRC   135
Other IRC sites   136
Commercial Internet   139

4 Information sources   152
Mailbase User Reference Card   152
IETF/RARE catalog of network training materials   159
Kevin Savetz's booklist   209
UK commercial domains   248
International Internet providers   283
JANET – acceptable use   286

Index   290

CHAPTER

Overview

This book takes a look at the Internet from a UK perspective. It is not intended to be a guide to 'The Internet, the Universe and Everything', though it is a good starting point. Many Internet books published in the last year attempt to do that, and many come close to succeeding. Most of these books have been published from the USA and have an undeniable US bias. The point of this book is to start to redress that balance, to point to UK access providers, to resources and tools that have a UK element to them.

There is a real sense that many Internet resources have no real geographical home. It does not matter much whether the FTP (File Transfer Protocol) site you use is in Manchester or Des Moines, it is the content that counts. On the other hand, due to unavoidable technical constraints, such as the fact that there is never enough bandwidth for us all to use the sites in Des Moines simultaneously, it is often better to use a UK site, if only to save your own time.

There are also, obviously, many resources that do have a particular bearing on the UK. I have attempted to bring a lot of them together in this book. Many Usenet groups either relate directly to the UK, or to UK events. I have not been too fanatical in my gathering of such resources – a line has to be drawn somewhere.

Only connect!

The Internet is an American 'thing'. Not! It is huge and modern and concerned with computers, it is complex and fast-moving and alien, it is self-opinionated, loud and dangerous. It must be American. So much has been written recently about this Internet, with its roots in the US industrial-military complex and its associated academic-research industry. Since the election of President Clinton and vice-President Al Gore with his talk of the 'information superhighway', there has been an exponential growth in media coverage of the Internet, let alone growth in the thing itself.

To many observers, even those with much computer knowledge, the Internet must seem to have arrived from nowhere. In the last year there has been an explosion of coverage in the popular and specialist press. It is has been almost impossible to open any publication without reading about the Information Superhighway or cyberspace. From the most populist newspapers to the most specialist and unlikely magazines, the Internet has been covered to one degree or another. However, to think that this extensive coverage has given the reading public an understanding of the Internet would be completely wrong. Many articles are superficial to the point of inanity or confused by the vastness of the subject. The truth is, the Internet is huge and varied. Anyone coming to it fresh has to grapple with a whole range of concepts and tools. The journalists writing about it have, on the whole, had no specialist knowledge and have relied on individuals to explain parts to them. Their readers may have had their appetites wetted, but the whole picture has been left unclear.

The Internet has not come from nowhere, it has been built piece on painstaking piece by dedicated individuals from all walks of life. Over many years a dream of unfettered access to powerful communication tools has been realized. There never was a masterplan. Most of the parts of the Internet have been put into place on a wing and a prayer, funded from academic research budgets and a desire to move forward. Whole sections of the Internet, tools we take for granted, have been defined and built by a few visionaries, often working in their own time with no reward.

The Internet is literally a network of networks. It has no beginning, no middle and no end. It is not controlled or owned by any company, government or organization. It is an example of co-operation and communal provision without equal, insofar as it spans the globe, respecting no borders or political divisions.

The Internet allows us to move information around the globe from site to site and from individual to individual with no restrictions. Once access has been gained, there are no time charges, no concept of 'long distance' or 'peak rate'. High-capacity networks are ours, each part passing our request on to the next until, generally, we are presented with the results of our commands.

This unfettered access and freedom has benefited almost all those who have come to use it. We will see later what a huge range of organizations, individuals, companies and institutions have made access to the Internet a vital part of their operating methods.

The Internet has a culture of co-operation and support. There is no history of greed or profiteering, and new users are guided and supported by those who have been 'on' for longer (though this may be only a matter of weeks). Internet denizens also have a culture of offering information services, ranging from personal offerings to huge academic databases. In almost all cases those offering these services have benefited in many ways from making the effort.

The Internet is changing. Original network acceptable use rules did not allow commercial traffic to pass. Over the last couple of years this has rapidly become unrealistic, as traffic is routed around increasingly complex networks and as more and more users come on from commercial sites. In August 1991 the number of commercial networks surpassed the number of non-commercial for the first time. A result of this shift is the increasing amount of commercial services on the Internet. However, there is still a culture of offering free access to services, partly because there are difficulties monitoring and charging for use.

The Internet is complex, difficult, frustrating and prone to breakage. It was not 'designed' with users in mind and users have to come to terms with its idiosyncrasies. Hardened computer users are regularly reduced to tears trying to set up access and use the services. In the recent past universities were the main access providers and they could at least control what their users encountered by setting up and documenting services. As more individuals come to set up their own access, there is obviously a lot of room for confusion, but changes such as the provision of installation kits and documentation have made it easier but not taken away all the trauma. Not so long ago the only books available to prospective Internet users were technical volumes that either explained in detail how to set up network systems or covered the existing global networks country by country. Recently a flood of publishing has been unleashed, making the Internet the most published subject of the 1990s. From new user guides to technical volumes, magazines articles, television programmes and specialist conferences all add to the deluge.

Why use the Internet?

You may be wondering why you need to use the Internet. After all, the computer on your desk can perform all the tasks you want it to. It is linked to a printer, to a CD-ROM, to large hard disks. You can buy CDs stuffed with information. Software is available from Shareware catalogs. Friends and colleagues can be phoned, letters can be written. The Internet, exciting though it may be, seems just too complex and sophisticated for everyday real world use, and isn't it just an American thing?

Take a look at this book – it is filled with reasons for using the Internet. The

Internet reflects the world, it is made up of people who exist in the real world. It is not a collection of computer users any more than radio is provided by a collection of radio fanatics. If you have an interest or need or desire, chances are the Internet will fill it. Out there somewhere there are others who know what you are talking about, who can help you, or give you something, or have what you want, or want what you have. Or who would be willing to pass some time, to chat or even (generally) to argue. The point is, the Internet makes it possible for the first time ever to meet those people, people who you would never in a lifetime normally come across. Think about it. In your everyday life, how many new people do you encounter a week? One? None? On the Internet you have the chance to encounter thousands or hundreds of thousands. You will never exchange the merest e-mail with most of them, just as you will never talk to any of the hundreds of thousands of individuals you pass every day on the pavements.

So how do you get to meet these people? Imagine that you could carry a number of signs that said 'I am interested in model railways, I'm studying metataxidermy, I want to know how to raise an orphaned rabbit, I just want to talk to someone' and that this sign could be seen by millions of people. Some of them would respond (though the responses would be variable, to say the least). Out of those who responded, some would just offer useful information. Some would engage you in a lasting conversation. And, some would turn out to be the sort of people you really like to get to know. Before you thought about it, you would find you had some new friends.

That is what the Internet is like. It is a collection of real people. You can send out your needs and desires and they will be responded to. This seems to me to be unique.

So what else do I get?

You could ask any of the several thousand individual Demon Internet account holders or any of the CIX conferencing system members. You could ask any of the small business persons or company members who have come to rely on the Internet. You could ask any of the estimated fifteen million users around the world. Or, you could ask yourself why the Internet has grown in such a short time to be the centre of so many users' lives.

You could join up with a local bulletin board that exchanges e-mail and Usenet with the wider Internet or you could buy a full leased line feed for your business and put everyone on twenty-four hours a day, start publishing your own information, start up a mailing list to discuss geranium cultivation or Russian aerobatics.

Having access to the Internet is like having access to a department store full of communication and information services. You do not need to use them all – and it is unlikely that you could. From the huge range available you select the items that are right for you and put them to work. E-mail is a universal choice, a basic building block for the Internet. It is much more extensive than the exchange of electronic mail between individuals. FTP allows access to huge stores of information software, archives and other files around the world. Telnet gives you the chance to use services such as bulletin boards and databases around the world without telecommunications charges. Internet Relay Chat is the CB Radio of the Internet, with thousands of channels covering all subjects and then some. Tools such as Gopher and WAIS offer information search capabilities of enormous power and imagination. The World Wide Web links information into a hypertext web – the user follows links around the globe by choosing which path to follow.

The UK has always been involved in Internet building: now there are more ways than ever to get on the Information Superhighway. The future is being built, but it is also a living, working everyday tool. Millions of individuals are finding the Internet indispensable. You may as well join them sooner than later.

JANET

The Internet grew quietly in the UK. JANET opened gateways to the international community long before there was a single Internet and built on those gateways as the Internet grew around the world. Students and staff could send mail through these gateways and, using arcane local software, could make contact with some services in other parts of the world.

The Internet is a global resource and users in the UK have much the same view of it as any other users around the world. That view is always shaped by the type of connection, the platform utilized and the software used. Someone using a dial-up bulletin board that exchanges e-mail into the Internet and provides access to Usenet is going to experience the Internet in much the same way, be they in Seattle or Scotland. A user on a high-bandwidth will have a very different experience from the dial-up user, but not from another high-bandwidth user on the other side of the globe. The main difference will be cultural and needs driven.

Internet access in the UK can be divided into three areas: commercial, academic and individual. Within the commercial and academic spheres, there are huge discrepancies. Individuals have a smaller range of choices, but depend largely on where they live for cost of access.

Academic Internet access historically meant university access. The Universities Funding Council 'taxed' the universities at source and re-distributed the money for computing and networking provision. This meant that, with few exceptions, university sites had proper JANET connections from early on – though how they distributed these internally was another matter. Policies ranged from very open to utterly elitist. The old polytechnics (the new universities) on the other hand benefited from no such socialistic policy and thus remained badly connected up until joining the ranks of universities. This situation is being slowly remedied, but there is a long way to go. Below this top level of education in the UK, the situation is much less satisfactory. Unlike in the US, there has been no concerted effort to bring higher education establishments online. They have been left to fend for themselves, making local arrangements where finance, vision and knowledge allowed. Schools and other educational establishments have not even figured on the map, though the efforts of companies such as Galviz, with their schools Internet scheme, may change this in the future.

Although it could not be said even a year ago, there is now almost something for everyone. From Pipex or (soon) BT providing high-powered fixed links down to Spuddy and his free Unix-fronted Internet access, we can all partake of the feast. Enthusiasts or entrepreneurs who have long run online services see the Internet as a value added service – expect many many more local providers to spring up fully formed in the near future.

GreenNet and POPTEL are providers to the roughly 'alternative' and developmental sector, from trade unions through organizations such as Amnesty and Greenpeace. For such organizations with dispersed memberships and information agendas, a system such as the Internet linked to local database and conferencing systems offers huge benefits of scale.

'Traditional' conferencing systems such as Compulink will soon broaden their offerings to full Internet access, or be swept away by faster moving setups. Although not as flexible as a full Internet feed from the desktop, a bulletin board type system offers support and a like-minded community. Until Internet support moves from being a black art to a profession, many individuals will want to explore the world through a friendly front end.

Commercial services

This time last year it was fairly rare to see a mention of the Internet in the UK press. Even the computer magazines did not have much interest in covering what was an arcane subject, difficult to explain to the average reader. Although many thousands of students and a growing range of business users had to come to terms with this global online world, access was on the whole difficult and expensive. The software used for exploration, text based and command line driven, kept all but the most hardened away from the systems.

The arrival of the Clinton/Gore team in the White House only served to accentuate what was already a hardening trend: the Internet was making waves. Populated by a huge range of inventive, creative, communicative and friendly people, it seemed to be a new continent: a space where almost anything was possible. The established tools such as FTP and Telnet started to give way to a new generation: powerful searching tools such as Archie; network search agents like Whois; information linking systems such as Gopher. With the beginning of the 90s, from an obscure Particle Physics research establishment in the heart of Europe, came the Internet's killer application, the first true multimedia tool, the World Wide Web.

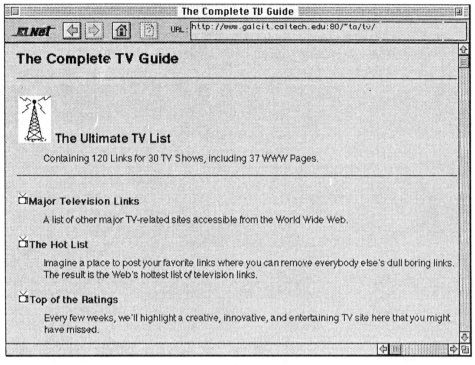

Hypermedia on the Internet: World Wide Web browser

Net developments in the UK

Will the Internet paradise be lost?

Author James Fallows predicts that as the Internet expands

something will have to give: either the government will stop paying, or politicians will notice that the government is paying and will impose controls, like those imposed by school boards on textbook content or by the regulators on radio and TV broadcasts. The Internet's low-visibility era of subsidized innocence will end, and the network will become as complicated as anything else. *Atlantic Monthly*, July 94

A fast-developing industry

A year ago there was very little that could be seriously considered an Internet 'industry' in the UK. For sure, there were a lot of people working in the area of networking, software, user-support and internetworking. However, most of these were employed within academic fields, where it had long been taken for granted that there was access to a national and global network, not necessarily the Internet. Companies such as Pipex and EUNet existed to provide Internet connections to large and medium companies, and UUCP dial-up connections could be bought from various suppliers outside academia. These connections were used only by the initiated and knowledgeable (or wealthy). There did not seem to be any pressing need to access the Internet. In fact, most people remained blissfully unaware.

The election of Clinton and Gore in 1992 set in motion the huge media coverage that raised the existence of the Internet in the UK public's consciousness. The term Information Superhighway was seized upon by various communications and entertainment industries around the world. US companies such as Disney and Paramount began to look at the potential of the coming communications revolution. They sought deals and mergers with telecommunications giants such as Sprint, MCI and AT&T in order to corner the market. A wave of optimism moved around the world and in its wake journalists discovered the potential of the subject.

Although it is undeniable that the Internet is a precursor of something that may be called an Information Superhighway, one should not get too excited at such an early stage. There are immense technological and financial hurdles to surmount in the coming years. The early Superhighway mania among American companies has already waned as the realities hit home.

Long before the mega-corps suddenly thought they had spotted a winner, many small companies were quietly building a business supplying Internet access to individual and small company users. These companies ranged from single site dial-in bulletin boards with an Internet feed to ambitious multi-state operations linked by commercial high-capacity backbones. As the large companies fought a high-profile war above their heads, these local providers got on with the learning curve that Internet provision had become.

In the UK a group of like-minded users of the Compulink conferencing system had come together to discuss how they could gain 'full' Internet access for themselves. This group split off to form Demon Internet Services, an organization that changed the face of UK Internet access for good.

What does Internet mean to the UK?

Although the Internet is a global resource, there is a huge importance attached to resource provision that has local and regional importance. The UK has been and remains at the forefront of advances in information provision; the academic community makes a lot of the running with new systems and processes. As we approach the 21st century, it is obvious that electronic information systems are crucial to any country's development. In the same way that the railways and later the motorways opened up economic development, the 'Information Super-highways' will encourage new industries and reshape our view of the world.

Even on a day to day basis, use of the Internet can reshape one's relationship with the world. Whether they are employees of a company that provides them with access, students who keep in touch from home or teleworkers, users can, from their village or tower-block, 'commute' to work in world centres. Using e-mail they can communicate on an equal basis with whoever they need to. These communications are fast and interactive. I know many people who now work from home, yet who have a knowledge and understanding and interaction with the world. These people can almost be said to work for 'Virtual Corporations', though this may not be how they see it.

Students and staff in education have access, from work and home, to huge amounts of research information, texts, library catalogs, course details and other minutiae of academic life. Students correspond with their tutors online; log-on to college information systems; check out developments and converse with their peers across the world. Staff can keep up with their subject; read research from around the world; contribute to debate and be published in more and more electronic journals. The Internet is an education in itself – increasingly it will become a subject of education, as the next generation of information workers comes online.

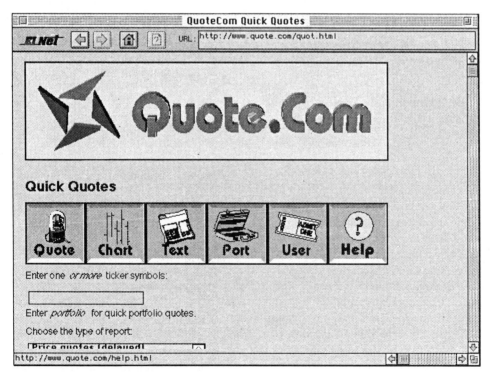

QuoteCom: stock-market quotes on the Web

A whole new field of distance education is opening up: students can take part in seminars; submit assignments; take tutorials and correspond with tutors all from hundreds or thousands of miles away. The multimedia capabilities of the Internet allow a rich and varied environment for distance students.

Commercial outfits have seen the Internet from a different aspect. There is a race on to discover how to make this goose lay the golden egg. The Internet has such a history and ingrained philosophy of free information, that commercial operations have had to work hard to make headway. There is a division between those who wish to provide pay-to-view services and those who see a more formal approach, such as linked advertising as the way to go. What is undeniable is that there will not be widespread opposition to commercial activity on the Internet, activity that a short time ago may have been impossible. The growth of commercial access providers has made this a reality, with traffic moving across non-academic networks whose 'acceptable use' policies would have made commercial services a non-starter.

Companies such as SCO and BT are experimenting with using World Wide Web servers and browsers in-house as information systems. It will not be long before they enter the wider commercial marketplace.

Companies that a short while ago would have built their own global networks at huge expense are now using the Internet to connect dispersed offices. Once they connect to the Internet and their employees have full access, they tend to see new possibilities for development. With players such as BT and Mercury seriously considering becoming Internet providers, it may not be long before the UK is the most 'wired' country in the world.

How extensive are the UK networks?

It is possible to look at current Internet provision from many different perspectives. Some networkers would claim that there are very few Internet access providers in the UK, others that there is a glut of services that will be difficult to sustain. The truth is complex. Compared with a very few years ago, there is a range of options for most Internet access needs. As with most things in life, the more you are prepared to pay, the wider your choices. At the same time, individuals and small companies have a choice of service and price level that is by far the best in Europe.

The current edition of *A Directory of Electronic Mail*, published by O'Reilly & Associates (ISBN 0-937175-15-3) lists four networks under United Kingdom (EUNet, GreenNet, JANET and Pipex) while the current *List of UK Internet Access Providers in the UK*, compiled by Paola Kathuria and available by anonymous FTP from ftp://ftp.demon.co.uk/pub/archives/uk-internet-list/, lists seventeen access providers which range from free Internet bulletin boards to network builders such as EUNet. Although there are many ways to define an Internet provider, the true total is certainly much higher and climbing. Research for this book has come up with over thirty providers, from the miniscule to the mighty JANET.

Internet provision in the UK is exploding. New providers will open up the market – this should be a benefit as the newcomers and established parties vie to provide local access and cheap plans. However, buying commercial access is fraught with hidden problems and costs. There is no simple way of comparing charges, as every company offers a completely different range of plans. Even when you can work out the best price, there are other considerations: what sort of network links do they have; what upgrade plans are there; what 'extras' can I expect; how easy is it for me to move my address? These may seem like arcane problems at the moment, but they will become all important as we become a nation of Information Superhighway providers.

The relative ease with which students have been able to explore the Internet for many years has inevitably led to demands for access after the three short years of their degree. Students who were encouraged to use this powerful global system, to meet and befriend other users and who have come to rely on its resources have complained long and hard on leaving college when realizing that there was no easy access in the wider world. Colleges have been unwilling for many reasons to allow alumni access to their systems. As the numbers of students learning about the Internet during their courses increased, the pressure for some sort of access outside has increased. They have taken the idea of access with them to companies and institutions that may have had no idea that the networks even existed. The recent explosion of interest and provision may well be traced to an itinerant ex-student population. In the US it has long been a recognized fact that high-flyers would not consider working for a company that has no Internet connection. As services have grown more powerful, the need and desire for more powerful connections has increased by leaps and bounds.

Commercial Internet provision in the UK was initiated by GBNet, now UKNet. Soon after the arrival of the Web, members of the UK CIX conferencing system got together to form Demon Internet Services. Desperate to provide cheap and simple dial-up full Internet access for themselves, they banded together and started selling 'the Internet for a tenner a month'. Success was instant: needing four hundred members to survive, they easily surpassed this. Within a short time they were part of the accelerating UK Internet scene. For the first time, Johanna Public could use the global networks from home for an easily affordable amount.

If we look to the US for a development model, we can see a huge spread of provision, with everyone from local Bulletin Boards (BBSs) to global corporations providing Internet connectivity. The maxim here is that, within reason, you get what you pay for. If you are an experienced computer user and you know your platform well, you could probably set up anything from scratch. Remember, once you have made the first contact with the Internet you have access to a huge, helpful and skilled community that is more than willing to help. On the other hand, if you are seduced by the lure of information and think you can buy a computer, set it up and go straight out onto the Information Superhighway tomorrow – think again. Remember when you first started to learn to drive and how you thought you would never get the hang of changing gear while decelerating into a roundabout during a rainstorm with a talkative passenger? You are going to go through it all again.

How Internet will change our lives

We are all publishers now

One of the first things that new users of the Internet realize is that they are not a passive consumer. Everyone on the net is a publisher, if only of their own words. From the moment when you first mail to a list or a Usenet group, your words are published on a global scale. You might think that you are talking to a small community and that no one outside the roc.basketweaving group could have any interest in your words. The net has a memory, a long and deep electronic memory. Everything you type and send into that electric darkness remains in some archive or other for a very, very long time. Your words will sooner or later be regurgitated in response to some arcane search command, some inquisitive depth search from a postgraduate student. You have started to publish.

On many levels the Internet allows us access to a huge global distribution system. Our impassioned outpourings can reach a huge audience. Small publications are made viable when there are no printing or distribution costs. Learned research or the imaginings of madness can be distributed without let or hinderance.

Online publishing

Online publishing can take many forms. Documents, such as articles, papers, letters, newsletters and the like, already in digital form once written or assembled on a word-processor, can be transmitted to mailing lists for instant dissemination. They can be placed in archives for later retrieval, or submitted to editors of other electronic publications for consideration. Specialist archives abound – and not just one place for each subject. Mirroring the real world, though in a slightly less inefficient manner, the libraries of cyberspace compete to maintain the most complete sets of electronic material. The Internet has already spawned several completely unique forms of publication, such as the Request for Comments (RFC) and Frequently Asked Questions (FAQ) lists. These FAQs are everywhere on the nets. Every subject has one – though finding them can sometimes be a chore. They are legion on Usenet. Most groups have them, and they should be regularly posted. Generally started by concerned individuals when the same questions came to be asked once too many times, they have become repositories of knowledge, structured to a masterplan and kept up to date with love and attention. Often passed from hand to hand like a sacred flame, they carry version numbers in the same manner as software. 'Newbies' in any area are advised to 'read the FAQs' before asking anything in a public forum – a rule honored as often in the breach as in the observance. The Internet FAQ, kept by Kevin Savetz, has recently been expanded and published as a paperback.

```
                      Welcome to the

     / ___)          *StarShip* 5-MINUTE Weekend Newscast
   / (              ~~~~~~~~~~~~~~~~~~~~~~~~~~~~~~~~~~~~~~~~
   / ___)
 / (__   very weekend the *StarShip* on GEnie presents a new 5-MINUTE Weekend
 (_____) Newscast in Communications Room 10 in the Real-Time Conference Area.
Featuring late-breaking stories from the Amiga community, these dynamic,
scrolling newscasts cycle every 5 minutes, so you can stop by between 6PM and
3AM Eastern time on Friday, or 3PM and 3AM Eastern time on Saturday or Sunday
and learn everything that happened during the preceding week. Industry news,
product announcements, upgrades, rumors, special *StarShip* activities, trade
show reports, GEnie usage tips, humor, recommended files to download...

        ... the works -- and it ONLY takes 5 minutes!

Each 5-MINUTE Weekend Newscast is available on *StarShip* Menu #10 during the
following week. Periodically, newscasts are combined and made available for
downloading from the *StarShip* Library.
```

Electronic Newsletter: Starship 5-minute broadcast

The ease with which the nets take and disseminate published information has encouraged many people to chance their arm as writers and publishers. Authors such as Bruce Sterling have taken to putting whole texts out on the nets alongside conventional book releases. It is asserted that such activity helps bookstore sales. Several of the more famous Internet documents, such as Brendan P. Kehoe's *Zen and the Art of the Internet* have come to be published as in the real world.

In addition to the distribution of texts across the Internet and all that that entails, a whole new discipline of Internet publisher seems to be emerging. The arrival of multimedia network tools such as Gopher and the World Wide Web has been so quick that no structure existed or evolved that could give a guide to new publishers. It is fairly simple to find a site that will carry your materials – the number of Web sites increases by several hundred a week. Publishing in these media is unlike anything that has gone before. There are pitfalls, but on the whole it is a hugely exciting time as we all struggle to come to terms with a publishing explosion.

The upshot of this is that we are all publishers. The old equations of money and distribution are going out the window. With some easily acquired knowledge and Internet access, we are able to pass international boundaries from our desktops. Much is being done with this already, but the next few years will bring unseen advances for us all.

Cityscape have recently made space on their Web server for a publication called *The Lynx Magazine.* You can read Lynx on the World Wide Web (WWW) at

    http://www.cityscape.co.uk/lynx/.

13

The first issue contains a full report from the first WWW Conference at Cern in Switzerland.

Who has access?

Robert Zakon forwards the following story:

I should point out that the Queen of England sent e-mail over the RSRE link into the proto-typical arpanet from London, via Malvern to the US, in around 1976 to open the link. This kind of predates any other head of state by rather a long time.

Queen Elizabeth was opening a new building at the Royal Signal and Radar Establishment (RSRE) at Malvern, Worcestershire in the UK. RSRE was heavily involved with the early definition of ADA, and therefore wanted direct access to Arpanet. For this reason, a 9.6 Kbps leased line was put in between RSRE and University College London (UCL), which was the end-point of the UK link. Between UCL and the British Telecom (the British Post Office) Earth Station in Goonhilly was a 64 Kbps digital communication channel. In the Goonhilly earthstation was a Honeywell 516 Satellite IMP, as part of the SATNET experiment, and at UCL a Honeywell 516 IMP. Other SATNET sites with SIMPs were earthstations in Germany, Norway, Italy, and the US.

At the time there were no good e-mail hosts in the UK, so that the Queen was given an account called HRHE2 on a TENEX at ISI. As part of the opening ceremony, she pressed a button, which sent a simple message to ISI by TELNET, and hence to other ARPA dignatories at ARPA (Washington), ISI, MIT, UCL and RSRE.

Although we do not see it now, access to telephone systems was for a long time restricted to those who lived near to an exchange and who could afford a connection. There is obviously a cost rationing mechanism in place for a lot of people even now – we do not have 100% telephone penetration.

Despite cuts of recent years, we still take the concept of public libraries very much for granted, accepting that we pay taxes and such services are provided in return.

In the UK so far there has not been much of a debate about what access we want the general population to have to the Internet. The Internet could be defined in many ways as a synthesis of public libraries and the telephone network. Some colleges do not give their students access to the Internet, citing various reasons for this, from cost to security. These restrictions do not arouse much concern, though we can imagine what would happen if the same colleges tried to restrict library usage for the same reasons.

The Internet is a powerful mechanism for education and communication. The Freenet movement in the US has started the ball rolling towards a public library of the next century. Perhaps our grandchildren will take Internet access for granted – or perhaps they will pay for what they want, suffer advertising for much of it and ignore what they do not need.

Spuddy's Xanadu system offers 'free' dial-in access to a powerful Internet system and many facilities. Run by one individual, it shows what can be done on a minimal budget. The Digital City project in Amsterdam is an example of a group

```
▤▤▤▤▤▤▤▤▤▤▤▤▤▤▤▤▤▤▤ Guest account on the WELL ▤▤▤▤▤▤▤▤▤▤▤▤▤▤ ▣
Topic 231:  Who Should Be On the Net?                                       ⬆
#  7: Eric S Theise (estheise)      Thu, Nov  5, '92  (17:04)       1 line
<space>=next page, <b>=prev page, <q>=quit reading
 Linked from Internet 231 to MIDS 45.

Topic 231:  Who Should Be On the Net?
#  8: I own my own packets (jdevoto)     Thu, Nov  5, '92  (23:37)      2 line
 It's another common misconception that the Internet is a "government
 paid-for network". The NSFNet is that, but not the Internet.

Topic 231:  Who Should Be On the Net?
#  9: Jerry (jmcarlin)      Fri, Nov  6, '92  (00:05)       5 lines


 To clarify -> there are commercial providers who sometimes a referred
 to as comprising "alternet". Theoretically, they are not supposed to
 pass packets to the releach network unless they meet the guidelines
 of NSF and the regional nets.

Topic 231:  Who Should Be On the Net?
# 10: Sgt. Poskanzer, Protocol Police (jef)      Fri, Nov  6, '92  (07:58)
 "Alternet" is the name of one of the many commercial Internet providers.
 I've also seen the term used, incorrectly, to refer to the alt.* netnews   ▤
<space>=next page, <b>=prev page, <q>=quit reading█                          ⬇
```

Internet conference on The Well

setting out to provide the general public with a way of using the Internet. Starting out with a desire to enable voters to have access to local election information, Digital City ended up with a newly written bulletin board and conferencing system with public access terminals in public libraries across Amsterdam.

GreenNet and the Institute for Global Communications

In the UK, GreenNet provides access to global networking with a radical agenda. Part of the Association for Progressive Communication (APC), GreenNet differs from other network access providers. It is used by many organizations from trade unions through to arts organizations to link up with members and other bodies around the world.

The Institute for Global Communications (IGC) provides computer networking tools for international communications and information exchange.

The IGC Networks, EcoNet, PeaceNet, ConflictNet, LaborNet, make up the world's only computer communications system dedicated solely to environmental preservation, peace and human rights. New technologies are helping these world wide communities co-operate more effectively and efficiently.

IGC's conferencing services offer easy-to-use tools in group communication and event co-ordination. Geographically dispersed people can communicate inexpensively on any subject. Whether you are administering an organization or distributing an urgent action alert, IGC conferences are an indispensable tool. Private conferences can be set up to facilitate internal group decision-making, task-sharing processes or sensitive communications. Public conferences are great for information sharing, newsletter distribution, legislative alerts and news services.

IGC regards international co-operation and partnership as essential in addressing peace and environmental problems. IGC maintains a major program to develop low-cost access to computer networking from outside the United States, especially from non-industrialized and Southern Hemisphere countries. The result of this program has been the APC which now includes low-cost computer networks in eight countries. IGC has played a major role in starting the Alternex (Brazil), Nicarao (Nicaragua) and GlasNet (Russia) non-profit computer networks, as well as in providing technical support to all of the partner networks. Current projects include developing computer networks for peace, environmental and international development organizations in Bolivia, Costa Rica, Ecuador, Uruguay and Kenya. The focus of the work is to empower local, indigenous organizations by transferring expertise and capacity in computer networking. Operation and management of a local APC node becomes the full responsibility of the local organization. All APC partners are independent organizations, and retain full control over their network.

Control and policing

Another stated reason for controlling access to the Internet is that untrammelled use of a global network by all and sundry is dangerous in itself. Threats of hacking, criminal activity and obscene e-mail are bandied about as if the simple postal or telephone systems are never used for such pursuits. Those who wish to control the Internet in this way soon run up against one truth: there is no-one in control who can stop users having access. The Internet is akin to a socialist project: it is co-operatively owned and run. Though locally controlled and policed, there is no Internet Parliament (yet) to lay down the law. Acceptable User Policies (AUPs) are going the way of all unenforceable laws. The recent massive influx of new Internet users has caused some strain on the fabric of such a co-operative endeavour. Some cracks are appearing as anti-social behaviour, by business and education as much as by individuals, multiplies. However, such problems are minor compared with the immensity of the system. It does not seem that control mechanisms are desirable or practicable. A more commercial Internet may change this in the future, but the rules will change as the Internet is commercialized anyway.

Problems: hackers, pornography

For quite a while almost without exception the first question that journalists wanted to talk about was pornography on the Internet. A simple subject that their readership could relate to, pornography and neo-nazi antics may have seemed to be the entire activity of the Internet to many outsiders. We seem to be passing that early fixation as the concept of the Internet moves from a small cliquey activity to a publicly acknowledged subject. While I still await the first subject-based Internet journalism, I know it is not far off. There is pornography on the Internet, though a definition of pornography is sometimes hard to come by. There are many hundreds of thousands of images that could be classified as such, from scanned in Page 3 images to hard core images. On the whole it is very difficult to find 'real' pornography. The recent exposure of a paedophile site at a UK university may have seemed to some as proof of the dangerous Internet, but in reality just shows how rare and obscure such sites are.

Hackers are another story, with some site managers running scared. All Internet sites will be probed by hackers looking for weak spots. The rate at which new sites have come onto the networks has made it inevitable that less-experienced administrators will leave security loopholes, and even very well run sites are not immune. The battle for secure systems is never-ending, with new sophistication being deployed on both sides. However, hackers rarely damage the systems that they enter, this privilege being left to crackers.

A more dangerous problem is the growing use of the Internet for commercial transactions. The sending of credit card details over the Internet is theoretically dangerous: 'sniffer' software can pick out the messages as they pass unencoded to the commercial sites. However, there is little evidence that this is happening in reality. Of the terabytes of traffic that passes daily over the nets, very little is intercepted for criminal purposes.

Parliament and the Internet

The US government has moved fast to codify their view of the Information Superhighway. Confidence in the future has been expressed by the speed with which government information and legal documentation has made its way onto the Internet. State legislatures have followed, making huge amounts of information available.

The 'Americans Communicating Electronically' Gopher provides one stop access to a variety of US government information – the National Health Security Act, National Information Infrastructure documents, North American Free Trade Agreement information and more.

```
gopher://gopher ace.esusda.gov
```

If you want to find out about White House goings on you have a huge choice. Start by sending the message

```
send info
```

to

```
publications@WhiteHouse.GOV
```

Overview

A White House Press Release Service is available at

```
gopher://wiretap.spies.com/Clinton
```

and contains press releases from the Clinton administration including briefings by Dee Dee Myers, Executive Orders, remarks during Photo Opportunities, remarks of Bill Clinton, briefings by George Stephanopolous.

The Internet Wiretap is at

```
gopher@wiretap.spies.com
```

Congress, the Supreme Court, the Patent Office, Social Security and myriad other governmental and semi-governmental organizations have put full information online. Combined with search tools, this opens up access to citizens in an unprecedented manner.

UK government information

The US culture of political openness contrasts wholly with the situation in the UK, where it is not currently possible to find any governmental information using the Internet. Worse than that, all press releases go by contract to a commercial information service, as David Shaw MP explains here, in a reply to a Usenet question:

```
David@dlshaw.demon.co.uk (David L Shaw)
Re: UK Press releases on the Internet

> Can anyone out there help, I am interested in getting
electronic copies of
> UK Government press releases if thats possible.
> Do we offer this service in the UK ??  If not WHY NOT ???
> also, are there any Government ftp sites where we can get >
hold of electronic articles of any political kind ??

Reply from David Shaw MP:
=====================================
I asked Parliamentary Questions of each Government Department
about this.
It seems that some time ago the Central Office of Information
contracted
with a company called Data-Star (owned by a Swiss Co.) to
provide a database of all UK Govt Press Releases. The search
costs are approx. £60 per hour.
The arrangement benefits the taxpayer by some £30,000 a year -
not large as total expenditure is over £300 Billion a year. It
appears to have been  set up when the only demand was from
lobby companies etc ie commercial.
```

```
I am not aware of any public Government FTP sites.
I am trying to explain the Internet to those who make the
decisions,
in order to see if consideration will be given to a free
public access
system in the future. Those on the Internet who would like a
free public
access service for Government press releases should write to
their own MP at House of Commons, London, SW1A 0AA
and ask that their MP brings it to the attention of Rt Hon
William Waldegrave who is the Minister responsible for Open
Government. It might help if the letter explains what the
Internet is as not all MPs know!
It may be that there is no copyright in UK Government Press
Releases (there is nothing on the bottom of the ones I have
seen) - indeed the press are encouraged to copy them!
Therefore, I suppose that there may be nothing in law to stop
an enterprising individual from collecting the Press Releases
from the COI and posting them to news groups.
-
David L Shaw MP    ||   Your Friendly MP on the Internet
```

Since that posting a report called 'Information Superhighways: Opportunities for public sector applications in the UK' has been released. Prepared for William Waldegrave and billed as a 'consultative report', it makes an attempt to set out the ground for a potential 'Information Superhighway'. The report is not about the Internet *per se*, although it nods in that direction and accepts that we already have some precursor to a superhighway. The report offers the Internet as one of three 'competing technologies', i.e. a high-capacity super-computer network, the 'Internet' or thirdly 'the commercial application of new, but extant, technologies'. On inspection these distinct strands seem to merge together somewhat: an example of a 'high-capacity super-computer network' is given as SuperJANET, which, although technologically distinct, is essentially part and parcel of the Internet. The thrust of the report is on what benefits and profits can be made from developments. There is little here that will come as any surprise to Internet users.

Unsurprisingly, given the nature of the government, there is little consideration of how a real change could be made or of how public sector action now could offer a vote of confidence in the whole adventure. An annexe lists government departments and what consumer service they could offer – on the whole information access, transmission of images and remote forms handling. There is no clarion call for these departments to offer such services.

The report certainly offers the first evidence that government has noticed this thing, the Internet, that has built up around us. It marks a move towards involvement, and if we make an assumption that the UK is at least two years behind the US in Internet type development, then we may yet see huge strides forward.

The report is available from CCTA, phone 071 217 3000 or by FTP from

```
ftp://ftp.demon.co.uk/pub/ccta/
```

Public interest: CommUnity

In the US the Electronic Freedom Foundation fights for cyberspace rights. In the UK a similar body with a much shorter history has been formed for the same defence of online rights.

CommUnity is the Computer Communicators' Association, a recently formed pressure group to represent the interest of the UK online community. It was initially formed in response to the threat of BBS licensing posed by the ELSPA (European Leisure Software Publishers Association) and FAST (Federation Against Software Theft) and other such organizations.

CommUnity aims to maintain and connect a membership which shares a common concern that access to technology, information and communication should be as freely available as possible. They will also monitor and inform press and media coverage of computer-based communications, responding to misinformation or prejudice with a coherent voice.

Other areas of work foreseen are fostering a better understanding of the issues underlying free and open telecommunications, and support for legal and structural approaches which ease the assimilation of new technologies.

Membership of CommUnity costs £5. Full information is available along with many more files from

```
ftp://ftp.demon.co.uk/archives/community
```

CommUnity, 89 Mayfair Avenue, Worcester Park, Surrey, KT4 7SJ

The Electronic Frontier Foundation

The Electronic Frontier Foundation (EFF) was founded in July of 1990 to ensure that the principles embodied in the US Constitution and the Bill of Rights are protected as new communications technologies emerge.

Since its inception, EFF has worked to shape communications infrastructure and the policies that govern it in order to maintain and enhance First Amendment, privacy and other democratic values. They believe that the overriding public goal must be the creation of Electronic Democracy.

For further information, send e-mail to either of these addresses:

```
ftp-help@eff.org
ask@eff.org
```

You can read the EFF Web pages at

```
http://www.eff.org/
```

or Gopher to

```
gopher://gopher.eff.org
```

Computer Professionals for Social Responsibility

CPSR was founded in 1981 by a group of computer scientists concerned about the use of computers in nuclear weapons systems. CPSR has since grown into a US based public-interest alliance of information technology professionals and other people. Currently, CPSR has 22 chapters in the US and affiliations with similar groups worldwide. The national office is in Palo Alto, California.

You can reach the CPSR Web pages at

```
http://cpsr.org/home
```

or gopher to them on

```
gopher://gopher.cpsr.org/
```

Their FTP site is at:

```
ftp://ftp.cpsr.org/cpsr/
```

Guide to the UK

A handy guide to the UK on the World Wide Web

Information on a range of UK cities and active maps of some, plus links to many other resources.

```
http://www.cs.ucl.ac.uk/misc/uk/intro.html
```

and is run by

```
mhandley@cs.ucl.ac.uk
```

You can take a guided tour, look at the UKCIA World Fact Book entry on the UK, today's weather map or read UK News from the VOGON News Service

Currently general information is available on: Scotland, North, Wales, Mid, Wales, South, Wales, North, Yorkshire, Cumbria (the Lake District), Dorset, Northumberland, Staffordshire. Information is also available on the following towns and cities (in alphabetic order): Bath, Birmingham, Bradford, Brighton, Bristol, Cambridge, Canterbury, Cardiff, Dundee, Durham, Edinburgh, Exeter, Glasgow, Guildford, Lichfield, London, Loughborough, Manchester, Newcastle, Norwich, Nottingham, Oxford, Sheffield, Stafford, Stoke, Southampton, Sunderland, Tamworth, Warwick, Watford and York.

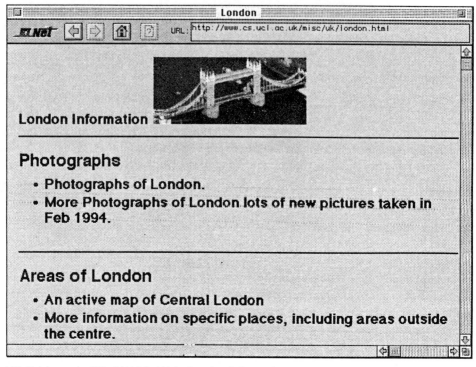

London Information

Photographs

- Photographs of London.
- More Photographs of London lots of new pictures taken in Feb 1994.

Areas of London

- An active map of Central London
- More information on specific places, including areas outside the centre.

UK Guide on the World Wide Web: London information

List of UK WWW servers

Another good listing of UK Web servers can be found at:

```
http://src.doc.ic.ac.uk/all-uk.html
```

This large listing is split into Commercial, Academic and Recreational sections and provides a good starting point for exploration.

CHAPTER

Using the Internet

Using the Internet is somewhat more complicated than firing up a piece of software and using it to interact with a seamless environment. The Internet is composed of a range of services and resources, and there is a range of tools available to exploit these. At first it seems impossible to work out what is what: how does gopher relate to e-mail; why do I need WAIS; what is finger; what is the difference between ARCHIE and FTP? After a steep learning curve, all the different tools will come into focus. You can then make decisions about which you need, when and how to use them. You will find that your e-mail package is crucial and Gopher is a powerful information seeking tool; that your World Wide Web browser is fun and FTP is a workhorse.

Luckily, all the tools you need are available from the Inernet itself, as are many many documents about them. Help and support comes from a huge variety of sources from Usenet groups to mailing lists to online documents. You are never alone with an Internet.

A client/server relationship

For a basic understanding of what you can do on the Internet, you need to know about the client/server relationship. The client is the intelligent bit that you instruct: your e-mail software, Gopher or finger application. The server is where the information resides that you want to find out about. It may be an archive that you query using WAIS; a bulletin board that you telnet to or a Veronica service. It is not important to know at any time what the client/server relationship is, but it helps to conceptualize the Internet if you know it exists.

Most Internet services use this model. Your clients will differ, depending on how you gain access to the Internet. If you have full 'hardwired' connectivity, you will most likely choose your own clients to run on your own machine. You may be offered a range by the institution that you work for, but with an Internet Protocol (IP) address you can really run what you want. If you use a shell account you may also have a choice of what you can run, but it may be more difficult to learn to install them. There will certainly be restrictions on what you can do. If you are a user of a bulletin board type account, you will have to use the clients provided by the people who run the board: simple Telnet, FTP and Gopher tools. Whatever you use, the client is under your control and the server, wherever it is, is provided by others. Between them we have the magic of the Internet.

Types of access

There are several different ways of connecting to the Internet. They range from simple terminal access through to full Internet connection, with many variations in between. There is no strict hierarchical progression between them, and several combinations are possible. It may be that some are not available or would be overkill for your needs. If you only want to exchange e-mail with the Internet you may do better having a simple UUCP feed or finding a bulletin board that will give you support and entertainment. On the other hand, you might want to become an information provider yourself, in which case you could acquire a full Internet feed – or look for a third party to provide publication facilities.

Terminal

Terminal-based Internet access is what you get when you are on a local network using a 'dumb' terminal to talk to a local computer. Terminal access is often provided in larger organizations who have large computers that are linked to the Internet. It is unlikely that you would have full Internet access from a terminal, though you should have e-mail capabilities. Terminals tend to be non-graphical interface machines and often use an arcane command line language to send commands to the main computer.

UUCP

UUCP is a method developed for computers to transfer information between themselves without humans having to intervene. It became a popular way of passing Internet information 'down the chain', and is still very useful (and cheap) if you want to collect e-mail and Usenet groups or even if you run a bulletin board and would like some Internet connectivity. UUCP services are provided by various companies such as ExNet in London.

Dial-up

Dial-up Internet access implies that you have a PC and a modem which you connect to your account on a remote machine. It may be that you have an account at work and your office provides a dial-in service so you can continue working from home, or that you are a student who uses the college computer from outside the college. Dial-in services also include 'shell accounts' with commercial companies. You buy access to a computer that you access by dialling in. You then have access to a 'shell' and to whatever software is available, for example Telnet, FTP and Gopher. You read e-mail while online and would need to separately upload and download any files that you FTP'd across to the 'shell'.

Bulletin boards

More and more bulletin boards are offering Internet access as part of the service. They range from small, individually run boards to large commercial services. Included in this section are services such as CIX, which prefers to call itself a 'conferencing system'. Bulletin board access to the Internet can be a good way to get started, with lots of support information, other users, specialist forums for help and a professional help-line. E-mail is read either online or, using an off-line reader, is collected and downloaded to be read and replied to while the connection is down. The huge American service, CompuServe, can exchange e-mail in and out of the Internet, but will charge you for the benefit of receiving e-mail.

Full Internet access

Full Internet access means you have an IP address for the machine that you are using. This machine will be directly connected to the Internet using IP connectivity, though this may be via a dial-up line using a protocol such as Point to Point Protocol (PPP) or Serial Line Internet Protocol (SLIP). If this access is from an academic or commercial site there is a high chance that you have access to a fairly high bandwidth. From a PC with its own Internet address you can run any Internet software such as full graphical versions of e-mail software, Gopher and World Wide Web browsers. You are also in a position to become an information provider over the Internet by running server software such as Gopher or a http

All resources are referred to using Universal Resource Locators (URLs), the Internet's common addressing ststem. Although they make it easy for me to point you in the right direction, you will need to interpret them for your own software.

URLs can and do apply to World Wide Web sites, Gopher sites, ftp sites, telnet addresses, maail sites and other resources. The example below uses an ftp site, but you will encounter all types in this book and on your Internet travels. You will have to learn to disentangle them for your own software, sometimes entering the parts manually, or changing directory after telnetting or ftp'ing to a site.

URLs offer a standardised form of Internet resource addressing and are simple to understand.

There are many types of URL, but they all start with the name of the service, the most common being ftp, gopher and http. Ftp and gopher are self explanatory, http is for World Wide Web browsers. Take, for example

ftp://ftp.demon.co.uk/pub/archive/guide.txt

The service name is followed by ://
So, for an ftp site, the URL would start with:

1   **ftp://**

between the :// and the next / comes the address of the site, in this case

2   **ftp.demon.co.uk**

this is the address that you will point your ftp software at. You will have to find out how to do this, which you probably already know. After the first single / comes the 'path' to the resource. For ftp sites this can be quite long winded. Here it is

3   **pub/archive/**

If we are pointing at a specific file, this will be the last part of the URL, here it is

4   **guide.txt**

Sometimes there will be no specific file, for example when you are pointed at a directory containing many interesting items.
Gopher sites are very similar. The URL directs you to a site and may or may not include a 'path' to the resource. You will have to find out how to navigate this path using your software.
World Wide Web sites are much more specific. They will always point to specific file, though this may just be the front page of a system. Some WWW URLs end in a / without a filename, but these default to a front page at the site.

(hypertext transport protocol) server for the World Wide Web. Obviously, this is not possible if you have a dial-up connection. Full Internet access in the UK is provided by a number of companies, from top-end providers such as Pipex and EUNet down to services such as Demon Internet Services 'Internet for a tenner a month' service.

IP software

Any connection beyond a shell or BBS type connection demands IP software, that is, software that uses the Internet Protocols. This is 'real' Internet software that runs from your desktop and allows you to partake of the full Internet menu.

PC and Windows

All Internet users need a TCP/IP (Transport Control Protocol/Internet Protocol) stack to allow their software to 'talk' via the Internet. Your can use other network protocols simultaneously with TCP/IP, such as Novell, LANtastic, or Windows for Workgroups network protocols.

The TCP/IP driver can be implemented in a variety of ways. Until recently, this was often a DOS TSR program loaded from the AUTOEXEC.BAT file.

Increasingly this layer of software is implemented as a Windows dynamic link library (DLL) or as a Windows virtual device driver (VxD), which does not require any modification of the boot files on the PC. The driver may be written to work with a specific network card, or it can be written to interface with a packet driver. In the latter case, a single TCP/IP driver can be used with any network card for which an associated packet driver is available. Thus, the packet driver specification eliminates the need for software vendors to customize their TCP/IP protocol stack for every network card on which it is used.

When a direct network connection is not available, Internet TCP/IP software can be used over serial lines to connect to a SLIP server that provides a connection to the Internet. SLIP does not require the drivers used for a direct network connection. The Trumpet Winsock shareware package to be described later has all SLIP functions internal to the TCP/IP driver, which is configured through a Windows dialog box.

Connecting to the Internet involves dialling the SLIP server using normal serial communications software and establishing a SLIP connection. Once the connection is established, TCP/IP software running on the PC can be used just as if the PC was connected directly to the Internet through a network card.

Clients run independently of whether the computer has a direct connection or a SLIP connection to the Internet. TCP/IP applications are frequently referred to as clients because they access a corresponding server.

Winsock

Until recently, each TCP/IP client had to be written to interface with a particular vendor's TCP/IP protocol stack. Clients that worked with one vendor's TCP/IP driver would not work with a driver from another vendor. This restriction was eliminated with the development of the Windows Sockets Application Programming Interface, otherwise known as the Winsock. Winsock works in the layer between the TCP/IP client and the TCP/IP protocol stack.

Winsock is a technical specification that defines a standard interface between a Windows TCP/IP client application (such as an FTP client or a Gopher client) and the underlying TCP/IP protocol stack.

When you launch a Winsock compliant client like HGopher, it calls procedures from the WINSOCK.DLL.

The WINSOCK.DLL file is not a generic file that can be used on any system. Each vendor of a TCP/IP protocol stack supplies a proprietary WINSOCK.DLL that works only with that vendor's TCP/IP stack.

The advantage of Winsock to the developer of a client is that the application will work with any vendor's Winsock implementation. Thus, the developer of an application such as a Gopher client has to understand the Winsock interface, but they do not have to know the details of each vendor's TCP/IP protocol stack in order to make the client application compatible with that stack. Winsock also eliminates the need for an application developer to include their own TCP/IP protocol stack within the application program itself.

Apple Mac users have always had the advantage of a standard TCP/IP stack MacTCP, written by Apple and used by all IP software. PC users, by contrast, have had a fragmented past where each application contained a built-in TCP/IP stack. Now, any Winsock compliant application will run with any vendor's TCP/IP protocol stack and accompanying WINSOCK.DLL.

Unfortunately, some commercial vendors of TCP/IP clients are not yet taking advantage of Winsock capabilities.

Installing Winsock

Trumpet Winsock is a TCP/IP protocol stack that includes basic clients such as Telnet, FTP, ping and Archie.

Full installation instructions are included in the ZIP file.

Trumpet Winsock is shareware and costs $20 to register.

Available by FTP from

```
ftp://ftp.utas.edu.au/pc/trumpet/winsock/twsk10a.zip
```
and
```
ftp://ftp.utas.edu.au/pc/trumpet/winsock/winapps.zip
```
or by Gopher from
```
gopher://info.utas.edu.au/UTas FTP
Archive/pc/trumpet/winsock
```

If you want to dial your SLIP server automatically, but you do not care to write your own dialling script for TCPMAN.EXE, a utility named DIALER provides a convenient means of dialling the phone and automatically starting the SLIP session. DIALER can be set up to automatically issue the commands and passwords needed to start the SLIP session. DIALER version 2.0A is available by FTP from

```
ftp.demon.co.uk/pub/ibmpc/windows/utilities/dialexe.zip
```

HGopher

This Gopher client has been sold and is no longer available from its author. He still distributes Version 2.3 which is quite functional and will continue to be available as shareware. Copies of version 2.4 may still be found at some anonymous FTP sites or at some Gopher sites.

Available by FTP from

```
lister.cc.ic.ac.uk/pub/wingopher/hgopher2.3.zip
```

or by Gopher from

```
gopher://gopher.ic.ac.uk/Networking/HGopher Information
Center/The Hgopher distribution
```

Trumpet for Windows

Internet news reader and POP mail client.

To read Internet news, you need access to an NNTP (Network News Transfer Protocol) server. To use the mail functions, you need an account on a POP (Post Office Protocol) mail server.

Available by FTP from:

```
ftp://ftp.utas.edu.au/pc/trumpet/wintrump/wtwsk10a.zip
```

or by Gopher

```
gopher://info.utas.edu.au under menu
item/pc/trumpet/wintrump
```

PC Eudora

To use this full featured mail client you will need an account on a POP mail server to send and receive mail at your PC, such as that sold by Cityscape. QUALCOMM sells a commercial version of Eudora for both Windows and the Macintosh.

Get it by anonymous FTP from:

```
ftp://ftp.qualcomm.com/quest/windows/eudora/1.4/
eudora14.exe
```

WS_FTP and WS_PING

Public domain FTP and ping clients

```
ftp://ftp.usma.edu in directory
/pub/msdos/winsock.files/ws_ftp.zip
ftp://ftp.usma.edu in directory
/pub/msdos/winsock.files/ws_ping.zip
```

NCSA Mosaic for Microsoft Windows

World Wide Web browser.

NCSA's Windows version of the software that is changing the world. Regularly updated, once you have it running keep an eye on the Mosaic Home Page.

Get it from

```
ftp://ftp.ncsa.uiuc.edu in directory
/PC/Mosaic/wmos20a5.zip
```

You can avoid the added complexity of installing Win32s and the substantial demands it places on your PC by reverting to Mosaic version 2.0 alpha 2. This version is still available from NCSA's FTP server in directory /PC/Mosaic/old.

CELLO

World Wide Web browser.

This Web client may be more stable than Mosaic, but it lacks Mosaic's convenient bookmark menus.

```
ftp://ftp.law.cornell.edu in directory
/pub/LII/Cello/cello.zip
```

Telnet

TELW.EXE is included with the Trumpet Winsock package in the WINAPPS.ZIP file. It is the first client that shareware users are likely to try. It is a minimal client with no configuration possibilities. It can be useful at times as a terminal/Telnet viewer in HGopher.

WinQVT/Net is an integrated package that includes Telnet, FTP, FTP server, mail and news reader clients. These client applications are normally launched from a console window. The Telnet client is probably the best shareware Winsock Telnet client available. You can select terminal emulations and customize the keyboard. The resizable Telnet window includes scrollback and session logging. A deficiency is that Telnet cannot be launched independently of the console window.

Available by FTP from:

```
ftp://biochemistry.bioc.cwru.edu/qvtws397.zip
```

or by Gopher from

```
gopher://biochemistry.cwru.edu under menu item/CWRU
Biochemistry FTP Archive/qvtnet
```

TRMPTEL

This can be used as a terminal/Telnet viewer with HGopher or with Mosaic and Cello. It is a very early release of a client that can be expected to become excellent in the near future.

FTP it from:

```
ftp://petros.psychol.utas.edu.au in directory
/pub/trumpet/trmptel/trmptel.exe
```

Other sources for Winsock information

Considerable information about the Winsock API, along with some application programs, is available at

```
sunsite.unc.edu in directory /pub/micro/pc-stuff/ms-
windows/winsock
```

Another good site for most software is

```
ftp://ftp.cica.indiana.edu/pub/pc/win3/winsock.
```

Usenet groups

The news groups

```
alt.winsock
```

```
comp.protocols.tcp-ip.ibmpc
```

carry discussions of the Winsock specification and Winsock compliant applications, as do the groups in the

```
comp.os.ms-windows
```

networking hierarchy.

Gopher software such as HGopher is discussed in

```
alt.gopher
```

```
comp.infosystems.gopher
```

Cello and Mosaic are discussed in the sections of the comp.infosystems.www hierarchy.

Mailing lists

Listserv WIN3-L@UICVM carries discussions about all topics relating to Windows, including Winsock applications.

A comprehensive list of FTPable Winsock applications is available. Send e-mail to

    info@lcs.com

with the

    Subject: FAQ.

and nothing else should be in the message.

An FAQ about TCP/IP on PC-compatible computers written by Bernard D. Adoba is posted monthly on

    comp.protocols.tcp-ip.ibmpc

You can get this by FTP from

    ftp://rtfm.mit.edu/pub/usenet-by-hierarchy/comp/protocols/tcp-
    ip/ibmpc/comp.protocols.tcp-ip.ibmpc_Frequently_Asked_Questions
    (FAQ).

and also as

    ftp://ibmtcp.zip/netcom2.netcom.com/pub/mailcom/IBMTCP.

An introduction to SLIP is available

    gopher.vt.edu/Computing Center.../Experimental file
    system/nyman/whatslip.txt.

Windows and TCP/IP for Internet access

Full information about the above Windows software and more is available in a document by Harry M. Kriz at the University Libraries Virginia Polytechnic Institute and State University.

    hmkriz@vt.edu

This document is available from

    ftp://nebula.lib.vt.edu in directory

    /pub/windows/winsock/wtcpip05.asc

The CSU San Marcos Windows Software Archive is available via URL at

    http://coyote.csusm.edu/cwis/winworld/winworld.html

Apple Macintosh

MacTCP

Apple Mac users have always had it easy when it comes to the TCP/IP stack. Although not perfect, there is only one to choose from – MacTCP from Apple themselves. As all software has had to use this stack there has never been any confusion about where to start. MacTCP is a commercial product from Apple, although in the

```
┌─────────────────────────────────────────────────────────────────────┐
│  ┌···Obtain Address:···┐  ┌············ IP Address:············┐     │
│  │  ◉ Manually         │  │  Class: [ B ]  Address: 158.152.9.252   │
│  │  ○ Server           │  │                                    │     │
│  │  ○ Dynamically      │  │    Subnet Mask: 255.255.0.0        │     │
│  │                     │  │  ┌────────────────┬──────────────┐ │     │
│  │                     │  │  │████████████████│██████████████│ │     │
│  │                     │  │    Net  |  Subnet  |  Node        │     │
│  │                     │  │  Bits:  16      0       16         │     │
│  └─────────────────────┘  │  Net:    [40600]       ☐ Lock     │     │
│  ┌·Routing Information:·┐  │  Subnet: [0        ]   ☐ Lock     │     │
│   Gateway Address:        │  Node:   [2556     ]   ☐ Lock     │     │
│  │                     │  └────────────────────────────────────┘     │
│  │ [158.152.1.65     ] │  ┌···Domain Name Server Information:···┐    │
│  └─────────────────────┘   Domain        IP Address  Default        │
│                           │[demon.co.uk] [158.152.1.65] ◉  ⇧│       │
│  ┌──────┐  ┌────────┐     │[.         ] [158.152.1.65]  ○   │       │
│  │  OK  │  │ Cancel │     │[.         ] [158.152.1.93]  ○  ⇩│       │
│  └──────┘  └────────┘     └──────────────────────────────────┘      │
└─────────────────────────────────────────────────────────────────────┘
```

MacTCP control panel window

past it has been licensed with various freeware and shareware products. These days it is increasingly available with third party products, for example with Adam Engst's book, *The Internet Starter Kit for Macintosh*. With the advent of System 7.5 for the Mac, Apple have bundled MacTCP into the operating system, thus offering a vote of confidence for the Internet and IP software.

InterSLIP and MacPPP

Using a dial-up full Internet connection calls for a connection made using either SLIP or PPP. These are the neat little pieces of software that sit between MacTCP and your service provider

If you are setting up a SLIP connection you can use a free package called InterSLIP to make the connection. InterSLIP comes with the Adam Engst book mentioned above and for this reason many people are tempted to use it. However, it needs some fairly complex configuration to get it to work. You can get scripts for specific services such as Demon, but on the whole you will be better off if you can use a PPP connection.

InterSLIP is available from

```
ftp://ftp.intercon.com/InterCon/
```

MacPPP

MacPPP is freely available and is something of an advance on SLIP connectivity. You should be able to get an installer from your service provider that will set up your script without intervention. Demon and CityScape provide such installers.

You can get MacPPP from

```
ftp://merit.edu/pub/ppp
```

NCSA Telnet

NCSA Telnet implements Telnet for the Mac in an easy to use package. Telnet needs no special knowledge to use, just the need to 'Telnet' to remote sites, such as information services. You can open multiple windows at the same time to different sites. A near perfect Telnet client.

NCSA Telnet is available from

```
ftp://ftp.ncsa.uiuc.edu/
```

Hytelnet

Hytelnet is an Internet information system that you can Telnet to across the Internet. You can also get a Hypercard version for the Mac. It is essentially a database with links to Internet resources. You can search it for interesting sites and then it will launch Telnet directly and attempt to log on to the resource. It is a good way of making a quick and simple recce of the Internet.

You can get Hytelnet for the Mac from

```
ftp://access.usask.ca/pub/hytelnet/mac/hytelnet6.5.sit.hqx
```

You will need Hypercard 2.1 or later or the Hypercard player.

Fetch (FTP)

Fetch is an excellent point and click FTP program that was developed at Dartmouth University. It makes it very easy to use anonymous FTP sites and uses a 'bookmark' system for regularly accessed sites.

Fetch is available at

```
ftp://ftp.dartmouth.edu/pub/mac/
```

TurboGopher

TurboGopher was developed at the University of Minnesota for easy cruising through Gopherspace. TurboGopher comes ready to run and is simple to use. However, you may like to change the 'home' Gopher site to one in the UK.

You can get the latest version of TurboGopher via Gopher from

```
gopher://boombox.micro.umn.edu/gopher/Macintosh-
TurboGopher/TurboGopher1.0.8b4
```

or FTP it from

```
ftp://boombox.micro.umn.edu/gopher/Macintosh-
TurboGopher/TurboGopher1.0.8b4
```

Mac Eudora

Eudora is a beautiful e-mail program that now exists in both freeware and commercial versions. Eudora needs a POP server to pick up mail, which can be a problem if you only have access to SMTP (Simple Mail Transfer Protocol), for example with a Demon account. However, there is now an excellent solution available for this in AddMail, which will pick up your SMTP mail and pass it on to Eudora with no intervention on your part. You can get Mac Eudora from

```
ftp://src.doc.ic.ac.uk/computing/systems/mac/eudora/
```

or from

```
ftp://ftp.demon.co.uk/pub/mac/MacTCP/eudora
```

AddMail

AddMail was written because the nicest Macintosh mail application, Eudora, is not able to directly receive mail by SMTP (although it sends via SMTP). Eudora can collect mail delivered by UUCP to the machine it is resident on. AddMail converts mail delivered by SMTP into a UUCP dropfile format which can then be picked up directly by Eudora and processed.

AddMail is available from Demon at

```
ftp://ftp.demon.co.uk/pub/Mac/Addmail
```

LeeMail

LeeMail is an SMTP mailer, which in theory makes it useful only in a fully connected site. However, many people use it, especially if they have a Demon account. The advent of AddMail has made LeeMail less important. It is available from

```
ftp://src.doc.ic.ac.uk/computing/systems/mac/umich/util
/comm/
```

or

```
ftp://ftp.demon.co.uk/pub/mac/leemail2/leemail1.24.cpt.
hqx
```

NCSA Mosaic for Mac

Mosaic is a World Wide Web browser developed at NCSA for Mac, PC and Unix platforms. This was the software that opened up WWW to a mass audience and made sense of it. After a long wait, version 2.x has been released with support for fill in forms, among other items. However, memory demands and instability make it a less than perfect program.

Available from

    ftp://ftp.luth.se/pub/infosystems/www/ncsa

or

    ftp://ftp.sunet.se/pub/mac/Mosaic

The Mosaic home page is at

    http://galaxy.einet.net/EINet/MacWeb/MacWebHome.html

MacWeb

MacWeb from EINet is currently available in an Alpha version for evaluation. This World Wide Web browser also handles forms and a lot more besides, and seems more stable than Mosaic at the moment.

Available from

    ftp://ftp.einet.net/einet/macweb/macweb0.98alpha.sea.hqx

The home page is at

    http://galaxy.einet.net/EINet/MacWeb/MacWebHome.html

Sumex archive

About the best archive of Mac software available on the Internet is the Info-Mac site. You can access this site through FTP, gopher and WWW.

The site is huge and is often very difficult to get into. Mirrors of it exist around the world. The main UK mirror is at Imperial College

    ftp://src.doc.ic.ac.uk/packages/info-mac

You can also use an FTP mail server at this site

    ftpmail@doc.ic.ac.uk

For full information about the archive and associated sites, Gopher to

    gopher://sumex-aim.Stanford.edu/info-mac/Help/Help

Amiga

Amiga Mosaic 1.2 is now available via FTP from

    ftp://max.physics.sunysb.edu/pub/amosaic/

or check the World Wide Web pages at

    http://insti.physics.sunysb.edu/AMosaic/

Amiga Mosaic is based on NCSA's Mosaic, but is not distributed by the University of Illinois or NCSA. To subscribe to the Amiga Mosaic mailing list, send mail to

```
witbrock@cmu.edu
```

To send a message to the mailing list, send to

```
amosaic@max.physics.sunysb.edu.
```

Amiga Mosaic works with either the PD AmiTCP 3.0beta2 or Commodore's AS225R2 software, or with DNET for those of you without SLIP connections. There is also the NoNet version which works if you have no networking at all and want to browse local HTML (Hyper-Text Markup Language) files.

Information about the Amiga IP stack, AmiTCP/IP 2.3, is available from amitcp-group@hut.fi

Amiga Mosaic requires Magic User Interface 2.0 to be installed also.

Amiga Mosaic uses the AmigaOS 3.0 DataTypes library for its external and inlined image decoding. This means that Amiga Mosaic can decode any image for which you have a DataType installed. You should at least install a GIF (Graphical Image Format) datatype to view most inlined images. Inlined X-Bitmaps (XBMs) are decoded internally. An XBM datatype will be provided in the future.

Amiga Information

News groups: Amiga Internet news groups

Introduction to the Amiga Family of computers.

```
news:comp.sys.amiga.announce
```

Amiga news.

```
news:comp.sys.amiga.reviews
```

Reviews of Amiga hardware and software, commercial and otherwise

```
news:comp.sys.amiga.applications
```

Applications

```
news:comp.sys.amiga.audio
```

Audio

```
news:comp.sys.amiga.datacomm
```

Datacomm

```
news:comp.sys.amiga.emulations
```

Emulations of PC clones, Macintoshes, C64s, and goodness only knows what else

```
news:comp.sys.amiga.games
```

Games

```
news:comp.sys.amiga.graphics
```

Graphics

```
news:comp.sys.amiga.hardware
```

Hardware

`news:comp.sys.amiga.multimedia`

Multimedia

`news:comp.sys.amiga.programmer`

Programmer

`news:comp.sys.amiga.marketplace`

If you want to buy or sell used Amiga stuff

`news:comp.sys.amiga.advocacy`

Advocacy where people rave on about the Amiga, and much more

`news:comp.sys.amiga.misc`

Where miscellaneous topics are discussed, more calmly

`news:comp.sys.amiga.introduction`

All of these groups can be read on the World Wide Web at

`http://www.cs.cmu.edu:8001/Web/People/mjw/Computer/`
`Amiga/NewsGroups.html`

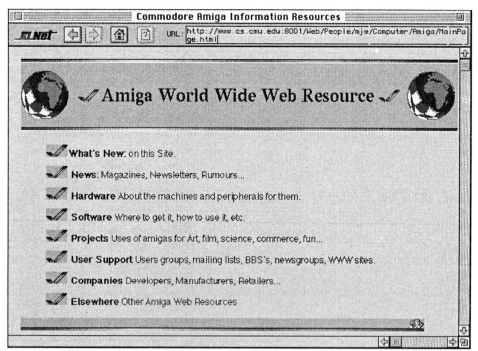

Amiga WWW Home page

A great Amiga home page is at

```
http://www.cs.cmu.edu:8001/Web/People/mjw/Computer/Amiga/
MainPage.html
```

Public Domain: some of the many sources of Amiga Public Domain, Shareware, Giftware, Freeware, GNU Software and other Amiga Picture, Sound, Music, Animation, Hypertext, and Multimedia Files

```
http://www.cs.cmu.edu:8001/Web/People/mjw/Computer/Amiga/
PDSites.html
```

Links: other Amiga Web resources

```
http://www.cs.cmu.edu:8001/Web/People/mjw/Computer/Amiga/
WWWResources.html
```

Bulletin Boards: every Amiga BBS in the world

```
http://www.cs.cmu.edu:8001/Web/People/mjw/Computer/Amiga/
AR/TW-WABL!_Sections/main.HTML
```

Amiga users groups

```
http://www.cs.cmu.edu:8001/Web/People/mjw/Computer/Amiga/
UserGroups.html
```

Reviews: the Amiga Software/Hardware Review Archive recent list and actual reviews

```
ftp://math.uh.edu/pub/Amiga/comp.sys.amiga.reviews/new/
NewSince30Days
```

Amiga Frequently Asked Questions file

```
http://www.cs.cmu.edu:8001/Web/People/mjw/Computer/Amiga/
AmigaFAQ_Sections/Main.html
```

Information about ArgoNauts Magazine for Amiga users

```
http://www.cs.cmu.edu:8001/Web/People/mjw/Computer/Amiga/
ArgoNaut.html
```

Hardware: information about specific Amiga models and peripherals

```
http://www.cs.cmu.edu:8001/Web/People/mjw/Computer/Amiga/
Hardware.html
```

Who connects?

There is not a huge choice in the UK for anyone wanting Internet access. Although companies have been offering various routes in ever since there has been an Internet, it is only very recently that small to medium users have had any sort of choice beyond UUCP access. The coming of Demon pushed Internet access downwards to individuals, provided of course that they lived within a local call of one of Demon's dial in points. Many people initially were prepared to make long distance calls to gain Internet access, but this is not really a happy solution. The success of Demon at the lower end of the market has brought other players in, most notably Cityscape who are an offshoot of Pipex, one of the largest Internet providers.

Cityscape set out to provide a widely spread set of dial in points, and with investment behind them have come up with an initial six points. The race between Cityscape and Demon is hotting up – with beneficial results for users in parts of the country that have no local access. It will not be long before most urban areas have a local dial-up point.

There are several Internet providers who have set out to build their own networks and sell Internet access via these on a number of levels. All of these providers are members of the CIX, the Commercial Internet Exchange. As the Internet is by definition a network of networks, this is hardly surprising. If no one built a network, there would not be any networks to join together. Every provider has to find someone to connect to, and most traffic in the UK goes through one of the big suppliers somewhere down the line.

Pipex and EUNet are two of the main providers, with Pipex putting a lot of money raised by its parent, Unipalm, into building a coherent network and linking into continental and global partners.

JANET is obviously the largest network in the UK, with a large client base consisting of the universities. For years the university budgets were top sliced to fund the academic network, with the result that good connectivity found its way to most sites. Unfortunately, for years only computing and science faculties at most sites were interested and prepared to invest their own money in local infrastructure. This has resulted in arts and humanities being left way behind in the network league. The Internet has become more and more of a medium, demanding content providers to drive it. The systems operators who invented the tools and resources need to relinquish some control to designers, theorists and publishers.

Conferencing plus

AppleLink

AppleLink, currently being replaced by e-World, is Apple's expensive and limited online service. Considered essential for developers and dealers, it does contain a wealth of useful information – if you can find it. Internet access is limited to e-mail exchange. If you have access via work it is a start, but not really much use if you want any sort of Internet access.

Compulink

Compulink, previously known as CIX, is a veteran of the UK online scene, offering multiple conferences on all subjects under the sun. If you want a basic Internet service with a lot of support, this is the sort of system for you. They reject the term Bulletin Board for the service, with some justification. Internet access is limited but usable, with Usenet groups and full e-mail. You will meet a lot of people here, and it is fairly cheap, though as they have time-based charges, not as cheap or as much fun as a full dial-up Internet feed. Compulink has the feeling of a club, and if you are a clubby type you may enjoy this – to others it will be a nightmare. You can Telnet in at

    cix.compulink.co.uk

which means cheap access from around the world, assuming you have some other means of getting on the Internet.

CompuServe

CompuServe (CIS) are making great efforts to be seen as part of, if not THE, Informaion Superhighway. Their current slogan, 'Driving the SuperHighway' gives the impression that they are out there in the forefront of Internet development. In fact, although it has over a million subscribers, CIS is very badly connected to the Internet. Until very recently they had no interest whatsoever in making any effort to provide connectivity. E-mail can be passed back and forth fairly easily, but CompuServe users have to pay for the privilege of receiving it.

CIS has recently attached itself to the Internet via Telnet, that is, you can now Telnet to your CIS account from the Internet. CompuServe Information Service Fee-Based Services

    telnet://compuserve.com

This gateway allows members to access the CompuServe Information Service directly from the Internet. However, this plunges you back into a text version of CompuServe, negating any benefit that the graphical interfaces which are available may give them. Anyone reading CIS advertising and buying an account to 'drive the SuperHighway' will be confused to say the least. However, if you are a CompuServe user, there are a number of excellent information areas that relate to the Internet and Information Superhighway matters. No doubt CompuServe will expand their offerings in the near future – watch this space.

Internet provision for individuals and small companies

Until a year or so back and the advent of Demon, individuals or small companies who wanted to use the Internet had almost no choice – pay hugely or forget it. The arrival of Demon changed all of that with the famous 'Internet for a tenner a month' dial-up SLIP or PPP service. Suddenly hundreds and now thousands of people could gain full access to every Internet tool and service available. Of course this has caused many problems, some of them the result of an over successful service. Demon have at times struggled to keep up with demand. That said, a new world has opened up and its success has brought other players into the field. Cityscape's much more recent service uses Pipex's network of POPs, as does the BBC's nascent Networking Club. All in all, cheap and effective Internet access has never looked better in the UK.

Educational sector

JANET

The University sector network in the UK, the Joint Academic Network (JANET), has been growing and mutating since the 1970s. Originally built as an X.25 network, it long intended to migrate to an internationally agreed standard known as OSI. However, during OSI's protracted gestation period the Internet by *force majeure* became an unstoppable force. In 1991 JANET introduced an Internet Protocol (IP) service known as JIPS. This has proved so successful, it now looks likely that JANET will become a full IP network, that is a full part of the Internet.

Since the old polytechnics became universities, the membership of JANET has grown dramatically. Colleges of Higher Education, research institutes and some libraries are members of JANET. Recent growth has included industrial research units and commercial suppliers. There is a steadily increasing amount of traffic between the commercial Internet providers and JANET, traffic that has lead to concern in some quarters about funding and commercialization factors.

Edex

In the US more and more schools have started to come onto the Internet, encouraged by the government which has an ambitious plan to create a full educational network. In the UK the situation is somewhat different. Things are starting to change, although underfunding and constant changes in services have somewhat undermined early confidence in online services.

Schools in the UK do not have much choice in Internet provision, though obviously they can use any commercial providers, albeit with security, cost and access qualifications.

The Education Exchange (Edex) has provided Internet access to schools since January 1994. The service gives schools an Internet node address and access from a local number in most urban locations. Forums, discussion groups and lessons in sending e-mail are all free and are organized as part of the service.

The education department at the BBC has launched an ambitious plan to offer Internet access and bulletin board support to thousands of individuals throughout the UK during 1994. Pipex, full IP Internet accounts will be offered for under £15 a month. Pipex will be building a nationwide network of POPs to support this ambitious move. Although launched as an educational and informational service, it is bound to have many attractions for individuals. It seems there will be no bar to buying in and ignoring the BBC element to acquire a full supported Internet feed.

Choosing a provider

Choosing what sort of connection you want can seem daunting, though I suspect that many people know before they start what they want. Cost is a deciding factor, though there are other considerations such as speed, ease of use and support. You may only want to exchange e-mail with other users. E-mail is the most successful online service and Internet access means that you can exchange e-mail with users on thousands of networks that are not strictly part of the Internet as well as with users directly on the Internet. It may be that you only ever will need to send and receive mail from people who use commercial systems such as CompuServe or that you want to be able to contact users on a huge variety of systems. Generally, Internet mail access will give you ultimate flexibility. Just having access to a bulletin board in your area that offers Internet e-mail exchange may be worth its weight in gold. On the other hand, if you have a CompuServe account and think this will do for all you e-mail exchange, remember that CompuServe charge for all 'external' mail delivered to you.

You can do a lot more with Internet e-mail than just exchange words. Any files such as images, texts, software can in theory be 'attached' to the mail. Files can also be retrieved from anonymous FTP sites by the use of FTP mail servers. You can also use most other Internet tools such as Gopher and World Wide Web via e-mail, though this is a slow method.

UK Internet providers' list

The following listing covers every organisation that provides Internet access in the UK. Internet access here is defined as a minimum of e-mail exchange between the user and other Internet connected individuals. For many people, this will be all that is wanted, and there are some very good minimal providers about, from local bulletin boards to CompuServe and Exnet. However, most people will want access to more tools than e-mail – that is what makes the Internet a living, vital resource. These listings are not exhaustive, and it is very difficult trying to find like to compare with like. I have attempted to give an outline idea of what is on offer by choosing a range of services to check for each company. Further information is listed in a generic Info box.

Internet Access

This section checks for nine services that you might expect an Internet provider to give you access to. Obviously, full access providers will by definition allow you access to all of these and more. A positive result here does not mean that the provider runs these services, just that you will be able to access them from the service. There are also many services that are provided which are not listed here. See the Info. box for more information.

Service access

This is a listing of how you use the services provided. There is no listing for the means of connectivity to the service, it is assumed that this will be via a dial-up phone line or, sometimes, via a dedicated line.

BBS/Shell indicates a 'log-on' type service of some sort, where you will be able to make choices from a menu, or use a local operating system.

UUCP indicates that the provider offers access using UUCP software to collect mail and/or Usenet news.

SLIP/PPP indicates that the provider is offering a SLIP or PPP line. That is, you will become a part of the Internet using connectivity software, and you will have your own IP address.

TELNET indicates that you can reach this service using Telnet, for example if you have another account elsewhere.

Other services

PDN. This indicates that the service is available via a public data network such as Tymnet or Dialplus. These allow you to make long-distance calls at a substantially cheaper rate. Charges for the PDN are usually added on to the provider's charges, though sometimes they are inclusive.

Leased line. The provider can offer a 'leased line' service. The leased line is generally provided by BT, for which you pay an installation and rental charge. You will also pay the provider a charge for 'plugging in' this line to the Internet. Leased lines generally run at 64K.

Domain registration. This indicates that the provider is willing to register you a high-level domain, usually for a fee.

Consultancy. The provider company can provide some form of consultancy related to Internet connectivity.

User sub-domain. This relates to providers such as Demon and Cityscape who provide you with a domain under their registerd domain. For example, Demon customers become 'username.demon.co.uk'. The user chooses the 'username' part of the address. They then use anyname@username.demon.co.uk.

Online Contact

AnonFTP indicates the provider runs an FTP site which contains full information. This can be accessed using FTP software and the login name and password of anon.

Gopher indicates the existence of a Gopher site with further information.

World Wide Web indicates the existence of a World Wide Web site.

Dial-Up gives the number for a dial-up service, where you may be able to see a demo or join the service. Default settings for your comms program are 8-N-1 unless indicated.

Local access points

These are the STD area codes that you can use to access this service. You will have to check whether this is a local or long-distance call for you. Some BBS and Shell access providers use a Public Data Network (PDN) for long distance callers. With a PDN you call a local number and reach the service you want over a cheaper data network. BT's service is called Dialplus and costs about three pence a minute for use. Services such as GreenNet and Edex will add the Dialplus charges onto your bill automatically. You can get a list of all Dialplus local numbers from BT at 0800 282 444 or from any service that uses it.

Choosing a provider

Choosing a provider can look daunting. However, there are almost certainly a number of decisions you can make immediately – thus eliminating many of the available choices. After that it is down to choice between services.

You can see from the following list that there is a range of commercial (and not so commercial) providers now operating – and more are joining in almost weekly. This Internet UK list attempts to cover any system that offers Internet e-mail exchange upwards.

Although our choice here in the UK is growing, you will still find that whatever your demands, you will end up with a choice between a couple of providers. Even there, you will find that competition is hard to find – as similar services are sold very differently.

Cityscape		Internet access		Service access	
Cityscape Internet Services Ltd		USENET	Y	BBS/SHELL	N
59 Wycliffe Rd		TELNET	Y	UUCP	Y
Cambridge		FTP	Y	SLIP/PPP	Y
CB1 3JE		GOPHER	Y	TELNET	N
UK		WWW	Y		
		IRC	Y	**Other services**	
Voice:	0223 566950	ARCHIE	Y	PDN	N
Fax:	0223 566951	MUD	Y	LEASED LINE	N
E-mail	sales@cityscape.co.uk	WAIS	Y	DOMAIN REGISTRATION	Y
				CONSULTANCY	Y
				USER SUB-DOMAIN	Y

Online contact		Local access points
WWW	http://www.cityscape.co.uk	London, Edinburgh, Manchester, Bristol, Birmingham, Cambridge

Rates	Other information
£50 initial charge/£180 p.a. for IP gold £400 p.a. for e-mail MHS gateway £999 first year/£599 subsequent years	SLIP, PPP, e-mail, UUCP, news feed, mail feed, WWW, FTP, telnet, indirect FTP, user groups

Demon

		Internet access		Service access	
Demon Internet Ltd		USENET	Y	BBS/SHELL	N
42 Hendon Lane		TELNET	Y	UUCP	N
London		FTP	Y	SLIP/PPP	Y
N3 1TT		GOPHER	Y	TELNET	Y
UK		WWW	Y		
		IRC	Y	**Other services**	
Voice:	0813490063	ARCHIE	Y	PDN	N
Fax:		MUD	Y	LEASED LINE	Y
E-mail	internet@demon.net	WAIS	Y	DOMAIN REGISTRATION	Y
				CONSULTANCY	Y
				USER SUB-DOMAIN	Y

Online contact

ANONFTP   ftp.demon.co.uk

Local access points

London, Warrington, Edinburgh, Reading

Rates

£12.50 joining fee £10 per month + VAT collected monthly from credited card. Companies pay annually in advance

Other information

mail feed, news feed, OLRs, ftp SLIP.PPP.leased line, irc open ftp archive, telnet

Direct Connection

		Internet access		Service access	
		USENET	Y	BBS/SHELL	Y
		TELNET	Y	UUCP	Y
		FTP	Y	SLIP/PPP	Y
		GOPHER	Y	TELNET	Y
		WWW	Y		
		IRC		**Other services**	
Voice:	081317 0100	ARCHIE		PDN	N
Fax:		MUD		LEASED LINE	N
E-mail	helpdesk@dircon.co.uk	WAIS		DOMAIN REGISTRATION	N
				CONSULTANCY	N
				USER SUB-DOMAIN	N

Rates

Various levels from £10 per month + VAT

Other information

Telnet, ftp, E-mail, Usenet (multiple OLRs), gopher, archie, WWW, FAX gateway, IRC, computer newswire, shell or meun driven, Hytenet, SLIP/PPP (with POP or SMTP), terminal access, FTP space, Batch FTP, conferencing, chat, off-line news and E-mail. (Helldiver, QWK, ZipNews), UUCP (mail/news) feeds, rolgin

Direct Line

		Internet access		Service access	
UK		USENET	Y	BBS/SHELL	Y
		TELNET	N	UUCP	N
		GOPHER	N	SLIP/PPP	N
		FTP	N	TELNET	N
		WWW	N		
		IRC	N	**Other services**	
Voice:		ARCHIE	N	PDN	N
Fax:		MUD	N	LEASED LINE	N
E-mail	sysop@ps.com	WAIS	N	DOMAIN REGISTRATION	N
				CONSULTANCY	N
				USER SUB-DOMAIN	N

Online contact

Local access points

081

Rates

£25 + VAT for full system and Internet access
All + VAT

Other information

Mail feed, News feed, QWK Offline system. Up to date local file areas for DOS, Windows, OS/2, Mac, Z88 & Psion. Newsbytes, Sat news, Satellite Journal, Soft & hardware sales, RIP/Ansi/Mono graphics, games

EUNet

Kent R & D Business Centre
Giles Lane
Canterbury
CT2 7PB
UK

Voice: 0227 475497
Fax: 0227 227 475478
E-mail sales@britain. eu.net

Internet access		Service access	
USENET	Y	BBS/SHELL	N
TELNET		UUCP	Y
FTP		SLIP/PPP	Y
GOPHER		TELNET	Y
WWW		**Other services**	
IRC			
ARCHIE		PDN	N
MUD		LEASED LINE	Y
WAIS		DOMAIN REGISTRATION	Y
		CONSULTANCY	Y
		USER SUB-DOMAIN	N

Online contact

Local access points

Birmingham, Bracknell, Cambridge, Canterbury, Glasgow, London

Rates

IP DIAL-UP: £150 per month/£300 setup
all + VAT

Other information

Part of EUNet, trans-global Internet access provider. In-house
network

Exnet

37 Honley Road
Catford
London
SE6 2HY
UK

Voice: 081 244 0077
Fax: 081 244 0078
E-mail info@exnet.com

Internet access		Service access	
USENET	Y	BBS/SHELL	Y
TELNET	Y	UUCP	Y
FTP	Y	SLIP/PPP	N
GOPHER	Y	TELNET	N
WWW	N	**Other services**	
IRC	N		
ARCHIE	Y	PDN	N
MUD	N	LEASED LINE	N
WAIS	N	DOMAIN REGISTRATION	N
		CONSULTANCY	N
		USER SUB-DOMAIN	N

Online contact

Local access points

081

Rates

Basic: £60 p.a. UUCP: £100 p.a.
Full feed: £300 p.a. All + VAT

Other information

Shell, mail feed, newsfeed, USENET, e-mail. FTPmail, batched ftp (soon),
user groups, UUCP, menu, NTP, terminal access, special arrangments
for overseas clients, archie, gopher, FTP and telnet

Greennet

23 Bevenden Street
London
N1 6BH

Voice: 071 608 3040
Fax: 071 253 0801
E-mail suppot@gn.apc.org

Internet access		Service access	
USENET	Y	BBS/SHELL	Y
TELNET	Y	UUCP	Y
FTP	Y	SLIP/PPP	N
GOPHER	Y	TELNET	N
WWW	N	**Other services**	
IRC	N		
ARCHIE	N	PDN	Y
MUD	N	LEASED LINE	N
WAIS	N	DOMAIN REGISTRATION	N
		CONSULTANCY	N
		USER SUB-DOMAIN	N

Online contact

DIAL UP 071 608 2622

Local access points

Rates

Non-commercial: registration £15;
monthly £5; connect 4 or 6p per minute
Commercial: registration £30;
monthly £30; connect 10p per minute

Other information

E- mail, conferenc, WAIS, Telnet, menu, Usenet, indirect FTP,
fax, off-peak, gopher. Part of the Association of progressive
Communications (APC)

Infocom Interactive

The Davinson group International, UKmail
White Bridge House
Old Bath Road
Charvil
RG10 9QJ
UK
Voice: 0850 920041
Fax: 0734 320988
E-mail

Internet access

USENET	Y
TELNET	N
GOPHER	N
WWW	N
IRC	N
ARCHIE	N
MUD	N
WAIS	N

Service access

BBS/SHELL	Y
UUCP	Y
SLIP/PPP	N
TELNET	N

Other services

PDN	N
LEASED LINE	N
DOMAIN REGISTRATION	Y
CONSULTANCY	Y
USER SUB-DOMAIN	Y

Rates

Contact UKmail for full details

Other information

UUCP Feeds to single-user/multi-user sites. MX Forwarding, Domain Registration (UK or Worlwide) 'AUTO NEWS', FREE UUCP software download for Acorn, Amiga, Atari,IBM. Mac & Unix Systems. use 'getuucp' to access a menu driven download server.interactive bbs access offering teletext, menu front-end, offline MAIL/NEWS

On-line

Online Entertainment Ltd
642 Lea Bridge Road
London
E10 6AP
UK

Voice: 081 558 6114
Fax: 081 558 391
E-mail jon™on-line.co.uk4

Internet access

USENET	Y
TELNET	Y
FTP	Y
GOPHER	N
WWW	N
IRC	N
ARCHIE	N
MUD	N
WAIS	N

Service access

BBS/SHELL	Y
UUCP	N
SLIP/PPP	N
TELNET	N

Other services

PDN	N
LEASED LINE	N
DOMAIN REGISTRATION	N
CONSULTANCY	N
USER SUB-DOMAIN	N

Rates

Full membership: £9.99 per month
or £2.20 per hour non subscribers

Other information

Menu front-end, indirect ftp, telnet, bbs, Usenet, e-mail, OLRs, chat system, games

PC User Group Connect

Voice: info@ibmpcug.co.uk
Fax:
E-mail

Internet access

USENET	Y
TELNET	Y
FTP	Y
GOPHER	Y
WWW	Y
IRC	Y
ARCHIE	N
MUD	Y
WAIS	N

Service access

BBS/SHELL	Y
UUCP	Y
SLIP/PPP	N
TELNET	N

Other services

PDN	N
LEASED LINE	N
DOMAIN REGISTRATION	N
CONSULTANCY	N
USER SUB-DOMAIN	N

Online contact

Local access points

081

Rates

Non-members, e-mail, FTP & Telnet
£65 + vat
£10 joining fee

Other information

Ftp, telnet, bbs, irc, feeds, World Wide Web, gopher, open ftp Archive, UUCP, Batch FTP movie database server movie@ibmpcug.co.uk, games including a mud and chat

PC User Group Winnet

UK

Internet access		Service access	
USENET	N	BBS/SHELL	N
TELNET	N	UUCP	N
FTP	N	SLIP/PPP	N
GOPHER	N	TELNET	N
WWW	N		
IRC	N	**Other services**	
ARCHIE	N	PDN	N
MUD	N	LEASED LINE	N
WAIS	N	DOMAIN REGISTRATION	N
		CONSULTANCY	N
		USER SUB-DOMAIN	Y

Voice: 081 863 1191
Fax:
E-mail help@win-uk.net

Online contact

ANONFTP	ftp.ibmpcug.co.uk/pub/winnet/

Local access points

London

Rates

£3.25 per hour + VAT

Other information

WinNET software for Windows e-mail system. Simple to use

Pipex

Pipex Ltd
216 Cambridge Science Park
Milton Road
Cambridge
CB4 4WA
UK

Internet access		Service access	
USENET	Y	BBS/SHELL	N
TELNET	Y	UUCP	N
FTP	Y	SLIP/PPP	Y
GOPHER	Y	TELNET	Y
WWW	Y		
IRC	Y	**Other services**	
ARCHIE	Y	PDN	N
MUD	Y	LEASED LINE	Y
WAIS	Y	DOMAIN REGISTRATION	Y
		CONSULTANCY	Y
		USER SUB-DOMAIN	N

Voice: 0223 250120
Fax: 0223 250121
E-mail pipex@pipex.net

Online contact

ANONFTP	ftp.pipex.net/pub/FAQ/	WWW	http://www.pipex.net

Rates

Contact Pipex for full information

Other information

Leased lines, routers, modems, encryption, network management, mail feed, news feed, Usenet, e-mail, radio, mail, Windows mail reader, X.400 ADMD, X.25, batch FTP, FTP, indirect FTP Telnet, PAD. rlogin, SLIP, PPP, fax gateway, gopher, WAIS, IRC, WWW, FTP space, ISDN, UUCP, NTP, PSS, Class B & Class C registrations, Domain Name registration, Third-Party on-line services, consultancy

Sound and Vision

Internet access		Service access	
USENET	Y	BBS/SHELL	Y
TELNET	N	UUCP	N
FTP	N	SLIP/PPP	N
GOPHER	N	TELNET	N
WWW	N		
IRC	N	**Other services**	
ARCHIE	N	PDN	N
MUD	N	LEASED LINE	N
WAIS	N	DOMAIN REGISTRATION	N
		CONSULTANCY	N
		USER SUB-DOMAIN	N

Voice: 0932 253131
Fax:
E-mail rob@sound.demon.co.uk

Online contact

Local access points

0932

Rates

£10 + VAT per annum for e-mail/usenet + minimal BBS access

Other information

Huge BBS, Usenet and Internet E-mail feeds

Specialix

Specialix International
3 Wintersells Road
Byfleet
KT14 7LF
UK

Voice:	0932 354354
Fax:	0932 352781
E-mail	keith@specialix.co.uk

Internet access

USENET	Y
TELNET	N
FTP	N
GOPHER	N
WWW	N
IRC	N
ARCHIE	N
MUD	N
WAIS	N

Service access

BBS/SHELL	N
UUCP	Y
SLIP/PPP	N
TELNET	N

Other services

PDN	N
LEASED LINE	N
DOMAIN REGISTRATION	N
CONSULTANCY	N
USER SUB-DOMAIN	N

Local Access Points

0932

Rates

£200 per year

Other information

Provide full Usenet feed, no other service

Spud's Xanadu

Voice:	
Fax:	
E-mail	

Internet access

USENET	Y
TELNET	N
FTP	N
GOPHER	N
WWW	N
IRC	Y
ARCHIE	Y
MUD	Y
WAIS	Y

Service access

BBS/SHELL	Y
UUCP	Y
SLIP/PPP	N
TELNET	Y

Other services

PDN	N
LEASED LINE	N
DOMAIN REGISTRATION	N
CONSULTANCY	N
USER SUB-DOMAIN	N

Online contact

Dialup   0203 364436/362560

Local access points

0203

Rates

Free

Other information

Shell, menu front-end, Usenet, e-mail, OLRs, FTPmail, FAX gateway,
bbs, games, chat system

Hackney Host

info@ibmpcug.co.uk

Voice:	
Fax:	
E-mail	

Internet access

USENET
TELNET
FTP
GOPHER
WWW
IRC
ARCHIE
MUD
WAIS

Service access

BBS/SHELL
UUCP
SLIP/PPP
TELNET

Other services

PDN
LEASED LINE
DOMAIN REGISTRATION
CONSULTANCY
USER SUB-DOMAIN

Online contact

Local access points

081

Strathclyde Host

Internet access	Service access
USENET	BBS/SHELL
TELNET	UUCP
FTP	SLIP/PPP
GOPHER	TELNET
WWW	
IRC	**Other services**
ARCHIE	PDN
MUD	LEASED LINE
WAIS	DOMAIN REGISTRATION
	CONSULTANCY
	USER SUB-DOMAIN

Voice:
Fax:
E-mail

Online contact

Local access points

Rates

Other information

Manchester Host

30 Naples Street
Manchester
M4 4DB
UK

Internet access		Service access	
USENET	N	BBS/SHELL	Y
TELNET	N	UUCP	N
FTP	N	SLIP/PPP	N
GOPHER	N	TELNET	N
WWW	N		
IRC		**Other services**	
ARCHIE		PDN	Y
MUD		LEASED LINE	N
WAIS		DOMAIN REGISTRATION	N
		CONSULTANCY	Y
		USER SUB-DOMAIN	N

Voice: 061 839 4212
Fax: 061 839 4214
E-mail   admin@mcr1.geonet.de

Local access points

DialPlus

Rates

Registration £25
Monthley fee £10 including £4 usage
12 p.m. peak 08p p.m. off-peak

Other information

Part of the Poptel network and linked to GeoNet. Access to bulletin boards, databases etc.

Janet

Internet access	Service access
USENET	BBS/SHELL
TELNET	UUCP
FTP	SLIP/PPP
GOPHER	TELNET
WWW	
IRC	**Other services**
ARCHIE	PDN
MUD	LEASED LINE
WAIS	DOMAIN REGISTRATION
	CONSULTANCY
	USER SUB-DOMAIN

Voice:
Fax:
E-mail

Local access points

All universities, many higher education Institutes, research establishments etc.

Rates

N/a

Compulink

Compulink Information Exchange
The Sanctuary
Oakhill Grove
Surbiton
KT6 6DU
UK
Voice: 081 390 8446
Fax: 081 390 6561
E-mail cixadmin@cix.compulink.co.uk

Internet access

USENET	Y
TELNET	Y
FTP	Y
GOPHER	Y
WWW	Y
IRC	Y
ARCHIE	Y
MUD	N
WAIS	N

Service access

BBS/SHELL	Y
UUCP	N
SLIP/PPP	N
TELNET	Y

Other services

PDN	N
LEASED LINE	N
DOMAIN REGISTRATION	Y
CONSULTANCY	Y
USER SUB-DOMAIN	Y

Online contact

ANONFTP	cix.compulink.co.uk
WWW	http://cix.compulink.co.uk
DIALUP	081 390 1244

Local access points

081

Rates

£25 registration (includes manual)
£2.40 per hour/off peak
£3.20 per hour/peak
£6.25 monthly minimum in advance

Other information

CIX is a conferencing system, like a bulletin board. Internet access is from the system with acces to telnet, ftp, ping, finger. There is a fair amount of support available from specialist forums. Files that are ftp'd have to be subsequently downloaded using Zmodem etc. Access is available via telnet from the Internet

Compuserve

Compuserve Information Services
1 Redcliffe Street
PO Box 676
Bristol   BS99 1YN
UK

Voice: 0800 298 458
Fax:
E-mail 70006.101@compuserve.com

Internet access

USENET	N
TELNET	Y
FTP	N
GOPHER	N
WWW	N
IRC	N
ARCHIE	N
MUD	N
WAIS	N

Service access

BBS/SHELL	N
UUCP	N
SLIP/PPP	N
TELNET	N

Other services

PDN	
LEASED LINE	N
DOMAIN REGISTRATION	N
CONSULTANCY	N
USER SUB-DOMAIN	N

Online contact

Local access aoints

See chapter 4

Rates

$8.95 per month basic
free connect for basic service
comms surcharge via Compuserve numbers in UK and Europe – free offpeaks /$7.70 per hour peak

Other information

Huge American bulletin board system with 1.5 million users. CIS has long exchanged information with the Internet, but only recently has moved to open itself further. You can now telnet to Compuserve

Embassy BBS

Voice:
Fax:
E-mail

Internet access

USENET	
TELNET	
FTP	
GOPHER	
WWW	
IRC	
ARCHIE	
MUD	
WAIS	

Service access

BBS/SHELL	Y
UUCP	
SLIP/PPP	
TELNET	Y

Other services

PDN	
LEASED LINE	
DOMAIN REGISTRATION	
CONSULTANCY	
USER SUB-DOMAIN	

Novalink

Internet access		Service access	
USENET		BBS/SHELL	
TELNET		UUCP	
FTP		SLIP/PPP	
GOPHER		TELNET	
WWW			
IRC		**Other services**	
ARCHIE		PDN	
MUD		LEASED LINE	
WAIS		DOMAIN REGISTRATION	
		CONSULTANCY	
		USER SUB-DOMAIN	

Voice:
Fax:
E-mail

Online contact   **Local access points**

Rates   **Other information**

Psilink

Performance Systems International, Inc.
510 Huntmar Park Drive
Herndon
22070
USA

Voice: +1 703 620 6651
Fax: +1 703 620 4586
E-mail

Internet access		Service access	
USENET	Y	BBS/SHELL	N
TELNET	N	UUCP	N
FTP	Y	SLIP/PPP	N
GOPHER	N	TELNET	N
WWW	N		
IRC		**Other services**	
ARCHIE		PDN	N
MUD		LEASED LINE	N
WAIS		DOMAIN REGISTRATION	N
		CONSULTANCY	N
		USER SUB-DOMAIN	N

Online contact

ANONFTP   ftp://ftp.psi.com/psilink/

Local access points

071 437 4393   017 437 4055

Rates

$18 per hour, minimum 5 minutes charge

Other information

US based Internet access systems for PCs. 2400 baud access

BBC Networking Club

Internet access		Service access	
USENET	Y	BBS/SHELL	Y
TELNET	Y	UUCP	N
FTP	Y	SLIP/PPP	Y
GOPHER	Y	TELNET	Y
WWW	Y		
IRC		**Other services**	
ARCHIE		PDN	N
MUD		LEASED LINE	N
WAIS		DOMAIN REGISTRATION	N
		CONSULTANCY	N
		USER SUB-DOMAIN	N

Voice:
Fax:
E-mail   info@bbcnc.co.uk

Online contact

ANONFTP   ftp.bbcnc.co.uk
WWW   http://www.bbcnc.co.uk/

Local access points

Edex

The Education Exchange
2 Stroud Road
Wimbledon Park
SW19 8DQ
UK

Voice:	081 944 8021
Fax:	081 944 5029
E-mail	info@galviz.co.uk

Internet access

USENET	Y
TELNET	Y
FTP	Y
GOPHER	N
WWW	N
IRC	N
ARCHIE	N
MUD	N
WAIS	N

Service access

BBS/SHELL	Y
UUCP	N
SLIP/PPP	N
TELNET	Y

Other services

PDN	Y
LEASED LINE	N
DOMAIN REGISTRATION	N
CONSULTANCY	N
USER SUB-DOMAIN	N

Online contact

DIAL UP	081 944 8026

Rates

£70 per year full service + £2.20 per hour

Local access points

DialPlus

Other information

File Library and Database access services; cheaper rate for Special Needs Establishments; schools projects available

Motiv Systems Ltd

22 Hills Road
Cambridge
CB2 1JP
UK

Voice:	0223 576318
Fax:	0223 576319
E-mail	motiv@motiv.demon.co.uk

Internet access

USENET	Y
TELNET	Y
FTP	Y
GOPHER	Y
WWW	Y
IRC	Y
ARCHIE	Y
MUD	Y
WAIS	Y

Service access

BBS/SHELL	N
UUCP	N
SLIP/PPP	Y
TELNET	N

Other services

PDN	N
LEASED LINE	Y
DOMAIN REGISTRATION	Y
CONSULTANCY	Y
USER SUB-DOMAIN	N

Rates

Other information

Consultancy; integration of LANs with Internet: resale of Demon services to clients

CNS

Brooklands Close
Sunbury-on-Thames
TW16 7DX
UK

Voice:	+44 932 814 800
Fax:	+44 932 814 808
E-mail	cns@chernikeeff.co.uk

Internet access

USENET
TELNET
FTP
GOPHER
WWW
IRC
ARCHIE
MUD
WAIS

Service access

BBS/SHELL
UUCP
SLIP/PPP
TELNET

Other services

PDN
LEASED LINE
DOMAIN REGISTRATION
CONSULTANCY
USER SUB-DOMAIN

Mercury

Data Network Services
1 Riverbank Way
Great West Road
Brentford
TW8 9RS
UK
Voice: +44 81 914 6174
Fax: +44 81 914 6040
E-mail

Internet access

USENET	
TELNET	
FTP	
GOPHER	
WWW	
IRC	
ARCHIE	
MUD	
WAIS	

Service access

BBS/SHELL	
UUCP	
SLIP/PPP	
TELNET	

Other services

PDN	
LEASED LINE	
DOMAIN REGISTRATION	
CONSULTANCY	
USER SUB-DOMAIN	

Rates

Other information

Data Network Services, address as above

Applelink

UK

Voice:
Fax:
E-mail

Internet access

USENET	N
TELNET	N
FTP	N
GOPHER	N
WWW	N
IRC	N
ARCHIE	N
MUD	N
WAIS	N

Service access

BBS/SHELL	Y
UUCP	N
SLIP/PPP	N
TELNET	N

Other services

PDN	Y
LEASED LINE	N
DOMAIN REGISTRATION	N
CONSULTANCY	N
USER SUB-DOMAIN	N

Rates

Other information

See also e-world which will replace AppleLink during 1995

BT

UK

Voice:
Fax:
E-mail

Internet access

USENET	Y
TELNET	Y
FTP	Y
GOPHER	Y
WWW	Y
IRC	Y
ARCHIE	Y
MUD	Y
WAIS	Y

Service access

BBS/SHELL	N
UUCP	N
SLIP/PPP	Y
TELNET	N

Other services

PDN	Y
LEASED LINE	Y
DOMAIN REGISTRATION	Y
CONSULTANCY	N
USER SUB-DOMAIN	N

Online contact

Local access points

London, Leeds

Rates

Other information

Service to start Autumn 1994. Leased lines

Dungeon Network

3 Hazel Close
Mildenhall
IP28 7HU
UK

Voice: +44-638-711550
Fax:
E-mail info@dungeon.com

Internet access

USENET	Y
TELNET	Y
FTP	Y
GOPHER	Y
WWW	Y
IRC	Y
ARCHIE	Y
MUD	Y
WAIS	Y

Service access

BBS/SHELL	N
UUCP	N
SLIP/PPP	Y
TELNET	N

Other services

PDN	N
LEASED LINE	Y
DOMAIN REGISTRATION	N
CONSULTANCY	N
USER SUB-DOMAIN	Y

Online contact

ANONFTP	ftp.dungeon.com

Local access points

Cambridge

Rates

£14 per month standard service
£11.67 if paid in advance

Other information

Full usenet feed, Clarinet

E-world

UK

Voice:
Fax:
E-mail

Internet access

USENET
TELNET
FTP
GOPHER
WWW
IRC
ARCHIE
MUD
WAIS

Service access

BBS/SHELL
UUCP
SLIP/PPP
TELNET

Other services

PDN
LEASED LINE
DOMAIN REGISTRATION
CONSULTANCY
USER SUB-DOMAIN

Rates

Other information

Apple' replacement for AppleLink

Microland Internet

Trevan Designs Ltd
P O Box 13
Aldershot
GU12 6YX
UK

Voice: 0252 258841
Fax: 0252 25841
E-mail support@trevan.co.uk

Internet access

USENET	Y
TELNET	Y
FTP	Y
GOPHER	Y
WWW	Y
IRC	Y
ARCHIE	Y
MUD	Y
WAIS	Y

Service access

BBS/SHELL	Y
UUCP	Y
SLIP/PPP	Y
TELNET	N

Other services

PDN	N
LEASED LINE	Y
DOMAIN REGISTRATION	N
CONSULTANCY	N
USER SUB-DOMAIN	N

Online contact

DAILUP	0483 725905

Local access points

0891

Rates

Premium rate number or

Other information

Full Internet service via premium rate 0891 or subscriptions service; BBS

Kirklees Host

Field House
15 Wellington Road
Dewsbury
WF13 1HF
UK

Voice: 0924 457070
Fax: 0924 457072
E-mail admin™geo2.poptel.org

Internet access

USENET	Y
TELNET	Y
FTP	Y
GOPHER	Y
WWW	Y
IRC	Y
ARCHIE	Y
MUD	Y
WAIS	Y

Service access

BBS/SHELL	Y
UUCP	Y
SLIP/PPP	Y
TELNET	Y

Other services

PDN	Y
LEASED LINE	Y
DOMAIN REGISTRATION	N
CONSULTANCY	Y
USER SUB-DOMAIN	Y

Online contact

DIALUP	Guest accounts available

Local access points

Soft Solution-Poptel

25 Downham Road
London
N1 5AA
UK

Voice: 071 249 2948
Fax: 071 254 1102
E-mail poptel@geo2.poptel.org

Internet access

USENET	Y
TELNET	Y
FTP	Y
GOPHER	Y
WWW	Y
IRC	Y
ARCHIE	Y
MUD	N
WAIS	Y

Service access

BBS/SHELL	Y
UUCP	Y
SLIP/PPP	Y
TELNET	Y

Other services

PDN	Y
LEASED LINE	Y
DOMAIN REGISTRATION	N
CONSULTANCY	Y
USER SUB-DOMAIN	Y

Online contact

ANONFTP	Planned
GOPHER	Planned

Local access points

Rates

Contact Poptel

Other information

Provider of online services and full consultancy to not-for-profit sector.
Linked to GeoNet. Good database access and datbase publishing services

---

Ireland On-Line

UK

Voice:
Fax:
E-mail

Internet access

USENET	Y
TELNET	Y
FTP	Y
GOPHER	Y
WWW	Y
IRC	Y
ARCHIE	Y
MUD	Y
WAIS	Y

Service access

BBS/SHELL	Y
UUCP	Y
SLIP/PPP	N
TELNET	Y

Other services

PDN	N
LEASED LINE	N
DOMAIN REGISTRATION	N
CONSULTANCY	N
USER SUB-DOMAIN	N

Rates

From £25 per year

Other information

Eunet Traveller

Kruislaan 409
1098 S J
Amsterdam
The Netherlands

Voice:	+31 20 592 5109
Fax:	+31 20 592 5163
E-mail	traveller@EU.net

Internet access

USENET	N
TELNET	N
FTP	N
GOPHER	N
WWW	N
IRC	N
ARCHIE	N
MUD	N
WAIS	N

Service access

BBS/SHELL	Y
UUCP	N
SLIP/PPP	N
TELNET	N

Other services

PDN	Y
LEASED LINE	N
DOMAIN REGISTRATION	N
CONSULTANCY	N
USER SUB-DOMAIN	N

Rates

Sign-up fee of ECU 30
ECU 30 per minute
Includes 3 hours connection time
ECU 10 per hour

Other information

Dial-up access to your Internet access account from around Europe.
Not TCP/IP but uses comms package to connect – then whatever, e.g.
telnet or ftp. No use of IP packages from your machine over ET

Tools, resources and services

Information tools are the powerhouses of the Internet. Learning the ins and outs of the tools, what software to use, where the prime resources are and how to build your own powerlists is a crucial stage. Here, each tool is introduced and related to the Internet as a whole. UK specific resources relating to that tool are listed, followed by more specific information available from around the Internet.

Once you have set up an Internet connection of your choice, you by definition have access to many of the resources of the global Internet. How you see and interact with these resources will depend on what connection you have and what software you are using. All new Internet users go through a time of confusion as they try to find dry land amid the heaving sea. This can be a time of panic, confusion and despair. It does pass though and before long services such as e-mail and FTP become second nature to the intrepid surfer. It is little short of amazing how much of a relief it can be to start receiving e-mail or to FTP your first file. From the stability of these platforms, users can survey the mighty oceans and make decisions about where they would like to go next.

UK flavour Internet

You might be interested in gossip, in databases or in the World Wide Web. You might decide to research using mailing lists or to hang out in some of the seedier Usenet groups. Your Internet life will certainly start to consist of a honed selection from all the available tools. Although there seem to be a huge variety of softwares, all Internet users come to an understanding with the beast. They take from it what they need and leave the rest for others to fathom. I often think the co-operative phrase 'to each according to their needs, from each according to their abilities' is a good description of the prevailing ethos of the nets.

From utter newbie (newcomer), you will find yourself before long offering help, encouragement and advice to newer newbies. If you are at the start stage this may seem far-fetched, but I can assure you it will happen. You will bring to the nets your own knowledge and expertise and almost without realizing it you will be drawn in to a spirit of helpful co-opertion. Or, you may be the Donald Trump of the Internet – but somehow it never seems to work like that.

General network information

There is a huge amount of general information out there – how to connect, how to find software, how to communicate. From Training Materials projects through to idiosyncratic information lists, these are some of the best starting points. The famous December and Yanoff lists are essentials which will give you a ready reckoner from whence all else flows. FTP and print them out for quick reference. Frequently Asked Question (FAQ) lists are available on every subject imaginable and should generally be your first stop for information.

Clearinghouse Internet Resource Guides

The Clearinghouse for Subject-Oriented Internet Resource Guides is a joint effort of the University of Michigan's University Library and the School of Information and Library Studies (SILS). Its goal is to collect and make widely available guides to Internet resources which are subject-oriented. These guides are produced by members of the Internet community and by SILS students who participate in the Internet Resource Discovery project.

Many useful guides to Internet resources are organized by format or by information delivery tool. For example, guides have been produced which solely describe Listservs, or online library catalogs. However, as the scope of available information on the Internet broadens and as the numbers of formats and delivery systems grow, it becomes increasingly necessary to organize information by subject.

Many Internet users are more likely to search for information by subject than by a specific tool or format.

Subject organization also provides a context for Internet resources and a means for comparing them.

Internet trainers can combine these guides with their own teaching skills and general knowledge of the Internet. This allows trainers to reach audiences they may previously have shied away from due to a lack of subject expertise.

System builders can use these guides to help determine what resources exist and which of those are of sufficient quality to include in their systems. For example, a Gopher server administrator could use a guide as a 'blueprint' for designing a Gopher branch on a specific subject. Because the guides are not tied to a specific format, a World Wide Web administrator may find the same guide useful.

You can FTP these guides from

```
ftp://una.hh.lib.umich.edu/inetdirsstacks
```

or by gopher at

```
gopher://una.hh.lib.umich.edu/11/inetdirs
gopher://gopher.lib.umich.edu/What's New and Featured
Resources/Clearinghouse
```

Access these guides on the World Wide Web at

```
http://http2.sils.umich.edu/~lou/chhome.html or
http://www.lib.umich.edu/chhome.html
```

UK resource list in Turbogopher

Questions and comments to Louis Rosenfeld

`i-guides@umich.edu`

December's Guide to Internet Resources

This is the first crucial guide to the Internet

`ftp://ftp.rpi.edu/pub/communications`

Also available on the World Wide Web in the following parts:
Information sources

`http://www.rpi.edu/Internet/Guides/decemj/icmc/toc2.html`

Internet tools

`http://www.rpi.edu/Internet/Guides/decemj/itools/toc2.html`

E-mail guide

How to get e-mail from network to network

`ftp://csd4.csd.uwm.edu/pub/internetwork-mail/guide`

FTP sites

A list of anonymous FTP sites is available from

`ftp://ftp.ucsc.edu/public/ftpsites`
`http://www.ii.uib.no/~magnus/paml.html`

InterNIC Gopher

InterNIC is the main information store for the Internet. This is a gateway to a huge
amount of information including FTP archives, Gopher servers and other pointers

`gopher://is.internic.net/`

Kevin Hughes' *Entering the World-Wide Web: A Guide to Cyberspace*

This is available at

`http://www.eit.com/web/www.guide/`

Or FTP it from

`ftp://ftp.eit.com/pub/web.guide/` directory.

The Guide is intended to be used as a beginner's guide to the World-Wide Web in
a hands-on sort of way and offers answers to many basic questions about the Web.
Web statistics, software pointers, information on hypertext and hypermedia and
other topics are covered.

`kevinh@eit.com`

Mailing lists list

This is a list of news groups and mailing lists all over the Internet. It is a large file, however, so approach with caution

```
ftp://ftp.sura.net/pub/nic/interest-groups.txt
```

Merit Internet Cruise

A great interactive tour of the Internet for Mac or PC is available at

```
ftp://nic.merit.edu/internet/resources/MERIT INTERNET CRUISE
```

This is a very colourful interactive tour comparing the Internet to the ocean. It covers an introduction to FTP, Gopher, Telnet, Archie, WAIS, e-mail. The Windows version requires an IBM-compatible PC, XGA or XGA-compatible adaptor set to display 256 colours at 640 x 480; Microsoft Windows version 3.1; about 1.5 MB disk space; 2 Mb RAM minimum.

The Mac version requires a Mac II or higher; a colour monitor; a high-density disk drive; system 6.07 or higher; approximately 2 Mb disk space; 4 Mb of RAM.

The file comes in .hqx format which means it is in binhex format. You need a utility such as BinHex 4.0, Compact Pro, or a Stuffit program to make it of use to you. This is a very approachable list for Web browsers.

Training Materials Gopher

This is an experimental Gopher server set up to promote and encourage network training. Trainmat is an initiative of the Network Training Materials Project, a joint enterprise of NISP (Networked Information Services Project) and ITTI (Information Technology Training Initiative), based at the University of Newcastle upon Tyne, UK.

Through the Trainmat Gopher, the Network Training Materials Project aims to make it easy for trainers to access a range of network training materials which they may then use as models, or which they may adapt for their own training programmes. Users may also find much of the material of interest.

The primary training materials being made available on this gopher are those produced by the Network Training Materials Project in its Network Training Pack. The Network Training Pack is a multi-format, multi-purpose set of generic materials produced primarily to assist and encourage UK user-support staff to provide network training to the UK academic community. However, the materials may be used and adapted by anyone, provided that the source is acknowledged and that they are not sold on or used for commercial gain.

Freely distributable software for use is available at

```
gopher://gopher.tuda.ncl.ac.uk/trainmat/Training aids/software
```

The Network Training Pack is also available for anonymous FTP retrieval from

```
ftp://tuda.ncl.ac.uk/pub/network-training
```

The data is maintained by Margaret Isaacs
```
Margaret.Isaacs@newcastle.ac.uk
```

Yanoff's List

This is the other 'crucial' guide to the Internet
```
ftp://csd4.csd.uwm.edu/Remote Information Services/Special
Internet Connections
```

Zen and the art of the Internet

Original and best, Brendan Kehoe's introduction to the Internet. Now a published book, but still available on the Internet in several formats
```
ftp://ftp.cs.widener.edu/pub/zen
```

Tools of the trade

Local knowledge in a global village

Any Internet user will have some need for more local resources – whether this be a site or service information point or specific support files. The Internet may have been sold to you as a gateway to the world and indeed it is, but you exist within a set of hierarchies and need to use this tool to relate to them. Finding mail addresses in the UK and Europe, reading local or regional Usenet groups, logging on to UK bulletin boards or information services or knowing where the European Gopher entry point is can save a lot of time and wallowing. By the nature of the global Internet, this sort of information can be difficult to track down, especially if no one tells you it is there to begin with.

E-mail

What is e-mail?

E-mail is so basic to electronic communications that most users will know they want it before they join any system. It is the common building block of all Internet activity – millions of messages flow across the Internet every day. These may be long formal letters, short chatty notes, long working whole texts or anything in between. E-mail can carry digital files, which in effect means you can send anything you have on your computer across the networks to anyone else who has a mail address. Though this may be limited by the type of software and connection the sender and receiver is using, it is a common and growing feature.

The Internet is a powerful system and will often pass mail across the world in a matter of minutes, allowing a type of ongoing conversation to develop. On the other hand, due to the 'store and forward' system, you know that any mail you sent will be kept somewhere until the intended recipient decides to read it. No more telephone tag or forgotten details. E-mail can be printed out, quoted on reply, forwarded to others or deleted. It is often wise to remember this when writing!

Every user of e-mail has to use some form of e-mail software to send it. What you can use depends on the connection you have and the platform you are working from. If you use a log-in or terminal-based system, chances are you will be reliant on a text-based system provided centrally. For example, a bulletin board will have its own internal e-mail software that you will have to learn to use. If you have an open connection by way of SLIP/PPP or LAN (Local Area Network), for example, you are likely to have a choice of possible e-mail software. This could range from a text-based simple mailer to a fully featured graphical interface system such as Eudora from Qualcomm. Eudora is able to sort mail into folders, attach documents, reply using alias names, quote previous messages, send to users' mailing lists and has many other wonderful features. Despite all of these possibilities, e-mail still consists of sending text files across the networks to be read at the other end.

Finding addresses

A question of all Internet users at an early stage is 'Where's the Phone Book?'. It is a good question, unfortunately there is no easy answer. It is in the nature of the Internet that no one built it, no one owns it and no one has enough of a financial interest to collate and publish a complete directory of e-mail addresses. It would be a huge task, even on a country by country or domain by domain basis, as users come and go, accounts open and close and networks expand at a frightening rate. Active Internet users can easily acquire multiple addresses – I currently have at least six, only one of which do I really use. Such a directory would hold the following information: names; addresses; telephone numbers; fax numbers; user IDs. You can see it is not a simple matter of putting together a small quantity of information. Having said that, there is obviously a need for a directory and as the basis of all this is computers, it does not take too much knowledge to assume computers could handle all this quite easily.

There are several ongoing projects to register and make available directories of users such as White Pages and Yellow Pages for commercial addresses. These are variously more or less useful and can be accessed through a variety of tools such as e-mail (obviously), finger, Gopher, WAIS and WWW.

UK and European e-mail resources

UK Whois servers
You can use Whois servers at the following addresses to find people.

Imperial College

> `src.doc.ic.ac.uk`

Loughborough University

> `whois.lut.ac.uk`

EUNet runs a Whois database on

> `whois.ripe.net`

Its contents are focused on people who are active in networking.

Paradise

Paradise is an X500 Directory Service run by the Cosine project for the European Research and Development community. The Paradise project is an attempt to co-ordinate and make available all electronic directory information.

You can contact Paradise by Telnetting to:

> `paradise.ulcc.ac.uk`

or by dialling direct to

> `+44 71 405 4222`

In both the 'simple' and 'power' searching modes, you will be asked to answer a short sequence of questions as below. Once you have entered the details of your query the program will try and find the entry for which you are looking. You will be prompted to enter a person's NAME, their DEPARTMENT (optional), the ORGANIZATION they work for and the COUNTRY in which the organization is based.

Online HELP is available to explain in more detail how to use the Directory Service. Please type ?INTRO (or ?intro) if you are not familiar with the Directory Service.

> ```
> Type ? for HELP with the current question you are being asked.
> ??for HELP on HELP - this lists the various help screens
> available.
> ```

Type q to quit the Directory Service.

Type Control-C to abandon the current query.

Simple Look-ups is the best mode if you are looking for a specific person, department or organization, although some browsing is also possible if you cannot initially find the entry for which you are looking. You will be offered a small number (3 or 4) of prompts to identify the entry you wish to find. Once you have selected this mode of querying there are large number of help screens available to guide you if you need help. If the information is available, the results should be delivered within seconds.

Paradise HelpDesk

+44 71 405 8400 x432

Fax: +44 71 242 1845

> `helpdesk@paradise.ulcc.ac.uk`

Written information about Paradise can be obtained from:

    info-server@paradise.ulcc.ac.uk

or

        Paradise Project,
        University College London, Computer Science,
        Gower Street, London WC1E 6BT, UK

Sending faxes: Faxnet
For full information about Faxnet, send the message

    help

to

    info@awa.com

General mail resources

How to e-mail
An introductory document is available from

    ftp://ftp.sura.net/pub/nic/network.service.guides/how.to.email.
    guide

Finding people
Read the FAQ 'How to find people's E-mail addresses', available from

    mail-server@rtfm.mit.edu

by sending

    send usenet/news.answers/finding-addresses

This document is posted regularly to the Usenet group news.answers.
    There is another long document specifically for finding college students' e-mail addresses. It is also posted to news.answers. You can also get the file from

    ftp://rtfm.mit.edu:/pub/usenet/soc.college/Student_Email_Addres
    sesor

To get it using e-mail, send the message

    send usenet/soc.college/Student_Email_Addresses

to

    mail-server@rtfm.mit.edu

InterNIC via e-mail
To get information from InterNIC via e-mail, first send the message

    help

to

    mailserv@internic.net

Whois

The computer networking administration and research in Europe List of Internet Whois servers is at

```
ftp://sipb.mit.edu:/pub/whois/whois-servers.list
```

The data in this list are also available via Gopher.

```
gopher://sipb.mit.edu:70
```

Choose the selection 'Internet Whois servers'. The Whois-server entries are accessible in the sipb.mit.edu Gopher server. These are automatically updated whenever this file is changed.

InterNetwork Mail Guide

This is posted to the newsgroups

```
comp.mail.misc
news.newusers.questions
```

Usenet user list

You can search a list of people who have posted to Usenet lists at any time in the past. This is a huge number of people and is constantly growing. Send an e-mail message saying

```
send usenet-addresses/name
```

to

```
mail-server@pit-manager.mit.edu
```

/name should be one or more space-separated words for which you want to search; since the search is fuzzy (i.e. all of the words you specify do not have to match). You can list any words you think might appear in the address, including first and last name, possible username and possible components of the host name (e.g. 'ac' for a person who you think is at a UK academic site).

You can make multiple requests on separate lines of the same message.

The usenet-addresses database is accessible via WAIS (see below) on two different hosts

```
pit-manager.mit.edu
cedar.cic.net
```

In both cases, the database is called 'usenet-addresses' and is on port 210.

For more details about how to use the database, send the mail message

```
send usenet-addresses/help
```

College e-mail Addresses FAQ

The College e-mail Addresses FAQ is posted to the newsgroups

```
soc.college
soc.net-people
news.answers
```

Tips on using soc.net-people is available from

```
ftp://pit-manager.mit.edu/pub/usenet/news.answers/college-
email/part1 & 2
ftp://pub/usenet/comp.mail.misc/Inter-Network_Mail_Guide
ftp:/pub/usenet/soc.net-people/Tips_on_using_soc.net-
people_[l.m._27_04_92]
```

The guide is also available from the mail-server

```
mail-server@pit-manager.mit.edu
```

by sending a mail message containing any or all of

```
send usenet/news.answers/college-email/part1
send usenet/news.answers/college-email/part2
send usenet/comp.mail.misc/Inter-Network_Mail_Guide
send usenet/soc.net-people/Tips_on_using_soc.net-
people_[l.m._27_04_92]
```

Send a message containing the message

```
help to get general information about the mail server.
```

Sending anonymous mail

It is possible to send anonymous mail by aiming a mail message at an anony-mizer. This will forward your mail to the intended destination with a spurious address added. To find out how to use it send the message:

```
help
```

to

```
anonymus+ping@tygra.mic
```

or

```
help@anon.penet.fi
```

E-mail FTP

To retreive documents from anonymous FTP sites using e-mail, start by mailing the message

```
help
```

to

```
ftpmail@decwrl.dec.com
```

Email Gopher

To use a Gopher server by way of e-mail, start by sending the command

```
help
```

to

```
gophermail@ncc.go.jp
```

E-mail WWW

To view World Wide Web pages by e-mail, start by sending the message

```
www URL
```

to

```
listserv@info.cern.ch
```

You can ask for specific Web pages if you know their address, i.e.

```
send http://www.wired.com/
send http://pass.wayne.edu/res-ad.html
```

Mailing lists

What are mailing lists?

Once you have set up and mastered your e-mail software, you have access to the world of mailing lists. Mailing lists are a classic network service offering a range of services to anyone who can get e-mail in and out of the Internet. Almost all networks have long offered Internet mail exchange to their users, though some such as CompuServe insist on charging for incoming mail. This can quickly add up, especially if you use mail lists to retrieve documents and files.

Mailing lists work on a simple premise: you are added to a list; you receive all mailings sent to that list; you send your own mailings to the list or reply to other members' mailings. All this is automated in software and each list has its own address. There are many variations on this simple premise: lists can be open or you may have to ask to be added; you may be able to send anything to a list or it may be for distributing items only; you may get a constant flow of mailings or opt for a digest of postings once a day. Some lists have very few members, others thousands. Some lists carry general chit-chat, some are reserved for portentous announcements.

You usually join a list by sending a short message to a general machine address. With the Mailbase system, this is always mailbase@mailbase.ac.uk. With Listservs it will usually be like listserv@somewhere.place.edu.

All mailing lists have an 'owner', some have several. The owner may 'moderate' the list, that is, read all submissions before sending them on to the list, or rejecting them, or they may not even read the list, being content to have set it up and let it find its own way. There is often much discussion on mailing lists as to whether moderation is needed or not and many disagreements as to whether it is 'a good thing'.

There are thousands of lists and it does not take much to start finding them. You can get a copy of the entire Listserv list of lists from any Listserv address, but it is huge. The Mailbase list of lists is much more manageable and covers many UK and global subjects.

You will often come across references to lists in your Internet travels – a question posted to the appropriate Usenet area will usually give good results.

Many lists are bi-directionally gated to Usenet, which means that a mailing list and a Usenet group are 'slaved' together. Any mailing to either is passed on to the other – increasing the distribution massively.

Mailbase

Mailbase is the UK's indigenous list serving software. It was developed at the University of Newcastle and is run by the Newcastle-based Networked Information Services Project (NISP). This national service is funded by the Information Systems Committee of the Universities funding council for groups within the UK higher education and research community. It is largely an academic service, though most lists have their fair share of non-academic members, which makes it more interesting.

Mailbase is described as 'an electronic group information exchange service'. It offers its users two main facilities via electronic mail:

- Discussion of topics using electronic mailing lists. Being a member of a particular list is like sitting in a discussion. You can join in, or merely observe.
- File archives associated with a discussion list and about Mailbase in general are available via e-mail.

Mailbase also runs a Gopher server and a World Wide Web server. There are now over six hundred lists available some of these are closed lists which are only available for specific groups. Mailbase regularly opens new lists at the requests of individuals and groups from academic sites.

A typical Mailbase day in April 1994

```
126 Megabytes of mail were processed
588 commands were successfully processed
253 messages were sent to distribution lists
36 messages were sent to the Mailbase helpline
108 new members joined Mailbase
There were 248 new subscriptions to lists
49 subscriptions ended
1 new list was set up
4 new files were added
74 files were retrieved by e-mail
64 files were retrieved by FTP
There were 292 connections to the Mailbase gopher
1951 files were retrieved from the Mailbase gopher
```

Mailbase Help

Mailbase is extremely efficient at supplying users and potential users with information about itself. All commands are sent to mailbase@mailbase.ac.uk, from an initial 'help' to complex orders for files and archived documents. Mailbase also supply printed documentation by post on request. Start by sending

```
help
```

to

```
mailbase@mailbase.ac.uk
```

A printed reference card is available from Mailbase. To get one, send your full postal address by e-mail to

```
mailbase-helpline@uk.ac.mailbase
```

A plain text version of the card is available by sending

```
send mailbase user-card
```

Mailbase Online service

The Mailbase online service has a 'documents' section which allows the user to read current documentation. You cannot retrieve documents with this service, but it allows you to browse before retrieving via e-mail.

To access Mailbase Online, Telnet to

```
telnet://mailbase.ac.uk
```

Login as 'guest' and use the password 'mailbase'. If you are in doubt when asked for a terminal type, try 'vt100'. This service has been experiencing heavy load and may be down at times.

A reference card describing how to use this service is available

```
send mailbase on-line-card
```

by e-mail to

```
mailbase@mailbase.ac.uk
```

Mailbase Gopher

You can Gopher to

```
gopher://mailbase.ac.uk/
```

or check the Web site at

```
http://
```

Listserv

The original mailing list service is called Listserv. This was originally written to run on IBM mainframes, but has since been re-written for many different platforms and is pervasive globally. Listserv offers many options which are sent as commands to the listserv@ address. For full information, send the line to any Listserv machine, e.g.

Listserv for Unix

Recently released, a prototype is already working on SunOS, HP-UX and AIX(R). General availability will vary among the various Unix brands. This software supposedly offers full compatibility with the original (VM) Listserv. Not all functions are available in the first release, but with very few exceptions those that are are totally compatible with the original Listserv.

L-Soft intends to support all the brands of unix(R) for which there is enough demand to offset the additional support and development costs.

An evaluation copy is available. Send mail to

    SALES@LSOFT.COM

UK Mailbase lists

You can get a full list of all the Mailbase groups by sending the command

    lists full

to

    mailbase@mailbase.ac.uk

To join any other list, send the command

    JOIN <list_name> <your_first_name> <your_last_name>

where list_name is the list you wish to join, your_first_name is your first name and your_last_name is your last name

to

    mailbase@mailbase.ac.uk

For example, if Johanna Smith wanted to join av-comms, she would send the line

    join av-comms Johanna Smith

to the e-mail address

    mailbase@mailbase.ac.uk

The mailbase system would add her name to the list and send her an acknowledgement in return. After that, to contribute to the discussion she would send her e-mail to

    av-comms@mailbase.ac.uk

Mailbase Lists

There are over 600 Mailbase lists currently in operation. This is a selected subset of those. Many Mailbase lists are 'closed', that is, membership is restricted by the owner, or highly specialized to the academic community.

academic-industry-relations

For exchange of information and ideas related to an International Study Group on Academic–Industry Relations. Current topics within the ISG are spin-off companies, strategic science centres and bridging institutions like FhG and TNO, but all interested in the topic are welcome.

admin-info
This list aims to provide a means for communication and information dissemination amongst the HE administration community. It is run by the JANET User Group for Administrators (JUGA).

admin-student
This list aims to provide a means of communication and information dissemination for HE administrators interested in student matters. It is run by the JANET User Group for Administrators (JUGA).

admin-medical
admin-medical is a list open to all administrators involved in medical education and research, particularly those with responsibility for Medical or Health care Schools and Faculties. The list is designed to facilitate the exchange of news, information and advice between users.

admin-planning
This list is for the benefit of those working in academic, financial or space planning in UK universities and colleges and others interested in these areas.

agocg-animation
This is a list for the discussion of the topic of animation.

Issues such as the scope of the topic; the need for central evaluation and provision of hardware and software; your own set up and experiences with hardware and software are all of interest.

airpollution-biology
This list will enable groups to discuss aspects of the biological/environmental impacts of air pollution. Topics will include biochemistry, physiology, ecology, genetics and an understanding of the processes underlying the reponses to air pollutants.

american-studies
This is an open list for primarily UK academics working in American Studies. Subgroups may be added later.

arch-theory
Arch-theory list is for discussions and exchange of information in archaeological theory in Europe: social theory, material culture, epistemology, the past in the present, cultural identity, perspectives from anthropology and history. Contributions are welcome in French, German, English.

aroma-trials
This list discusses the scientific investigation of claims of aromatherapy and related areas of olfaction. The design, analysis and interpretation of studies

will all be appropriate topics for discussion. Unsubstantiated comments are appropriate only if they are used to generate testable claims.

artnet
ARTNET will provide a forum for the discussion of ART that is concerned with: network; installation; project; communication; temporary; ad-hoc; transient; mobile; time-based; formless; de-centred. I call this Peripatetic art.

av-comms
The av-comms list has been set up to provide an e-mail forum for members of the UK academic community to discuss matters relating to real-time interactive audio and video communications.

built-environment
This is a list for the discussion of issues within the built environment; encompassing building, surveying, architecture and civil/mechanical/services engineering.

business-information-all
Business-Information-All is a forum for teachers and researchers working in the areas of business information management, business information systems or business information technology. It was set up after the conference Business Information Technology – the First Seven Years.

census-publications
This is an open, moderated list containing details of census research reports and other publications. Some of these documents are available in ASCII format as files and can be obtained by sending the appropriate command (see MAILBASE userguide for details).

census-news
This is an open list to which anyone can subscribe and contribute. It is for items of news about census datasets and census research and for circulating details of conferences and workshops relevant to the census community.

census-analysis
This is a public discussion list to which anyone can subscribe and contribute. It is a forum for discussing problems and solutions and exchanging ideas about use of census data and related research.

cm-collab-learning
This list is for people interested in computer-mediated collaborative learning (CMCL). It is a place to discuss issues and share our individual experiences of supporting learners/learning in this way. It is a forum to discuss CMCL in terms of both technological tools and methodologies.

coastal-research
For the exchange of news and views in the context of the SERC. Coastal Research Programme. This is concerned with the field, experimental and theoretical study

of waves, currents, sediments, structures, mixing and pollution in the coastal environment.

comparative-literature
Comparative-literature intends to provide a forum for all who are interested in the study of literature without confinement to national or linguistic boundaries and in relation to other disciplines. It will advertise the activities of the British Comparative Literature Association (BCLA).

computers-and-psychology
This list is a forum for discussion on all psychological aspects of computers. For example, human–computer interaction, computers and learning, computers and careers guidance. It includes comments, queries, research, literature, articles and conferences, etc.

cti-acc-business
CTI-acc-business is for the use of those interested in the use of computers in the teaching of Accounting Finance and Management. It has been set up by the CTI Centre for accounting finance and management at the School of Information Systems, University of East Anglia.

cti-acc-region
CTI-acc-business is for the use of those interested in the use of computers in the teaching of accounting finance and management. It has been set up by the CTI Centre for Accounting Finance and Management at the School of Information Systems, University of East Anglia.

cti-econ
This list was set up by the CTI Centre for Computing in Economics to provide an electronic discussion group for academic economists. Its purpose is to share information on workshops, seminars and conferences, new research and job vacancies. Members may also use it to ask questions of other members.

cti-psychology
For psychology lecturers using educational technology. This list disseminates information from the CTI Centre for Psychology and circulates enquiries about software and teaching practice to UK psychology departments.

cti-maths
A discussion group for mathematicians, particularly those interested in the use of computers or the teaching of mathematics in higher education.

cti-law
A discussion group for lawyers, especially those interested in the use of information technology within legal teaching.

cti-music
This list is run by the CTI (Computers in Teaching Initiative) Centre for Music and

is open to anyone working in university music departments. It is intended for discussion of university-level music teaching and research, whether or not computers are involved.

cti-engineering
This is a (moderated) rapid response forum of usage and development of software for engineering education, providing advice and guidance to academic engineers on all aspects of computer aided engineering education and associated new technologies.

cti-geog
This open list is available for everyone interested in the CTI Centre for Geography and its work in promoting the use of IT in teaching geography in higher education. We welcome postings likely to be of interest to geography teachers in the HE sector who use computers in their teaching.

cvnet-uk
A UK branch of the worldwide CVNET list, for people in colour and vision research in the UK.

war-research-sources
To co-ordinate the location of online and on-shelf research sources for the study of war, peace and defence related issues.

military-history
Aspects of military history including strategy, equipment, civil–military relations and the role of the civilian.

defence-technology
Scientific and technological development of weapons and related systems.

design-research
A general discussion and information exchange for academic staff and postgraduate students involved in design research. Contributions are welcome in the following areas: research methods, conferences, publications, current research, course descriptions, research training and resource issues.

distributed-ai
This list is for all researchers who are interested in Distributed Artificial Intelligence and enables them to exchange ideas, to discuss hot issues and problems, to ask and answer questions and to share experience in DAI research and experiments.

east-west-research
East-West-Research, set up under the ESRC's East West Programme, is a forum for the discussion of research problems and findings in relation to all aspects of social, economic and political transformation in Central and Eastern Europe and the former Soviet Union.

engineering-design
This list supports researchers at the five national Engineering Design Centres.

englit-victorian
Forum for discussion of research topics in Victorian Literature and related fields.

enterprise-he
For discussion of issues and activities related to the Enterprise in Higher Education programme funded by the UK Department of Employment; and for discussion of other activities which have similar objectives in curriculum development, personal transferable skills, learning at work, etc.

evrs
The European Virtual Reality Society e-mailing list.

extraterrestrials
This list is for all those who, from within whatever academic or scientific discipline, are interested in discoveries and speculations concerning the existence and nature of extraterrestrial life and in particular of extraterrestrial intelligent life.

f-email
F-EMAIL is for information and discussion on gender differences in use of computer communication, noting both a prevalent view that internetworking is a predominantly male domain, but also some suggestions that females may in fact be better suited to computer mediated communication (CMC).

fonetiks
Mailing list for 'foNETiks', a monthly electronic newsletter containing news about meetings, new positions and a range of other areas of interest to those studying and working in the areas of phonetics, phonology and speech science.

forced-migration
This mailing list aims to encourage greater exchange of information and to promote discussion on the problem of refugees and other victims of forced migration/involuntary resettlement, including those of development projects which lead to their forcible uprooting.

france-media
This list is intended to facilitate the exchange of ideas and information between researchers interested in the French broadcasting media.

gis-articles
This is a public moderated list containing details of any research reports and other publications that contributors may wish to make available for distribution within the GIS (Geographical Information Systems) community. Papers for distribution should be in a format suitable for machine reading, i.e. ASCII (and/or possibly Rich Text Format).

history-vasco
VASCO is a list for discussion and exchange of information on all aspects of the study of the Portuguese Discoveries of the fifteenth and sixteenth centuries, organized by the Centre for the Study of the Portuguese Discoveries, Linacre College Oxford.

history-teaching
Run by the Computers in Teaching Initiative Centre for History with Archaeology and Art History, for the exchange of information about the use of computers in teaching, including datasets, software and teaching methods.

history-news
History-news is a news service run by the Computers in Teaching Initiative Centre for History with Archaeology and Art History and replaces a bulletin board of the same name.

history-sources
History-sources is to co-ordinate the collection of online and written sources for the National Information Services and Systems (NISS)/Bulletin Board for Libraries (BUBL) Subject Tree project. Online sources will be included as Gopher or WWW pointers while off-line sources will be WAIS archived.

humgrad
This list is intended for all postgraduate students in humanities subjects. It is a means of exchanging ideas and questions on any aspect of the humanities, especially (though not exclusively) when connected with the use of computers.

iberia
IBERIA provides a forum for the dissemination of information and the discussion of matters of common concern among subject specialists, librarians, academic staff, postgraduate students and others in the field of Spanish and Portuguese studies.

ipr-science
Intellectual property–science. This list covers intellectual property in science, academic–industry links, sociological/ethical/legal analyses, inventiveness and exploitability (e.g. via patents). Information, bibliographies, news, research-in-progress, meetings, etc. All welcome.

irnes
Communication channel for members of the Interdisciplinary Research Network on the Environment and Society. IRNES is open to all those who have an interest in the interplay between the ecosystem and its sub-unit that we call society. The network is made up of young researchers in this field.

itti-networks
This list is for discussion of the training needed for use of the JANET network and its services. Input to the list will be a determining element in the assessment

of user requirements by the ITTI Network Training Materials Project and in the content of the Training Pack to be produced.

jmcci-pilot

A forum for researchers/practitioners of environmental/conservation policy to contribute to the planning/collation of resources and establishing a (virtual) conservation centre in the name of John Muir. Internet is to be used as a core technology for access to such resources on a global scale.

law-europe

An open list for the discussion of European law.

law-family

An open list for the discussion of family law.

law-public

A list for the discussion of issues around public/constitutional law.

law-economics

A list for the discussion of issues around law and economics.

lis-scitech

Run by the Universities Science and Technology Librarians' Group for librarians in all types of organization, the list is for discussion of problems, issues, services, information sources in the science and technology area (particularly networked sources). Emphasis is on UK practice.

lis-maps

Lis-maps is a forum for discussing news, ideas, issues, policies and practices related to map and spatial data librarianship. Topics can be broad ranging including: acquisition; cataloging; use; information retrieval; management of metadata; relationship to GIS & RS; collaborative work; conservation.

mac-ademic-uk

Intended for all end-users of Macintosh systems. Request information on system and software problems, availability of software solutions, or provide info on software titles particularly useful to the academic community. Complementary to MAC-SUPPORTERS (a closed list for Macintosh Support Staff).

mailbase-news

News and information about Mailbase. Formerly named NISP (the Networked Information Services Project).

modern-british-fiction

Discussion includes all post-war fiction originating in the British Isles, though specific attention is aimed at recent publications.

neuron-uk

Neuron-UK is a list (in digest form) dealing with all aspects of neural networks in Europe and the USA (and any type of network or neuromorphic system).

new-lists
When a new list starts on the Mailbase system the details are posted to this list. It is an open moderated list.

niss-news
The list is used to broadcast news and information about NISS services and activities. NISS online services currently include the NISS Gateway, NISSBB, NISS-PAC and NISSWAIS.

paranormal
This list welcomes serious discussion of what is variously called parapsychology, psychical research or the study of the paranormal: theoretical and philosophical issues; practical and experimental projects; publications, conferences and relevant items in the printed and broadcast media.

primatology
This list provides a discussion forum for issues arising from the study of human and non-human primates. Research news and views across the spectrum of field and laboratory-based work concerned with monkeys, apes and social anthropology are welcome.

psych-couns
Psych-couns is a mail list for students and researchers in counselling psychology, counselling and psychotherapy and others who wish to discuss theoretical and research issues in counselling psychology.

psychiatry
Many research findings and viewpoints in psychiatry are controversial, leaving a gulf between those pursuing radically different approaches to mental illness. This forum will act as a bridge between those taking a biomedical approach and those taking a psychodynamic approach.

depression
This forum exists for scholarly discussion of issues related to mood disorders in clinical and research settings. Integrative biological–psychological contributions are particularly welcome. Topics include causation, correlates, consequences, co-morbidity, treatment/prevention, etc.

helplessness
Learned Helplessness and Explanatory Style was created to discuss the latest research on animals and humans, biological substratum, depression, anxiety, prevention, CAVE, politics, children, personal control, health, battering, bereavement, PTSD (post traumatic stress disorder), sex differences, pessimism, work, heritability.

traumatic-stress
This list promotes the investigation, assessment and treatment of the immediate and long-term psychosocial, biophysiological and existential consequences of high-

ly stressful (traumatic) events. Of special interest are efforts to identify a cure of PTSD.

public-health
This list provides a discussion forum and information resource for those working in epidemiology and public health. It aims to facilitate information-sharing, (e.g. workshops, seminars, conferences and new research) and promote links, collaborative working, joint problem-solving and mutual support.

religious-studies-uk
This list is primarily for UK academics, graduates and librarians working within the field of religious studies. Focusing on the current representation and development of the subject, it encourages the discussion of problems and opportunities regarding teaching, research, resources, etc.

ecotheol
A forum for discussion of ecological theology. The goal of the list is to enable academic discussion of environmental issues from a theological or ethical perspective. Open to all traditions, contributions are welcome from those in other disciplines, including philosophy and the social sciences.

liturgy
LITURGY is intended as a discussion on all aspects of the academic study of Christian liturgy. The list does not confine itself to any single historical period, geographical area or denomination. Contributions are therefore welcome from scholars in all fields of theology and history.

religious-pluralism
The aim of this list is to facilitate a discussion of contemporary issues relating to the Christian theology of world religions. Particular attention will be on religious pluralism and inter-religious dialog. The list is open to contributors from any perspective.

russia-telecoms
To discuss ways in which electronic communication facilities for educational and research uses between Russia and the rest of the world can be improved.

russian-studies
This list is for members of the UK academic community studying all aspects of the former Soviet Union and Eastern Europe.

school-management
For discussion of education in schools, in particular their management and government and the curriculum. To provide a forum for those concerned with these issues, whether as researchers, educators or governors. The focus is principally British schools, but is open to evidence from other systems.

science-education
A forum for academics engaged in the study of science education. The list will

consider practical and theoretical issues relating to the teaching of science and the professional development of science educators at all levels. The list will have a research focus.

superjanet-applications
A list for the discussion of SuperJANET applications.

telework
For discussion of matters relating to teleworking, telecommuting, distance working and location-independent working.

uk-nextstep-users
Discussion group for users of the NeXTSTEP environment on either NeXT or other hardware. The group is intended to supplement, rather than replace, the various NeXT groups operating in the US and elsewhere and to provide a particular forum for UK users, both academic and otherwise.

web-support
For the discussion of issues relating to the World Wide Web, Web browsers (Mosaic and Cello in particular), Web servers (MacHTTP and serweb), the HTML language, HTML documents and editors, across Macintosh, DOS and Unix platforms in particular.

unite
UNITE is an acronym for User Network Interface To Everything. This list is a focus for discussion on the concept of a total solution interface with user friendly, desktop-integrated, access to ALL network services. Information exchange on existing systems which approach this ideal is encouraged.

windows-nt
This list is an unmoderated list for discussions of issues regarding Windows NT. The list is looked after by the European Microsoft Windows NT Academic Centre (EMWAC) based at the University of Edinburgh.

Information sources

NetTools
A document covering many network tools, including Listserv, is available in electronic format.
Mail the command

```
GET NETTOOLS MEMO
```

to

```
listserv@earncc.bitnet
```

Listserv info
For information on Listservs mail the command

```
        INFO
```
to any Listserv, for example
```
        listserv@bitnic.
```

List of Lists

To get a copy of the List of Lists send the mail message
```
        lists global
```
to ANY listserv address. The list is huge, over 1.2 Mb, so you can be specific and specify a subject thus, replacing <subject> with any word
```
        lists global /<subject>
```

Publicly accessible mailing lists (PAML)

Publicly accessible mailing lists. A definitive summary is available from
```
        mail-server@ftfm.mit.edu
```
Send the message
```
        send USENET/news.lists/P_A_M_L,_P_1_5
        send USENET/news.lists/P_A_M_L,_P_2_5
        send USENET/news.lists/P_A_M_L,_P_3_5
        send USENET/news.lists/P_A_M_L,_P_4_5
        send USENET/news.lists/P_A_M_L,_P_5_5
```

PAML by anonymous FTP

You can get the same lists by anonymous FTP from
```
        ftp://rtfm.mit.edu/pub/USENET/news.lists/P_A_M_L*
```

Usenet News

What is Usenet News

Usenet, also known as 'The News', is a worldwide information exchange and communications system, based on 'newsgroups'. It is often referred to as a 'bulletin board' system, though this is a somewhat erroneous description. You subscribe to Usenet groups on an individual basis using one of many newsreaders. There are many thousands of groups, divided between a range of hierarchical areas. You 'read' Usenet groups and 'post' replies or new 'articles' to them.

Items posted to Usenet groups from anywhere in the world are passed around until they are available everywhere. Users 'read' their list of groups as often as they wish, but articles are removed from the server when they reach a certain age, almost always less then two weeks.

You may find that your site takes a range of Usenet groups and you can read them locally. All JANET sites have access to Usenet. If you use a 'full' Internet provider you will have to decide which software to use and then point it at a news server. All Internet service providers should be able to tell you where to get your News feed from.

Categories

All Usenet groups have a name that relates to their position in the global hierarchy. There are several major categories:

```
biz.      Business topics
comp.     Computer subjects
misc.     Miscellaneous
news.     Internet and Usenet information
rec.      Recreational subjects
sci.      Scientific subjects
soc.      Sociological subjects
talk.     Debates
alt.      Everything else
```

Apart from these 'global' areas, there are many that have a national, regional or local relevance, such as the uk. groups.

Getting a full list of newsgroups

There are two ways of getting the current list of newsgroups:
Get it by anonymous FTP from

`ftp.demon.co.uk:/pub/news/active.zip.`

Or, telnet to news.demon.co.uk on port 119. Log the session to a file and type LIST and press return. Type QUIT when it finishes.

The first method is probably easier, but the list on ftp.demon.co.uk does not get updated very often. The second method gets you the latest data.

UK newsgroups

uk.announce
uk.net.news
uk.telecom
   `Telecommunications information and chat`
uk.bcs.announce
   `British Computer Society announcements`
uk.bcs.misc
   `BCS bits and pieces`
uk.environment
   `Eco netting`
uk.events
   `What's On`
uk.finance

Money, money, money
uk.forsale
Bring and buy sale
uk.ikbs
uk.jips
JANET Internet service
uk.jobs
Gissa job. I could do that
uk.jobs.d
uk.jobs.offered
uk.jobs.wanted
uk.legal
Law n Order
uk.lisp
uk.misc
uk.net.maps
UK networking maps
uk.org.community
uk.org.starlink.announce
uk.org.starlink.hardware
uk.org.starlink.misc
uk.org.starlink.research
uk.org.starlink.software
uk.politics
Set the world to rights
uk.radio.amateur
Hamming it up
uk.singles
Online singles bar - enter who dares
uk.sources
uk.sun
Holidays, I mean Sun Workstations, etc.
uk.test
uk.tex
uk.transport
Planes, trains and automobiles
uk.ukuug
uk.wic
ukmail.general
ukmail.info
ukmail.test
mail.uktex

Miscellaneous newsgroups

lon.misc
  London
cam.misc
  Cambridge
cam.sug
  Sun user group
cam.lists.4ad
  Indie record label, 4AD
scot.announce
  Scotland announcements
scot.birds
  Birds of a Scottish feather
scot.environment
  Scotecology
scot.followup
scot.general
  Scottish things
scot.test
rec.arts.tv.uk
  Best of UK television, generally as seen by the rest of the world
soc.culture.british
  Culture what culture
alt.comedy.british
alt.comedy.british.blackadder
  Blackadder for beginners
alt.fan.british-accent
  Wierd. Fans of british accents - which one?
alt.politics.british
  General british politics (see uk.politics)
alt.politics.europe.misc
  European politics
alt.satellite.tv.europe
  Satellite TV over Europe
bit.listserv.e-europe
  European mailing lists
alt.fan.douglas-adams
  The internet, the Universe and everything
alt.fan.monty-python
  Online parrot sketches
alt.fan.vic-reeves
  Vic Reeves

```
╔════════════════════ √READ THIS, DOUGLAS ADAMS ════════════════════╗
║ Author: Arm600                                                     ║
║ Organization: One one one, me me me.                               ║
║ Sat, 6 Aug 1994 20:31:39 GMT                                       ║
╟────────────────────────────────────────────────────────────────── ║
║|                                                                   ║
║  Douglas Adams...                                                  ║
║   I know you read this newsgroup. Well you must do if you're reading this.
║                                                                    ║
║  Could you please email me... I'd like to know your views on science fiction,
║ mustic, chaos and the Internet (among other things) for a small-readership cult
║ magazine article.                                                  ║
║                                                                    ║
║  And if you're not Douglas Adams (ie a nosy alt.fan.douglas-adams subscriber
║ :-) then can you tell me Douglas's email address?                  ║
║                                                                    ║
║  Thanks in anticipation of any reply. :)                          ║
║                                                                    ║
║ Arm600                                                             ║
║ ------                                                             ║
║ arm600@mstuart.demon.co.uk                                         ║
║ "Holy Zarquon Singing Fish"                                        ║
╚════════════════════════════════════════════════════════════════════╝
```

Mail to alt.fan.douglas-adams Usenet group

alt.fan.wodehouse
    PG
alt.music.pink-floyd
    Never trust a hippie
list.ukipnet
list.dialupip

Demon newsgroups
demon.adverts
demon.adverts.d
demon.announce
    Demon Internet Services service announcements
demon.answers
demon.ip.discoveries
    Discuss what you've discovered on the nets
demon.ip.cppnews
demon.ip.developers
demon.ip.support
    General internet support
demon.ip.support.amiga
demon.ip.support.archimedes
demon.ip.support.atari
demon.ip.support.mac
    Support for Apple Mac based Internet users

demon.ip.support.other
demon.ip.support.pc
demon.ip.support.pc.announce   <moderated>
demon.ip.support.unix
demon.ip.winsock
demon.ip.winsock.dics
demon.ip.www
demon.local
   Wide ranging discussions
demon.news
demon.pops
   For discussion of Demon dial-up points
demon.sales   <moderated>
demon.sales.d
demon.security
demon.security.keys
demon.service
demon.test

Pipex newsgroups

pipex.admin
pipex.dialup
pipex.info
pipex.news
pipex.techs
pipex.tickets
pipex.dialup
   For discussion of Pipex dial-up points

EUNet newsgroups

eunet.aviation
eunet.bugs.4bsd
eunet.bugs.uucp
eunet.checkgroups   <moderated>
eunet.esprit
eunet.esprit.eurochip
eunet.europen
eunet.euug
eunet.general
eunet.jokes
eunet.micro.acorn
eunet.misc
eunet.newprod
eunet.news

eunet.news.group
eunet.politics
eunet.sources
eunet.test
eunet.works
exnet-ibmpcug.misc
exnet.answers
exnet.sys
misc.news.east-europe.rferl

Clarinet newsgroups

The Clarinet groups are commercial and only available on payment. There is a huge range of them and they are good for news and hot information. These cover Europe between them. Check clari. for samples. Mail xxx for further information.

clari.world.europe.alpine	\<moderated\>
clari.world.europe.balkans	\<moderated\>
clari.world.europe.benelux	\<moderated\>
clari.world.europe.central	\<moderated\>
clari.world.europe.eastern	\<moderated\>
clari.world.europe.france	\<moderated\>
clari.world.europe.germany	\<moderated\>
clari.world.europe.greece	\<moderated\>
clari.world.europe.iberia	\<moderated\>
clari.world.europe.ireland	\<moderated\>
clari.world.europe.italy	\<moderated\>
clari.world.europe.northern	\<moderated\>
clari.world.europe.russia	\<moderated\>
clari.world.europe.uk	\<moderated\>
clari.world.europe.union	\<moderated\>
clari.biz.market.report.europe	

Usenet information sources

Usenet World
```
ftp://wuarchive.wustl.edu/doc/misc/acn/acn4-5.txt.Z
```
What is Usenet?
An introduction to Usenet, available from
```
ftp://rtfm.mit.edu/pub/usenet/news.answers/what-is-usenet/part1
```
Usenet via Telnet
How to access Usenet groups via a Telnet connection
```
telnet://sol.ctr.columbia.edu:119
```

Anonymous FTP

What is FTP?

FTP is the File Transfer Protocol or the primary method of transferring files from one place to another over the Internet. Anonymous FTP is a way of offering and gaining access to archives of information without having to know any passwords or user IDs. The intention is to make files available to anyone in the manner of a public library, without offering free access to a whole machine. Some anonymous FTP archives are huge, such as wuarchive.wustl.edu at Washington University or the Simtel archive.

Anonymous FTP gives you access to an almost endless range of files, from software to documents, from datasets to artworks, from booklists to mail archives. Knowing where to go for specific types of files is part of building your personal map of the Internet. Some archives are so huge that you will never fathom the depths of them, others are very specific and will never grow to any kind of size. Some have a purely local relevance, others collect all items relating to a specific subject which may be of interest to users all around the world.

Due to the distributed nature of FTP sites, there exists a concept of mirrors. Large and complex sites are generally mirrored by other sites to reduce the load. For example, the Imperial College FTP site mirrors the US Simtel.

Anonymous (and any other kind) FTP connections can be made using any FTP software. This will depend on what system and platform you are using. It is, however, a simple method of making a connection. Assuming you are using a command line interface, you make a call to the address of an FTP site. You will be asked for Name: to which you answer 'anonymous'. You will then be asked for a Password, to which you respond with your e-mail address. This should gain you entry to the site.

```
Name: anonymous
Password: me@jimmie.ac.uk
```

Once you have entered the site, the prompt will change, generally to an

```
>ftp
```

As you are now using another operating system, it helps to know a few commands, i.e. how to get around. Typing

```
dir
```

should get you a list of files or sub-directories in the current area. To change to another directory, use

```
cd directoryname
```

To get a file use the word get

```
get thefile
```

There are many other commands available. To see a list, use

```
help
```

You can also use dedicated software to make your task a lot easier. For example, on the Mac you have a choice of Fetch or Xferit, both of which implement point and click FTP.

UK FTP sites

University of Birmingham, School of Computer Science
ftp://ftp.cs.bham.ac.uk
hostmaster@cs.bham.ac.uk
Usenet archives: comp.lang.pop & sci.cognitive; local research papers and software.

University of Bradford
ftp://ftp.brad.ac.uk
AU sound files; graphics (GIF, JPG); Married With Childen program guide; mods; MS-DOS.

University, Cambridge, CL
ftp://ftp.cl.cam.ac.uk
acquilex; bitmaps; hol; hvg; IEEE-TSC-EECS; Linux; m; niftp; nltools; pegasus; portal; shoestring.

Cambridge University, Engineering Department
ftp://svr-ftp.eng.cam.ac.uk
comp.speech archives & sources; ectl; reports; wernicke.

Cambridge University, Isaac Newton Institute for Mathematical Sciences
ftp://newton.newton.cam.ac.uk
Isaac Newton Institute courses, info, seminars; older files relating to cvi, egyptology, rsp.

Cambridge University, MRC APU
ftp://ftp.mrc-apu.cam.ac.uk
aim; amodeus; faces; hpr; Linux; NN; sum.

Cambridge University, MRC LMB
ftp://al.mrc-lmb.cam.ac.uk
jkb@mrc-lmb.cam.ac.uk
Some BBC utilities.

Demon Internet
ftp.demon.co.uk
4.3BSD; ACCU (/pub/cug); Amiga; Antivirus (comprehensive across all platforms); Archimedes; Atari; books; commercial demos; CP/M; CUG; Dialup IP, PGP and Usenet software; doc; games; GNU; ham-radio; images; Mac; mail; MS-DOS (Simtel 20); news; NeXt; NT; OS/2; perl; PGP; pick; PPP; roundhill; SCO; SLIP; Sun; trumphurst; Unix; Xenix; XWindows.

University of Edinburgh, Metereology Department
> `ftp://cumulus.met.ed.ac.uk`

root@met.ed.ac.uk
Computer Aided Learning in Metereology software; Meteosat3 and Meteosat4 images.

University of Edinburgh
> `ftp://ftp.ed.ac.uk`

a2ps; courses; EdLAN; emwac; GNU; IUSC; JIPS; lrtt; mail; mmaccess; maps; MFT; Motif FAQ; netdocs; PC-NFS; pdps; smrsh; Solaris; spooling; Sun: ecl, fixes, papers; UCSG; uniras; Unixhelp; whiteosi; X.400; X11 FAQ.

University of Edinburgh, AI Department
> `ftp://ftp.dai.ed.ac.uk`

AI (probably); cam; ga; papers; pga; siamakr.

University of Edinburgh, Cognitive Sciences Department
> `ftp://scott.cogsci.ed.ac.uk`

adger; ai2scheme; alpha; awb; cavedon; docs; elsnet; et; fracas; ginzburg; graphics; HCRC papers; htl htk; Mac; maptask; phonology; SISTA; statling; tagger; time-constraints; tvtwm; vogel; xerion; xxyx; yeats.

University of Edinburgh, Edinburgh Center for Parallel Computing (EPCC)
> `ftp://ftp.epcc.ed.ac.uk`

chimp; cs9; DCS; explorer; ifip; paramics; parintro; pul; RCS; rpl2; ss; th; tn; tr; ug; visualization.

EUnet Britain/UK
> `ftp.britain.eu.net`

comp.sources.x; docs; GNU; infosrv; ISO; ITR; misc; news; RFCs; Sun-dist/patches; uumap; X11R6; xcal.

University of Glasgow, Scotland, CS Department
> `ftp://ftp.dcs.gla.ac.uk`
> `ftp://ftp.dcs.ed.ac.uk`

support@dcs.gla.ac.uk
actress; Ansible; Avalanche; BCS; fide; flare; gist; glasgow-fp; haskell; hug94; iii; imis; Linux; Mac; merill; mail; NASA; news; pj-lester book; recipes; src; SF archives; theory; triangle; types; Acorn; BBC; Postscript utils.

Imperial College of Science, Technology and Medicine, CC
> `lister.cc.ic.ac.uk`

PC-elm; pem; prism; Win-elm; Win-gopher; Win-mime; X11.

Imperial College of Science, Technology and Medicine, Department of Computing
> `wombat.doc.ic.ac.uk`

Acorn Archimedes software in pub/acorn.

Imperial College of Science, Technology and Medicine, Department of Computing, SunSITE Northern Europe

`ftp://ftp.doc.ic.ac.uk`

Earth, the Universe and Everything. Huge site which also mirrors several other sites including Simtel. Aminet; biology; faces; geology; GNU; IAFA-SITEINFO; info; literary; media; mirrors: MS-DOS programs from the Simtel Software Repository (/pub/packages/simtel20), MS-DOS games from ftp.uml.edu (/computing/systems/ibmpc/msdos-games/Games), MS-Windows from ftp.cica.indiana.edu; politics; RFCs; Sun; TeX from ftp.tex.ac.uk; UKUUG; Unix; Usenet; weather.

Imperial College of Science, Technology and Medicine, London, Management School

`mscmga.ms.ic.ac.uk`

OR library, you have to know what you are looking for here or read the info.txt file.

University of Canterbury, Canterbury, Kent

`unix.hensa.ac.uk`

info; Linux (mirror of sunsite.unc.edu); maple; matlab; netlib; parallel; statlib; uunet.

Lancaster University

`micros.hensa.ac.uk`

comug; MS-DOS; DV (DesqView); news; OS/2; pc-blue; sig; windows; Archimedes; kermit; bbc computer.

University of Leeds, School of Computer Studies (SCS)

`agora.leeds.ac.uk`

support@scs.leeds.ac.uk

CP/M; DTM; rec.games.abstract; SCS items; SGI UK distribution.

Liverpool University, CS Department

`ftp.csc.liv.ac.uk`

tp@csc.liv.ac.uk

Ports to HP-UX machines (especially Series 700): including X11R4 clients, GNU, recreational software, text editors, sysadmin tools.

Manchester Computing Centre

`ftp.mcc.ac.uk`

386bsd (mirrors agate.Berkeley.EDU); NCSA telnet; X11R5; TeX; djgpp; f2c; Gnu (mirrors prep.ai.mit.edu); Linux stuff (and mirrors ftp.funet.fi); Mach 3.0; Minix; MS-DOS utils; Unix utils; MIDI files; Cubase archive.

Mantis Consultants Ltd

`ftp.mantis.co.uk`

alt.angst; alt.atheism; atari-lynx; cryptography; pictures; russell; utilities.

Oxford University
ftp://black.ox.ac.uk

Docs; IP; math; Oxford Text Archive; RFCs; seminar papers; crossword worldlists; CIA world fact book

ftp://camelot.cc.rl.ac.uk

Cute; MandR; open; reports; wg5

ftp://catless.ncl.ac.uk

X11 IRC client

ftp://ftp://cs.ucl.ac.uk
ftp://cells.cs.ucl.ac.uk

DIS CMIS/P.

Oxford University, Computing Laboratory (OUCL)
ftp://ftp.comlab.ox.ac.uk

archive-management@comlab.ox.ac.uk

CSP; documents; microprocessor cards; music research; OBJ forum; Occam; packages; programs; Transputer; Z forum.

Pipex
ftp.pipex.net

areacode; IRC; mail; maps; monthly; named; netinfo; news; OS/2; Perl; PIPEX info in /pub, Unipalm in /unipalm, Xtech in /xtech, Computer College in /compucol; RFCs; RFC-drafts; security; sendmail; src; stats; Sun-patches; techguide; telecom; terms; Unipalm; vendor; WWW.

University of Swansea
sunacm.swan.ac.uk

ACM info; Linux (kernel); LPMUD; Seti; SUCS.

TeX site
ftp.tex.ac.uk

TeX (root directory, mirrored by ftp.doc.ic.ac.uk).

University of Wolverhampton, School of Computing and Information Technology
scitsc.wlv.ac.uk

C programming course; ham-radio (no executables); Network info (incl. ftp-list); pictures (censored); RFCs.

Warwick University
ftp.warwick.ac.uk

C64; Computer Underground Digest (CuD) archives; fiction; games; GNU; HTML; MS-DOS; MUD related; Novell; SNMP; Solaris2; Statlib; TeX; usenet; X11.

University of York
ftp.york.ac.uk

distrib; Mac; PC; PC NFS; uniras.

Useful FTP sites information sources

Perry.Rovers' Anonymous FTP Sites Listing
(See also the related Frequently Asked Questions (FAQ) List.)
This list can be obtained by one of the following ways.
Send an e-mail message with no subject and in the body

```
send usenet/news.answers/ftp-list/faq
send usenet/news.answers/ftp-list/sitelist/part1
send usenet/news.answers/ftp-list/sitelist/part2
send usenet/news.answers/ftp-list/sitelist/part3
send usenet/news.answers/ftp-list/sitelist/part4
send usenet/news.answers/ftp-list/sitelist/part5
send usenet/news.answers/ftp-list/sitelist/part6
send usenet/news.answers/ftp-list/sitelist/part7
send usenet/news.answers/ftp-list/sitelist/part8
send usenet/news.answers/ftp-list/sitelist/part9
send usenet/news.answers/ftp-list/sitelist/part10
```

to

```
mail-server@rtfm.mit.edu
```

By anonymous FTP

```
ftp://rtfm.mit.edu/pub/usenet/new.answers/ftp-list/sitelist
```

and

```
ftp://rtfm.mit.edu/pub/usenet/news.answers/ftp-list/faq
```

for the ASCII FAQ List.
For a zip compressed version

```
ftp://garbo.uwasa.fi/pc/doc-net/ftp-list.zip
```

```
ftp://oak.oakland.edu/pub/msdos/info/ftp-list.zip
```

For a choice of formats

```
ftp://ftp.edu.tw/documents/networking/guides/ftp-list
directory.
```

Several formats are available, including a .Z and .gz version of the FAQ and sitelist.
The list is kept by Perry.Rovers

```
Perry.Rovers@kub.nl
```

InterNIC FTP

```
ftp://ds.internic.net/pub/InterNIC-info/
```

FTP FAQ

```
ftp://tfm.mit.edu/pub/usenet-by-group/new
```

FTP by e-mail

To find out about retrieving FTP files by e-mail, send the command

    help

to

    ftpmail@decwrl.dec.com

You will automatically get a document returned to you with full information.

Telnet

What is Telnet?

Telnet is the ability to 'log-on' to a remote site across the Internet. It connects your machine to any others across the Internet that allow public access or that you have an account on. You can also Telnet to sites where you can use other tools such as Gopher, World Wide Web or WAIS; library catalogs and bulletin boards around the world, including NISS and janet.news in the UK.

Telnet is available on all platforms, whether you are using a full Internet feed, in which case you would run Telnet on your desktop, or you are using a dial-up connection, where you use a telnet tool as provided by the service itself. Although it is a powerful Internet resource, it is harder to use for various reasons than newer tools. You will have to learn individual systems at each place that you visit. That said, access to Telnet at whatever level opens up access to a lot of the Internet.

Telnet is a general purpose tool that allows you to call across the Internet to any system that is running an information tool such as a bulletin board, library catalog, database or many other services. Making a Telnet call allows you to rummage around at the other end, using whatever commands are. For example, if you want to check the NISS Bulletin Board, you would Telnet to the address of the board. It is somewhat like making a phone call – you do not know how the call is routed, but if you know the number and the area code, it will get there.

UK Telnet sites

Telnet provides a useful way of accessing information on the Internet. All these systems are text based, which speeds up access but sometimes makes understanding how to navigate a bit problematic. Most of these sites now offer Gopher and/or WWW access to part or all of their services. If you have a local client for one of those, you might be better off using it. However, these systems are tried and tested and have given sterling service for years.

NISS – National Information Services and Systems

NISS provides a bulletin board style gateway to a range of academic services at

    telnet://niss.ac.uk

There is a lot here and it can take a number of visits to get the measure of it.

```
N I S S    G A T E W A Y   M A I N   M E N U
AA) NISS Bulletin Board
    (NISSBB - Traditional access)
AB) NISS Bulletin Board
    (NISSBB - Gopher access)
B)  NISS Public Access Collections
    (NISSPAC)
C)  NISSWAIS Service free text searching of selected databases
D)  NISS Newspapers and Journals Services
E)  NISS Gopher Services
R)  Library Catalogues (OPACs)
S)  Campus Information Systems
T)  Bibliographic Services
    (e.g. BUBL, FirstSearch, DIALOG)
U)  Directory Services
    (e.g. Yellow Pages, Paradise, WAIS)
V)  Archive Services
    (e.g. HENSA, Mailbase, BIRON)
W)  General Services
    (e.g. Guest-Telnet, ASK, JANET.NEWS)
```

HENSA – Higher Education National Software Archive

HENSA provides the main software archive site at

```
telnet://micros.hensa.ac.uk:hensa
```

A huge range of public domain and shareware for PCs, Macs, UNIX, X and many others. A slightly arcane system, but worth getting used to.

Useful commands

```
?             Lists the commands you can use
help          Enters interactive help system
news ?        For a list of latest news topics
```

SunSITE Northern Europe, Imperial CollegeArchive

SunSITE Northern Europe is located at the Department of Computing, Imperial College, London and is running on a SPARCserver 1000 with 6 CPUs and 34 Gb of disk space, kindly donated by Sun Microsystems. This is a truly huge archive site, with many mirrors of other sites around the world,

```
telnet://src.doc.ic.ac.uk
To access The Archive                login as sources
no password
To access Archie                     login as archie
no password
To abandon a login                   enter a control-D
Please email suggestions and questions to wizards@doc.ic.ac.uk
```

JANET news
The UK academic network information site. Lots of arcane addresses, strange information, plus some very useful items. Watch the dates of files: a lot of the information here is out of date.

        telnet://news.janet.ac.uk:INFO

Kings College Information Server
        telnet://info.kcl.ac.uk:INFO

Loughborough University Information Server
        telnet://info.lut.ac.uk

NISP - Networked Information Services Project
        telnet://mailbase.ac.uk:guest

Oxford University OUCS Information Service
        telnet://info.ox.ac.uk

Queen Mary & Westfield College Information Server
        telnet://alpha.qmw.ac.uk:info

University of Birmingham Campus Information Service
        telnet://info.bham.ac.uk

University of Bristol Information Server
        telnet://info.bristol.ac.uk:info

```
══════════════════════════ JANET News ══════════════════════════
 JANET news information service.                      Main-menu  ⬆

    1.  ADDRESSES   -JANET Addresses, NRS info, Site info, Mail info.

    2.  DOCUMENTS   -JANET documents, Network News, Starter pack, NRS Guide.

    3.  TECHNICAL   -Information on IP, Ether, Rainbow, X.29/Telnet, X25/TCP.

    4.  CONNECTIONS -Gateways info, IXI, JANET IP Service (JIPS).

    5.  NOC INFO    -Status of the JANET Network Operation Centres.

    6.  JANET INFO  -JANET stats, CERT Info, General JANET Information.

    7.  USER GROUPS -User Group information and minutes.

    8.  MISC        -CHEST, NISS, EYP, World Data Cntr.

    9.  JANET.NEWS  -Server help and information, Reporting faults.
 .  .   .   .   .   .   .       .   .   .       .   .   .   .   .
    Help                        Main-menu  Suggestion  Redisplay
    Contents                                           Quit
  Command?  ▮
```

Janet.news via Telnet

University of Edinburgh EdINFO
```
telnet://castle.ed.ac.uk:edinfo
```

University of Southampton Campus Information Service
```
telnet://info.soton.ac.uk:info
```

University of Wales, College of Cardiff Information Server
```
telnet://info.cf.ac.uk:info
```

University of York Information Server
```
telnet://info.york.ac.uk:INFO
```

BIRON
```
telnet://biron.essex.ac.uk:biron
```

Other Internet services

InterNIC Telnet
```
telnet://ds.internic.net:guest
```
CNI search
```
telnet://gopher.cni.org:brsuser
```
HPCWire
```
telnet://hpcwire.ans.net
```
Archie
```
telnet://archie.ans.net:archie
```
Gopher
```
telnet://onsultant.micro.umn.edu:gopher
```
Netfind
```
telnet://mudhoney.micro.umn.edu:netfind
```
Whois
```
telnet://rs.internic.net
```
White Pgs/PSI
```
telnet://wp.psi.net:fred
```
World Wide Web
```
telnet://info.cern.ch
```
CARL Systems
```
telnet://database.carl.org
```
Correct Time/NBS
```
telnet://india.colorado.edu:13
```
ENewsstand
```
telnet://enews.com:enews
```
Knowbot
```
telnet://info.cnri.reston.va.us:185
```
WorldWindow
```
telnet://library.wustl.edu
```

Internet bulletin board systems, interactive databases and Freenets

There are several systems you can establish a connection with that provide a var-iety of services/information. In some respects they resemble Campus Wide Infor-mation Systems, in others they are more like bulletin boards or interactive databases.

A file containing the most frequently asked questions about bulletin board sys-tems is available via anonymous FTP

```
ftp://polyslo.calpoly.edu/alt.bbs.faq
```

The Freenets

Freenets exist to provide public access to a local bulletin board and from there the Internet. Charges are minimal or free – much funding comes from business and fundraising activities. They are run on a voluntary basis and are controlled by the community they have been set up to serve. You can gain access as a guest to the services listed below. The Freenet movement is spreading across the world – maybe we will see them in the UK before long.

The organizing body for Freenets is the National Public Telecomputing Network. You can contact them by e-mail at

```
info@nptn.org
```
They have an anonymous FTP site at
```
ftp://ntpn.org/pub/info.nptn
```
and also a Gopher at
```
gopher://gopher.lib.utk.edu/Other-Internet-Resources/Freenet
Documents
```
Big Sky Telegraph – Dillon, Montana
```
telnet://192.231.192.1:bbs
```
Buffalo Free-Net – Buffalo, New York
```
telnet://freenet.buffalo.edu:freeport
```
CapAccess: National Capital Area Public Access Network
```
telnet://cap.gwu.edu
login:guest,visitor
```
CIAO! Free-Net – Trail, British Columbia, Canada
```
telnet://142.231.5.1:visitor
```
Cleveland Free-Net – Cleveland, Ohio
```
telnet://freenet-in-a.cwru.edu
login: Select #2 at first menu
```
Columbia Online Information Network (COIN) – Columbia, Missouri
```
telnet://bigcat.missouri.edu:guest
```
Dayton Free-Net – Dayton, Ohio
```
telnet://130.108.128.174:visitor
```
Denver Free-Net – Denver, Colorado
```
telnet://freenet.hsc.colorado.edu:guest
```
Erlangen Free-Net
```
telnet://131.188.192.11:gast
```

Heartland Free-Net – Peoria, Illinois
    telnet://heartland.bradley.edu:bbguest
Lorain County Free-Net – Elyria, Ohio
    telnet://freenet.lorain.oberlin.edu:guest
National Capital Free-Net – Ottawa, Canada
    telnet://freenet.carleton.ca:guest
Prairienet – Champaign-Urbana, Illinois
    telnet://prairienet.org:visitor
SENDIT, North Dakota
    telnet://sendit.nodak.edu
    login: bbs,sendit2me,visitor
Talawanda Learning Community Network
    telnet://tlcnet.muohio.edu:visitor
Tallahassee Free-Net – Tallahassee, Florida
    telnet://freenet.fsu.edu:visitor

```
========================= Cleveland Free-Net =========================


<<< CLEVELAND FREE-NET DIRECTORY >>>

  1 The Administration Building
  2 The Post Office
  3 Public Square
  4 The Courthouse & Government Center
  5 The Arts Building
  6 Science and Technology Center
  7 The Medical Arts Building
  8 The Schoolhouse (Academy One)
  9 The Community Center & Recreation Area
 10 The Business and Industrial Park
 11 The Library
 12 University Circle
 13 The Teleport
 14 The Communications Center
 15 NPTN/USA TODAY HEADLINE NEWS
----------------------------------------------------
h=Help, x=Exit Free-Net, "go help"=extended help

Your Choice ==>
```

Cleveland Freenet front menu

Toledo Free-Net
```
telnet://131.183.4.100
login: visitor,visitor
```
Traverse City Free-Net
```
telnet://leo.nmc.edu:visitor
```
Tristate Online – Cincinnati, Ohio
```
telnet://cbos.uc.edu
```
login sequence: cbos, visitor, 9999, <return>
   Victoria Free-Net – Victoria, British Columbia, Canada
```
telnet://freenet.victoria.bc.ca:guest
```
Youngstown Free-Net – Youngstown, Ohio
```
telnet://yfn.ysu.edu:visitor
```
Vaasa FreePort Bulletin Board, Finland
```
telnet://garbo.uwasa.fi:guest
```
Free-Net Erlangen – Nuernberg, Germany
```
telnet://freenet-a.fim.uni-erlangen.de:gast
```

Telnet information sources

How to Telnet
```
ftp://tp.sura.net/pub/nic/network.service.guides/how.to.telnet.
guide
```

Hytelnet

What is Hytelnet?

Hytelnet is a constantly updated reference system to Internet information systems worldwide. You can access Hytelnet on remote sites using Telnet, but it is better to run it on your own machine. It is designed to assist users in reaching all Internet accessible libraries, Freenets, Campus Wide Information Systems, BBSs and other information sites by Telnet, specifically those users who access Telnet via a modem or the ethernet from an IBM-compatible personal computer.

Hytelnet was originally written for librarians and has a whole section devoted to libraries.

Hytelnet is a great way to 'surf' parts of the Internet. It does a lot of the hard work for you, offering you lists of resources and then making the Telnet connections. It even tells you what the login name is for your chosen destination.

Note that, due to restrictions in the UK for Internet users outside JANET, you will not be able to use Hytelnet via a Telnet site to get onto JANET sites. This is because, although you can make one hop into JANET, you cannot make a double hop once you are there.

You can get Telnet access to Hytelnet at

```
telnet://info.mcc.ac.uk:hytelnet
```

```
telnet://rsl.ox.ac.uk:hytelnet
```

```
telnet://library.adelaide.edu.au:access
telnet://nctuccca.edu.tw:hytelnet
```

Sources of Hytelnet software

The various Hytelnet packages are widely available and it is recommended that they are installed locally and then kept up to date.

The Demon FTP site has the Mac version

```
ftp://ftp.demon.co.uk/pub/mac/hytelnet/hytelnet6.6.sea
```

The IBMPC version is available from

```
ftp://ftp.usask.ca/pub/hytelnet/pc/hyteln66.zip
```

The Amiga version is available from

```
ftp://uceng.uc.edu/pub/wuarchive/systems/amiga/boing/comms/netw
ork/tcpip/
```

Guide to Hytelnet

ftp://uceng.uc.edu/pub/wuarchive/doc/EFF/Net_info/Guidebooks/Hytelnet

Hytelnet Readme

ftp://ftp.usask.ca/pub/hytelnet/README

Hytelnet demo

telnet://access.usask.ca:hytelnet

Gopher

What is Gopher?

Gopher is an excellent information search and retrieval tool that takes all the above concepts one stage further. It was developed at the University of Minnesota and provides a menu-based view of the Internet, allowing you to chase subjects from site to site and to view or retrieve files that you find.

As with Telnet, you can run a version of Gopher on your desktop if you have a full (IP) connection to the Internet. Doing this will give you a graphical interface to Gopherspace. If you use a dial-up service such as CIX you will use their text-based service. You can also Telnet to third party Gopher servers.

Gopher has spread rapidly across the Internet due largely to its information handling capabilities. Each Gopher search starts with a 'home' Gopher. From there you expand the search outwards, following preset paths or hunting at random.

A good Gopheof UK Gophers may as well now point at this list directly. The link entry for it is the UK Gopher Server at

```
gopher://ukoln.bath.ac.uk/UK_Gopher_Servers
```

This Gopher is the UK 'point of entry' and has links to most UK Gopher servers including the Almac BBS, National software archive (HENSA), the JANET News Machine, LSE/AppleUK HE Social Sciences Gopher, Law Technology Centre Gopher, NURSING Gopher Service for Nurses, European Microsoft Windows NT Academic Centre, International Centre for Distance Learning and many others.

Using Gopher

As we have seen with other tools, there are different ways of using Gopher, depending on whether you have a full Internet connection or whether you use a dial-up connection to get on to the Internet. Gopher is extremely easy to use, whether you run a full (Graphical User Interface) version from your desktop or use a text Gopher client. You can use Telnet to get to a Gopher server at many sites around the world.

If you Telnet to

```
gopher://gopher.msu.edu
```

You can choose from three search tools: a search on the index of Gopher site names; the Veronica search engine and a high-level local search.

Choosing one of the menu numbers gives you a text box to fill. After searching on a word, we can look at any of the items, losing ourselves within Gopherspace as we search. At any time we can return up the hierarchy, backtracking until we find a new path to follow. Many of the results at a higher level will be further sites. We are in fact moving around the world from place to place. One of the beauties of Gopher is that all this disparate information is presented to us in a similar manner – we no longer have to worry about what tool we need to use. At some point we will arrive at individual files, be they texts (most likely), images, sounds, software or other files. Anything that can be found on a computer can be found in Gopherspace.

We can 'read' and save text files and download copies of other files for later reading and use. If we are using a more sophisticated browser, such as Turbo-Gopher on the Mac, we can choose to view images 'live', though we still have to wait for them to arrive before this is viewing them.

Bookmarks

During Gopher searches there are often times when you come across useful information via a very roundabout route. You can place bookmarks at these sites or documents for later easy return. 'a' adds an item to your list and 'd' deletes a bookmark.

More information

Gopher is capable of linking to many different kinds of information and to different levels of information. You can even find yourself making a Telnet call after choosing a menu item.

Gopher indicates what a particular item is. If you are using a graphical browser like TurboGopher you will be given iconic indicators. Text-based systems use '?' for a search engine; <TEL> for a Telnet link and/for a link to another menu.

UK Gopher list

The following list of UK Gopher servers is based on a list compiled by UKOLN who can be contacted at gopher@ukoln.bath.ac.uk.

The UKOLN list is the UK entry point for all Gophers worldwide. New UK Gophers can be registered with the European Gopher registration point by sending mail to

```
gopher@ebone.net
```

giving the name and e-mail address of the administrator, Gopher server name, host name and optionally a path.

The list is available at

```
gopher://ukoln.bath.ac.uk/UK_Gopher_Servers
```

It is compiled by Andy Powell

```
A.Powell@bath.ac.uk
```

Aston University
```
gopher://gopher.aston.ac.uk
```
Contact: g.owen@aston.ac.uk

Brunel University
```
gopher://gopher.brunel.ac.uk
```

Communications Research Group, Nottingham University
```
gopher://gopher.cs.nott.ac.uk
```
Contact: Marcus Roberts
mjr@cs.nott.ac.uk

Cranfield Institute of Technology
```
gopher://gopher.cranfield.ac.uk
```
Contact: Peter Lister
p.lister@cranfield.ac.uk
Contact: a.pibworth@cranfield.ac.uk

Dundee University Library
```
gopher://gopher.dundee.ac.uk
```
Contact: j.bagnall@dundee.ac.uk

EMBnet Bioinformation Resource
> `gopher://s-crim1.daresbury.ac.uk`
Contact: Alan Bleasby
ajb@seqnet.dl.ac.uk

Faculty of Mathematical Studies, Southampton
> `gopher://mir.maths.soton.ac.uk`
Contact: Jim Renshaw
jhr@maths.soton.ac.uk

HENSA micros (National Software Archive, Lancaster University)
> `gopher://micros.hensa.ac.uk`
Contact: hensa@micros.hensa.ac.uk
Contact: Martin Kalugin
pdmartin@central1.lancaster.ac.uk

HENSA Unix (National Software Archive, University of Kent)
> `gopher://unix.hensa.ac.uk`
Contact: David Clear
dac@ukc.ac.uk

Imperial College
> `gopher://gopher.ic.ac.uk`
Contact: Susan Feng
gopher@ic.ac.uk

Imperial College Gopher

Internet Gopher ©1991–1993 University of Minnesota.

📁 About this Gopher
📄 Message of the Day
📁 Imperial College Information
📁 Centre for Computing Services Information
📁 Library Services, References and Dictionaries
📁 Directory Services
📁 Networking
📁 Gopher World (other Gopher Servers, FAQ, Wais, etc.)
📁 Search GopherSpace

The Imperial College Gopher site

Imperial College London, Chemistry Department
gopher://argon.ch.ic.ac.uk
Contact: Henry Rzepa
h.rzepa@ic.ac.uk

Imperial College, Department of Computing
gopher://src.doc.ic.ac.uk
Contact: Lee McLoughlin
lmjm@doc.ic.ac.uk

UK Main FTP Archive, Imperial College
gopher://src.doc.ic.ac.uk
Contact: Lee McLoughlin
lmjm@doc.ic.ac.uk

JANET News Machine
gopher://news.janet.ac.uk
D.Salmon@jnt.ac.uk
Contact: David Salmon

LSE/AppleUK HE Social Sciences Gopher
gopher://158.143.96.100
Contact: Craig Whitehead
c.whitehead@lse.ac.uk

Liverpool University, Computer Science
gopher://gopher.csc.liv.ac.uk
Contact: gophermaster@csc.liv.ac.uk
Contact: Dave Shield
D.T.Shield@compsci.liverpool.ac.uk

UKOLN: The Office for Library and Information Networking
gopher://ukoln.bath.ac.uk
Contact: gopher@ukoln.bath.ac.uk

BUBL: The Bulletin Board for Libraries
gopher://ukoln.bath.ac.uk:7070
Contact: gopher@ukoln.bath.ac.uk

Oxford Brookes University
gopher://cs3.brookes.ac.uk
Contact: shewison@brookes.ac.uk
Contact: Hewison Sj
p0063886@cs3.oxford-brookes.ac.uk

Oxford University Libraries Board – OLIS
gopher://gopher.lib.ox.ac.uk
Contact: Jose_Marques@olis.lib.ox.ac.uk

Oxford University, Radcliffe Science Library
  gopher://rsl.ox.ac.uk
Contact: Dave Price
djp@rsl.ox.ac.uk

Queen Mary & Westfield College London
  gopher://gopher.qmw.ac.uk
Contact: info-admin@qmw.ac.uk

Queen Mary & Westfield College, Department of Computer Science, London
  gopher://gopher.dcs.qmw.ac.uk
Contact: amandla@dcs.qmw.ac.uk

Social Statistics Research Unit, City University
  gopher://ssru.city.ac.uk

Society for Computing, Durham University
  gopher://johnson.dur.ac.uk
Contact: dur.info@durham.ac.uk
Contact: Nigel Ellis
n.r.ellis@durham.ac.uk

UK Chemistry Database Service (Daresbury Laboratory)
  gopher://dlvb.daresbury.ac.uk

Mailbase (mailing list information)
  gopher://mailbase.ac.uk
Contact: mailbase-helpline@mailbase.ac.uk

UK TeX Archive
  gopher://ftp.tex.ac.uk
Contact: spqr@minster.york.ac.uk

University of Bath
  gopher://gopher.bath.ac.uk
Contact: gopher@bath.ac.uk
Contact: Andy Powell
A.Powell@bath.ac.uk

University of Birmingham
  gopher://gopher.bham.ac.uk
Contact: Glyn Simpson
g.simpson@bham.ac.uk
Contact: Roy Pearce
r.a.pearce@bham.ac.uk

University of Bradford Campus Wide Information Service
  gopher://gopher.brad.ac.uk
Contact: info-admin@bradford.ac.uk

University of Edinburgh
>   gopher://gopher.ed.ac.uk
>Contact: gopher@edinburgh.ac.uk

University of Manchester
>   gopher://uts.mcc.ac.uk
>Contact: Geoff Lane
>zzassgl@uts.mcc.ac.uk

University of Manchester and UMIST Information Server
>   gopher://info.mcc.ac.uk
>Contact: Mark Whidby
>m.whidby@mcc.ac.uk

University of Surrey, Department of Chemical and Process Engineering
>   gopher://gopher.cpe.surrey.ac.uk
>Contact: Andy Tate
>ces1at@surrey.ac.uk

University of Surrey
>   gopher://gopher.surrey.ac.uk
>Contact: Hans Litteck
>cus1hl@surrey.ac.uk

University of Warwick
>   gopher://gopher.csv.warwick.ac.uk
>Contact: Denis Anthony +44 203 524629
>cudma@warwick.ac.uk

IRIS Explorer Center Bulletin Board
>   gopher://nags2.nag.co.uk/visual/IE/iecbb

NAG Bulletin Board Services
>   gopher://nags2.nag.co.uk

University of Cambridge
>   gopher://gopher.cam.ac.uk
>Contact: John Line
>gopher-admin@ucs.cam.ac.uk

Durham University Campus Information Service
>   gopher://delphi.dur.ac.uk

Exeter University
>   gopher://cen.ex.ac.uk
>Contact: Howard Davies
>H.E.Davies@exeter.ac.uk
>Contact: Martin Myhill
>M.R.Myhill@exeter.ac.uk

Imperial College, Dictionary of Computing
> gopher://wombat.doc.ic.ac.uk
Contact: Denis Howe
dbh@doc.ic.ac.uk

Liverpool University HP-UX Software Archive
> gopher://ftp.csc.liv.ac.uk

Loughborough University Computer Studies
> gopher://alpha.lut.ac.uk
Contact: A.Schappo@lut.ac.uk

Loughborough University High Performance Networks
> gopher://agate.lut.ac.uk
Contact: Info.Server@lut.ac.uk

Loughborough University Computing Services
> gopher://hill.lut.ac.uk

Oxford University Computing Laboratory
> gopher://thom5.ecs.ox.ac.uk
Contact: support@comlab.ox.ac.uk

Oxford University Experimental Psychology
> gopher://ep1.psych.ox.ac.uk

Oxford University Molecular Biology Data Centre
> gopher://gopher.molbiol.ox.ac.uk
Contact: jasper@molbiol.ox.ac.uk

University of York, Electronics Department
> gopher://menu.crc.ac.uk

UK Human Genome Mapping Project
> gopher://gopher.ohm.york.ac.uk

Royal Postgraduate Medical School, Hammersmith Hospital
> gopher://mpcc2.rpms.ac.uk
Contact: Don-Carlso Abrams
c.abrams@rpms.ac.uk

University of Sunderland
> gopher://orac.sunderland.ac.uk
Contact: Dave Webster
root@orac.sundp.ac.uk

Kingston University
> gopher://gopher.king.ac.uk
Contact: J.Jabbar@king.ac.uk

Law Technology Centre Gopher
gopher://gopher.law.warwick.ac.uk
Contact: Colin Shaw
laraq@warwick.ac.uk

University of Newcastle upon Tyne experimental Gopher server
gopher://gopher.newcastle.ac.uk
Contact: Sarah Ghani
S.E.Ghani@newcastle.ac.uk

University of East Anglia, Information Systems
gopher://gopher.sys.uea.ac.uk
Contact: Shaun McCullagh
sm@sys.uea.ac.uk

University of Glasgow Information Service
gopher://info.gla.ac.uk
Contact: Alan Dawson
A.Dawson@compserv.gla.ac.uk

University of Birmingham, School of Computer Science
gopher://gopher.cs.bham.ac.uk
Contact: K.A.Marlow@computer-science.birmingham.ac.uk

University of Brighton
gopher://gopher.bton.ac.uk
Contact: gopheradmin@vms.bton.ac.uk

NURSING New Gopher Service for Nurses
gopher@warwick.ac.uk/crocus.csv.warwick.ac.uk:10001
Contact: Denis Anthony, unix support 0203 524629

Oxford University Top-Level Server
gopher://gopher.ox.ac.uk
Contact: Steve Jones (Oxford 273206)
saj@vax.ox.ac.uk

Newcastle University Theory of Condensed Matter Group
gopher://bragg.ncl.ac.uk
Contact: Jerry.Hagon@newcastle.ac.uk

University of Cambridge, Department of Engineering
gopher://gopher.eng.cam.ac.uk
Contact: Tim Love
gopher@eng.cam.ac.uk

University of Wales, Aberystwyth
gopher://deca.aber.ac.uk
Contact: Jeremy Perkins
jwp@aber.ac.uk

EMWAC: European Microsoft Windows NT Academic Centre
gopher://emwac-info.ed.ac.uk
Contact: emwac@ed.ac.uk

Colloid Group, Department of Chemistry, University of Surrey
gopher://odin.chem.surrey.ac.uk
Contact: Paul Mitchell
chs1pm@surrey.ac.uk

University of York
gopher://gopher.york.ac.uk
Contact: gopher@unix.york.ac.uk

Theory and Formal Methods, Department of Computing, Imperial College
gopher://theory.doc.ic.ac.uk
Contact: md@doc.ic.ac.uk (Mark Dawson)
Imperial College, Theory and Formal Methods

Sheffield Hallam University
gopher://gopher.shu.ac.uk
Contact: Dave Haywood
Liaison@shu.ac.uk

Queens University Belfast
gopher://jupiter.qub.ac.uk
Contact: George Munroe
CCG0073@v2.qub.ac.uk

Decanter Magazine
gopher://gopher.internet.com/collected/decanter:2100
Contact: raisch@internet.com

Network Training Materials Gopher
gopher://trainmat.ncl.ac.uk
Contact: Margaret.Isaacs@newcastle.ac.uk

Action for Blind People
gopher://able.afbp.org
Contact: Tony Holroyd
tony@afbp.org

UMDS: United Medical and Dental Schools Gopher
gopher://gopher.umds.ac.uk
Contact: Chris Sleep
csleep@miranda.umds.ac.uk

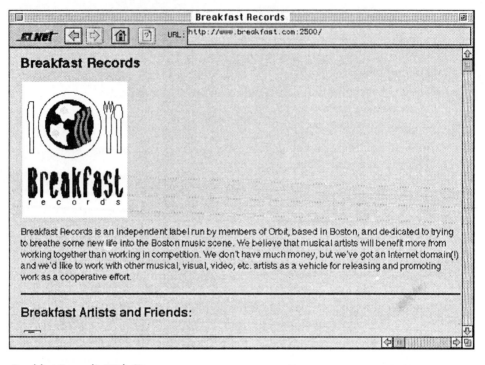

Breakfast Record's Web Site

University of Hull, Department of Computer Science
    gopher://gopher.dcs.hull.ac.uk
Contact: Brian Tompsett
bct@dcs.hull.ac.uk

South Bank University
    gopher://gopher.sbu.ac.uk
Contact: John Shanks
SHANKSJ@uk.ac.sbu.vax

Teesside University
    gopher://gopher.tees.ac.uk
Contact: 'Jon Smith, Library and Information Systems'
Jon.Smith@tees.ac.uk

De Montfort University Gopher Server
    gopher://gopher.dmu.ac.uk
Contact: Andy Humberston
iah@dmu.ac.uk

Daresbury Laboratory
> gopher://gopher.dl.ac.uk
Contact: P.Kummer@dl.ac.uk

University of Bradford Electronic Engineering Help System
> gopher://manuel.brad.ac.uk
Contact: David Loomes
djloomes@bradford.ac.uk

Society for Experimental Biology
> gopher://130.209.9.190
Contact: Julian Dow
gbaa02@udcf.gla.ac.uk

University of Wolverhampton, SCIT
> gopher://scitsc.wlv.ac.uk
Contact: Peter Burden
jphb@scitsc.wlv.ac.uk

University of Sheffield
> gopher://gopher2.shef.ac.uk
Contact: Paul Leman

> p.leman@sheffield.ac.uk

Ireland
The Irish point of entry is at
> gopher://Danann.hea.ie:70/Ireland/.Gopher/OtherGophers/Ireland

Useful UK gophers

Gopher Software Distribution
> gopher://boombox.micro.umn.edu/gopher
Almost every Gopher client is available here.

Usenet News at Aston University
> gopher://news.aston.ac.uk/
Every FAQ you are ever likely to want to read and many that you never would, plus search engines to help you in your quest. Excellent site.

Information sources available on Internet
> info.mcc.ac.uk/external/internet_uk

Satellite images of Europe
> gopher://merlot.welch.jhu.edu/images/

Imperial College FTP archive
> gopher://gopher.cam.ac.uk/
Gopher access to the most comprehensive UK FTP archives at ftp.doc.ic.ac.uk.

University of Bristol, Maths and Statistics Gopher
gopher://gopher.stats.bris.ac.uk

International Centre for Distance Learning
gopher://rowan.open.ac.uk

Kite Flying – Oxford Brookes University 1
gopher://gopher.cpe.surrey.ac.uk/GOPHER/KITES

Almac BBS Historic Scotland Gopher
gopher://almac.co.uk/scotland/historic

Manchester Metropolitan University Galleries and Museums
gopher://info.mcc.ac.uk/city/museums

The definitive list of UK sitcoms
gopher://info.mcc.ac.uk/miscellany/sitcom

Useful Gopher sites
Hierarchical Gopher information search site.

The University of Minnesota's Gopher
gopher://gopher.micro.umn.ed
The mother of all Gophers – where it all began.

Moon Travel Handbooks
gopher://gopher.moon.com:7000
Commercial travel book gopher.

Kevin's World
gopher://skynet.usask.ca
Welcome to Prarie Dog Town – Kevin's crazy world.

Project Gutenberg
gopher.tc.umn.edu/Libraries/Electronic Books
Hundreds of e-texts, many classic novels.

EnviroGopher
gopher://envirolink.org
Environmental information, green issues.

Virtual Reality Space
gopher://ftp.cc.utexas.edu/pub/output/vr:3003

Apple Computer Higher Education Gopher server
gopher://info.hed.apple.com
Gopher for the Apple Mac community.

```
╔══════════════════════════════════════════════════════════════╗
║ ▒▒▒══ Authors, Books, Periodicals, Zines (Factsheet Five lives here!) ══▒▒ ║
║ ▼   Internet Gopher ©1991-1993 University of Minnesota.       ║
╠══════════════════════════════════════════════════════════════╣
║ 📁Electronic Serials archive at CICNet                      ⬆ ║
║ 📁Factsheet Five, Electric                                    ║
║ 📁French Language Press Review                                ║
║ 📁FringeWare<tm>, Inc., Publishers of Fringe Ware Review      ║
║ 📄FYI France: the Grandes Ecole, on the Future, by Jack Kessler ║
║ 📁Gnosis Magazine – ToC, Back Issues and Guidelines          ║
║ 📁Natural Literacy Publishers – Environmental Publications    ║
║ 📁ND Magazine archives                                        ║
║ 📁Incunabula                                                  ║
║ 📁LOCUS Magazine – Tom Maddox reports on the Electronic Frontier ║
║ 📁MicroTimes                                                  ║
║ 📁Miscellaneous Cyberprose                                    ║
║ 📁MONDO 2000                                                  ║
║ 📁Online Zines                                                ║
║ 📁Poetry                                                      ║
║ 📁Whole Earth Review, the Magazine                           ║
║ 📁Wired Magazine                                             ║
║ 📁ZYZZYVA: the last word: west coast writers & artists      ⬇ ║
╚══════════════════════════════════════════════════════════════╝
```

Satillite image from gopher://merlot.welch.jhu.edu/images/

Telecom Information Exchange Services (TIES)
    gopher://info.itu.ch
    Network and telecomms information.

Roswell Electronic Computer Bookstore
    gopher://nstn.ns.ca/Other Gophers in Nova
    Scotia/Roswell Electronic Computer Bookstore.

Selected Public Domain Software Archives
    gopher://info.itu.ch/.1/Softarchives
    Pointers to a collection of public domain software archives.

Computer hardware and software companies
    gopher://info.itu.ch/.1/ITcompanies
    Computer companies that are running their own Gopher servers.

World Health Organisation, Regional Office for Europe
    gopher://gopher.who.dk

Gopher Jewels

Gopher servers around the world have grown at an amazing rate. A byproduct of this growth has been the difficulty of quickly locating sites and information that you need. Gopher Jewels is a project that attempts to get around this by building a hierarchical front end to all Gopher sites. It is not perfect and may well be slower than using other search methods for some purposes, but it does provide an excellent reference point. Like any information system, it does tend to reflect the priorities of the builders. Personally, I find it somewhat offensive to find 'fun-stuff' and 'multimedia' lumped into the same category, as if they were somehow logically related.

As Gopher Jewels themselves put it:

We offer this new approach to the Internet community as an alternative to the more traditional subject tree design. Although many of the features, individually, are not new, the combined set represents the best features found on sites around the world. We do not pretend to have the answer, but offer our solutions to navigating information by subject as an experiment in the evolution of information cataloging. Our focus is on locating information by subject and does not attempt to address the quality of the information we point to.

A new version of Gopher Jewels now offers the following changes and additions:

- Collapsed the top menu to one page
- Jughead search of all menus in Gopher Jewels
- Option to jump up one menu level from any directory
- Option to jump to the top menu from any directory
- Access tips in help documents
- Gopher Jewels list archives and Talk list archives
- Other gopher related archives are available
- Help and archives are searchable by WAIS

Gopher Jewels will also soon add sites in the United Kingdom, Australia and Israel.

Gopher Jewels is at

```
gopher://cwis.usc.edu/11/Other_Gophers_and_Information_
Resources/
```

Gopher Jewels WWW service – you can use Gopher Jewels via the World Wide Web at

```
http://galaxy.einet.net/gopher/gopher.html
```

or

```
http://galaxy.einet.net/GJ/index.html
```

Gopher Jewels List

A moderated mailing list for sharing interesting Gopher finds is GOPHER-JEW-ELS@EINET.NET.

The list owner/moderator is David Riggins

>   `david.riggins@tpoint.com`

To subscribe send the line

>   `SUBSCRIBE GOPHERJEWELS firstname lastname`

to

>   `LISTPROC@EINET.NET.`

Leave the Subject line blank.

An unmoderated list called

>   `GOPHERJEWELS-TALK@EINET.NET`

exists for new users to ask questions and get answers on using Gopher. You can also post inquiries for locating information, discuss issues such as information quality and content, Gopher features you would like to see and other related topics.

To subscribe send the line

>   `SUBSCRIBE GOPHERJEWELS-TALK firstname lastname`

to

>   `LISTPROC@EINET.NET`

Leave the Subject line blank

Gopher information services

Learning to use the network
>   `is.internic.net/infosource/getting-started/tools`

Gopherin
>   `ftp://ubvm.cc.buffalo.edu/gophern`

Gopher Readme
>   `ftp://boombox.micro.umn.edu/pub/gopher/00README`

Gopher FAQ
>   `ftp://rtfm.mit.edu/pub/usenet/news.answers/gopher-faq`

Gopher demo
>   `gopher://gopher/gopher.micro.umn.edu`

Gopher sites
>   `ftp/liberty.uc.wlu.edu/pub/lawlib/veronica.gopher.sites`

Gopher Telnet demo
>   `telnet://consultant.micro.umn.ed:gopher`

GopherCon 93 Conference Summary
>   `gopher://groucho.unidata.ucar.edu/systems/servers/gophercon93`

Gopher Software at Minnesota
>   `gopher://boombox.micro.umn.edu/`

Veronica

What is Veronica?

Very Easy Rodent-Oriented Net-wide Index to Computerized Archives.

Veronica offers a keyword search of most Gopher-server menus in the world. The search results can connect you directly to the data source. Currently, Veronica has over 12 million titles indexed.

Veronica is a search engine for Gopher. There is so much information now available by Gopher it has become extremely difficult to find references to specific subjects. Veronica is built into Gopher servers – you will notice it as you travel around, probably at the first Gopher site you visit. It is certainly one for your bookmarks list.

Veronica traverses Gopherspace daily and collects menu items, building an index of them. When you ask for a search, it builds a custom menu from this index. It is very similar to using Gopher itself, whatever your browser.

When you find a Veronica server, you will notice that there are many available places to search. They all contain the same information. You will soon find that at certain times, certain Veronica servers are too heavily used to get access to. Start with a server close to you – Imperial College runs one in the UK. If that does not work, move outwards to European servers. You will get results faster the closer the server is – but in the end it does not really matter which you use.

Veronica allows a more sophisticated searching than the simple entering of a word to check. Boolean searches allow the use of statements such as AND or NOT to hone searches. You can also use a * at the end of a word. For example, to search for children, childcare and chilterns you would use 'chil*'. To exclude terms like chilterns you would use 'chil* NOT chilt*'.

Where is Veronica?

There are currently four publicly-accessible Veronica servers. All of them can be accessed via the Veronica Gopher menu at

```
gopher://veronica.scs.unr.edu
```

If that server is down, try one of the other sites below which has a Gopher menu advertising Veronica searches.

UNR, Nevada, USA
```
gopher://veronica.scs.unr.edu/veronica
```

CNIDR, North Carolina, USA
```
gopher://wisteria.cnidr.org
```

NYSERNET, New York, USA
```
gopher://nysernet.org/Search the Internet
```

SERRA, Pisa, Italy
```
gopher://gopher.unipi.it/University of Pisa - Services
```

Veronica Information

Veronica FAQ

        gopher://veronica.scs.unr.edu/eronica/veronica-faq

Veronica blurb

        ftp://cs.dal.ca/pub/comp.archives/bionet.software/veronica

Veronica demo

        gopher://veronica.scs.unr.edu

WAIS (Wide Area Information Service)

What is WAIS?

Wide Area Information Service is another tool for information search and retrieval. Although a client-server tool like Gopher and WWW, the relationship between the client and server is somewhat different.

You choose which WAIS databases you wish to search and you specify the word or phrase that you are looking for.

WAIS is a networked information retrieval system. WAIS currently uses TCP/IP to connect client applications to information servers. Client applications are able to retrieve text or multimedia documents stored on the servers.

Client applications request documents using keywords. Servers search a full text index for the documents and return a list of documents containing the keyword. The client may then request the server to send a copy of any of the documents found.

WAIS was developed as a project of Thinking Machines, Apple Computer, Dow Jones and KPMG Peat Marwick. A version of WAIS that is freely redistributable is available with full source to the server, indexing software and many clients.

Thinking Machines no longer supports the publicly distributed WAIS [as of WAIS-8-b5.1]. Support and development of 'free' WAIS has been taken over by CNIDR (Clearinghouse for Networked Information Discovery and Retrieval).

Current CNIDR releases are called freeWAIS, to help reduce confusion.

        http://cnidr.org/welcome.html

Commercial development and support of WAIS is now available from WAIS, Inc. WAIS, Inc. was founded by many of the original developers of WAIS. Although WAIS, Inc. does sell commercial servers with extra features and full support, they continue to provide other freely redistributable tools.

        ftp://ftp.wais.com/pub/wais-inc-doc/wais-inc-company-story.txt

Thinking Machines runs a WAIS server, directory-of-servers.src, which is a 'white pages' of other WAIS servers. You can query this WAIS server to find other servers and new ones that pop up. When someone creates a server that they want others to know about, s/he registers that server with the directory-of-servers.

WAIS via Telnet

You can Telnet to a variety of Wais servers

```
telnet://quake.think.com:swais
telnet://swais.cwis.uci.edu:swais
telnet://sunsite.unc.edu:swais
telnet://nnsc.nsf.net:wais
telnet://info.funet.fi
```

WAIS information sources

Perhaps the best place to start is the WAIS white sheet available via anonymous FTP from

```
ftp://ftp.think.com/wais/wais-corporate-paper.text
```

This will give you a good idea of why people got interested in WAIS and a very simple overview of the WAIS architecture.

A bibliography of articles published on WAIS is available from

```
ftp://ftp.wais.com/pub/wais-inc-doc/bibliography.txt
```

Newsgroups

```
news:comp.infosystems.wais.
```

The newsgroup is regularly visited by the authors of WAIS and other experts on using both WAIS and other resources on the Internet.

Mailing lists include wais-interest, contact

```
wais-interest-request@think.com
```

This is a moderated list used to announce new releases for the Internet.

WAIS-discussion is a digested, moderated list on electronic publishing issues in general and Wide Area Information Servers in particular. There are postings every week or two. Contact

```
wais-discussion-request@think.com
```

WAIS-talk is an open list for implementors and developers. This is a technical list that is not meant to be used as a support list. Contact

```
wais-talk-request@think.com
```

Sig-wais-info is a list for announcements of meetings and presentations of the WAIS Special Interest Group. These face-to-face conferences provide useful demonstrations and talks on WAIS. Contact

```
sig-wais-info@cnidr.org
```

WAISCUST is for discussion among customers of WAIS Inc. It is not sponsored by WAIS Inc. and opinions expressed here are those of the individual posters.

To subscribe, send mail to listserv@rice.edu with the message

```
subscribe waiscust firstname lastname
```

CNIDR is releasing information on freeWAIS status, plans and operational hints via World Wide Web. This is perhaps the best way to get up-to-date information on freeWAIS.

```
<a HREF="http://kudzu.cnidr.org/cnidr_projects">CNIDR
Projects</a>
```

The United States Geological Survey has produced a number of training video tapes on the subject of Wide Area Information Servers. Information on their contents and availability is available with WWW.

```
<a
HREF="http://billings.nlm.nih.gov/current_news.dir/wais_tapes.h
tml">Tapes</a>
```

WAIS software

For the current release of the UNIX server and clients distribution of WAIS.

```
ftp://ftp.cnidr.org/pub/NIDR.tools/freeWAIS-0.3.tar.Z
```

RELEASE-NOTES

```
http://cnidr.org/cnidr_projects/freewais0.2.html
```

WAIStation.app – a NeXTstep based client interface for NeXT workstations.

```
ftp://ftp.think.com/wais/WAIStation-NeXT-1.9.6.tar.Z
```

WAIStation – a Macintosh interface client based on MacTCP. MacTCP must be obtained separately. Source to the client in THINK C is available from quake.-think.com:/wais/WAIStation-0-62-Sources.sit.hqx.

```
ftp://sunsite.unc.edu/pub/wais/clients/macintosh/WAIStation-0-
63.sit.hqx
```

This is a free Macintosh WAIS client that supports both WAIS and the new Z39.50 commercial servers. Requires wais-for-mac-1.1.sea.hqx A product of WAIS Inc. Source is also available from

```
ftp://ftp.wais.com:/pub/freeware/mac/src/wais-for-mac-1.1-
src.sea.hqx
```

HyperWais – A Macintosh Hypercard client interface. Requires System 7.0, MacTCP 1.1 and Hypercard 2.1 . Source is also available from

```
ftp://ftp.wais.com/pub/freeware/mac/HyperWais.sea.hqx
```

MacWAIS is a shareware product of MCC.

```
ftp://ftp.einet.net/einet/mac/macwais1.28.sea.hqx
```

Pcwais is an MS-DOS client interface based on Borland TurboVision and the Crynwr packet drivers.

```
ftp://sunsite.unc.edu/pub/packages/infosystems/wais/clients/ms-
dos/pcdist.zip
```

oacwais is an MS-DOS client interface based on FTP Software's PC/TCP. This must be obtained separately.

```
ftp://oac.hsc.uth.tmc.edu/public/dos/misc/oacwais.exe
```

Wwais is a Microsoft Windows 3.0 client interface based on Visual Basic and Novell's LAN Workplace for DOS. LAN Workplace for DOS must be obtained separately.

```
ftp://wuarchive.wustl.edu/systems/ibmpc/win3/util/wwais103.zip
```

WinWAIS is the USGS version of WAIS for Windows. Includes support for SLIP, ODI and CRYNWR packet drivers.

```
ftp://ridgisd.er.usgs.gov/software/wais/wnwais22a.zip
```

Source is also available from

```
ftp://ridgisd.er.usgs.gov:/software/wais/wnwsrc22.zip
```

WWW: World Wide Web

The World Wide Web is one of the youngest tools on the Internet, yet it has had a huge impact – probably changing the way we see and use global networking forever. A couple of years ago the total number of Web sites could probably be counted in the low tens – now it is counted in the hundred of thousands.

Several factors have contributed to this phenomenal growth - ease of use, availability of excellent software, the multimedia nature of the system. One of the main reasons is surely that the Web arrived at exactly the right time. With US politicians and business just noticing that the Internet had grown behind their backs, the Information Superhighway had been mooted as the answer to many ills. Despite the excellence ot other Internet tools, they did not have much instant appeal to newcomers. The World Wide Web and especially the Mosaic browsers from NCSA, changed all of that practically overnight.

UK WWW sites

3W Magazine
```
http://www.3w.com/3W/
```

ALIWEB
```
http://web.nexor.co.uk/aliweb/doc/aliweb.html
```

Amateur Radio
```
http://www.mcc.ac.uk/OtherPages/AmateurRadio.html
```

Apollo Advertising
```
http://apollo.co.uk/home.html
```

Archie
> http://web.nexor.co.uk/archie.html

Astronomy
> http://cast0.ast.cam.ac.uk/overview.html

BBCNetworking Club
> http://www.bbcnc.org.uk/

Birmingham SoCS Home Page
> http://www.cs.bham.ac.uk/

BLAST Database Searches at NCBI
> http://www.bio.cam.ac.uk/seqsrch/blast.html

Brunel Information Service
> http://http1.brunel.ac.uk:8080/

BUBL Information Service Web Server
> http://bubl.bath.ac.uk/BUBLHOME.html

Cambridge Astronomy
> http://cast0.ast.cam.ac.uk/

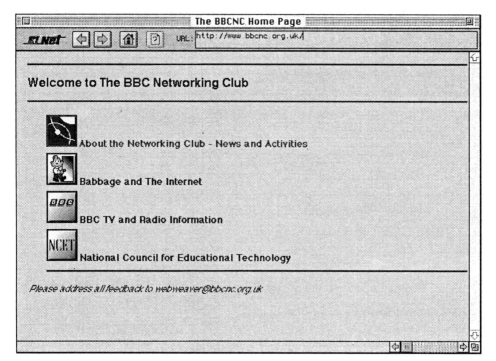

BBC Networking Club WWW site

Cambridge School of Biological Sciences
http://www.bio.cam.ac.uk/

Cambridge University Chemical Laboratory Home Page
http://www.ch.cam.ac.uk/

Cambridge, University of, Computer Laboratory Home Page
http://www.cl.cam.ac.uk/

Cardiff's usage statistics in graph form
http://www.cm.cf.ac.uk/htbin/Graphs/show_stats_graphs

Centre for Neural Networks
http://physig.ph.kcl.ac.uk/cnn/cnn.html

Charlie's Virtual Anthology
http://tardis.ed.ac.uk/~charlie/fictionhome.html

Chemistry at the University of Sheffield
http://www2.shef.ac.uk/chemistry/chemistry-home.html

City University
http://web.cs.city.ac.uk/documents/home.html

City University, Computer Science
http://web.cs.city.ac.uk/documents/city/informatics/cs/cs.html

CityScape Bar
http://www.cityscape.co.uk:81/bar/

CityScape Internet Services Home Page
http://www.cityscape.co.uk/

COMMA Hotlist Database – Subject Search
http://www.cm.cf.ac.uk/htbin/AndrewW/Hotlist/hot_list_search.csh

COMMA Information Server
http://www.cm.cf.ac.uk/

Commercial WWW for the UK and the world
http://mach.demon.co.uk:8000/mach.demon

Communications Research Group
http://web.cs.nott.ac.uk/crg.html

Communications Research Group, Nottingham
http://web.cs.nott.ac.uk/

Computer Graphics Unit – Research
http://info.mcc.ac.uk/CGU/CGU-research.html

Computing
http://web.doc.ic.ac.uk/bySubject/Computing/Overview.html

Computing Dictionary
http://wombat.doc.ic.ac.uk/

Control Group
http://www-control.eng.cam.ac.uk/

Csound Front Page
http://www.leeds.ac.uk/music/Man/c_front.html

Department of Chemistry, Imperial College.
http://www.ch.ic.ac.uk/

Department of Computer Science, University of Exeter
http://www.dcs.exeter.ac.uk/

Department of Computing, Imperial College, London.
http://www.doc.ic.ac.uk/

Durham/RAL HEP Databases – HEPDATA
http://cpt1.dur.ac.uk/HEPDATA

Ecosse Group Page
http://www.chemeng.ed.ac.uk/ecosse/

Edinburgh Chemical Engineering WWW Home Page
http://www.chemeng.ed.ac.uk/

ELSNET'S Home Page
http://www.cogsci.ed.ac.uk/elsnet/home.html

EMWAC Web Server
http://emwac.ed.ac.uk/html/top.html

Europe by map
http://www.tue.nl/maps.html

Fantasy Baseball Home Page
http://www.cm.cf.ac.uk/User/Gwyn.Price/fantasy_baseball.html

Fantasy World Cup web site
http://www.atm.ch.cam.ac.uk/sports/FGS/

Formal Methods
http://www.comlab.ox.ac.uk/archive/formal-methods.html

Galactic SNRs: Introduction
http://cast0.ast.cam.ac.uk/MRAO/snrs.intro.html

Hangman at COMMA in Cardiff
http://www.cm.cf.ac.uk/htbin/RobH/hangman?go

HENSA Archives - funded by JISC
http://www.hensa.ac.uk/

HENSA Web Cache
http://www.hensa.ac.uk/cache.html

Heriot-Watt University
http://vulcan.cee.hw.ac.uk:8080/

High-performance Networks and Distributed Systems Archive
http://hill.lut.ac.uk/DS-Archive/HighPerformanceNetworking.html

HST – UK Support Facility
http://cast0.ast.cam.ac.uk/HST/

Hypertext front-end to the rec.arts.movies (Cardiff UK)
http://www.cm.cf.ac.uk/Movies/moviequery.html

IECIRIS Explorer Center
http://www.nag.co.uk:70/1h/

Web movie browser at Cardiff

Image Processing Group at King's College London
http://physig.ph.kcl.ac.uk/ipg/Welcome.html

Indie/alternative music scene
http://web.cs.nott.ac.uk/Music/

Information on Sheffield Wednesday FC
http://web.cs.nott.ac.uk/Users/anb/Football/index.html

Information Technology Training Initiative
http://info.mcc.ac.uk/CGU/ITTI/ITTI.html

Institute for Computer-based Learning
http://www.icbl.hw.ac.uk/

Institute for Transport Studies home page
http://its02.leeds.ac.uk/

Institute of Astronomy
http://cast0.ast.cam.ac.uk/IOA/IOA.html

Interesting places in the Web
http://web.nexor.co.uk/places.html

ITTI Gravigs Project
http://info.mcc.ac.uk/CGU/ITTI/gravigs.html

J.R.R. Tolkien Information Page
http://www.math.uni-hamburg.de/.relippert/tolkien/rootpage.html

JumpStation Front Page
http://www.stir.ac.uk/jsbin/js

LaTeX2HTML Translator
http://cbl.leeds.ac.uk/nikos/tex2html/doc/latex2html/latex2html.html

Learned InfoNet
http://info.learned.co.uk/

Leeds University Department of Music
http://www.leeds.ac.uk/music.html

Leeds, University of
http://www.leeds.ac.uk/

Leeds, University of
http://gps.leeds.ac.uk/

Leeds, University of, Computing Service
http://www.leeds.ac.uk/ucs/ucs.html

Lemmings II Tribes
http://www.cm.cf.ac.uk/Latex/lemmings2/lemmings.html

Manchester, University of
http://info.mcc.ac.uk/UofM.html

Manchester, University of, CGU software
http://info.mcc.ac.uk/CGU/CGU-software.html

Manchester, University of, Computer Graphics Unit
http://info.mcc.ac.uk/CGU/CGU-intro.html

Martijn's Page
http://web.nexor.co.uk/mak/mak.html

Message of the Day
http://gauss.dur.ac.uk:8000

Midwifery
http://www.csv.warwick.ac.uk:8000/midwifery.html

Mirroring in the Web
http://web.nexor.co.uk/mirror/mirror.html

MRAO home page
http://cast0.ast.cam.ac.uk/MRAO/mrao.home.html

Nathan Hoover's Juggling Page
http://www.hal.com/~nathan/Juggling/

Networking: overview of information available
http://web.doc.ic.ac.uk/bySubject/Networking.html

New services from Cambridge Astronomy
http://cast0.ast.cam.ac.uk/whatsnew.html

Newcastle, University of, Department of Computer Science W3 server
http://dcs.www.ncl.ac.uk/

NEXOR
http://web.nexor.co.uk/welcome.html

Niel's Timelines and Scales of Measurement List
http://cast0.ast.cam.ac.uk/Xray_www/niel/scales.html

Nottingham Arabidopsis Stock Centre Home Page
http://nasc.life.nott.ac.uk/index.html

Nottingham, University of
http://www.nott.ac.uk/

Numerical Algorithms Group Ltd
http://www.nag.co.uk:70/

NURSE
```
http://www.csv.warwick.ac.uk:8000/default.html
```

Obituary Page
```
http://catless.ncl.ac.uk/Obituary/
```

Online Dictionary of Computing
```
http://wombat.doc.ic.ac.uk/
```

Open University ACS Information Store
```
http://acs-info.open.ac.uk/info-start.html
```

PASSWORD Project
```
http://web.nexor.co.uk/users/cjr/password.html
```

Pipex
```
http://www.pipex.net/
```

Preparation of Papers
```
http://cast0.ast.cam.ac.uk/documents/Journal.html
```

Puzzle (OLD VERSION)
```
http://www.cm.cf.ac.uk/AndysTestMenu/PuzzleDocument.html
```

Red Dwarf
```
http://http2.brunel.ac.uk:8080/red_dwarf/home.html
```

Redirection
```
http://cbl.leeds.ac.uk/
```

Requirements Engineering Newsletter Index
```
http://web.doc.ic.ac.uk/req-eng/index.html
```

Royal Greenwich Observatory
```
http://cast0.ast.cam.ac.uk/RGO/RGO.html
```

Rutherford Appleton Laboratory
```
http://www.rl.ac.uk/home.html
```

Satellite Images
```
http://web.nexor.co.uk/places/satelite.html
```

School of Chemistry
```
http://chem.leeds.ac.uk/default.html
```

Science Fiction TV series Guides
```
http://www.ee.surrey.ac.uk/Personal/sf.html
```

Sheffield Collegiate Cricket Club
```
http://www2.shef.ac.uk/chemistry/collegiate/collegiate-
home.html
```

Sheffield, University of
http://www2.shef.ac.uk/default.html

Simon Homepage
http://web.elec.qmw.ac.uk:12121/SIMON HOMEPAGE

Solid State Physics WEB Server (Experimental)
http://bragg.ncl.ac.uk/index.html

Southampton University Astronomy Group
http://sousun1.phys.soton.ac.uk/

Star Trek: Deep Space Nine
http://www.ee.surrey.ac.uk/Personal/STDS9/

Star Trek: Next Generation
http://www.ee.surrey.ac.uk/Personal/STTNG/

Strathclyde, University of, Home Page
http://www.strath.ac.uk/

Subjective Electronic Information Repository
http://cbl.leeds.ac.uk/nikos/doc/repository.html

Sunderland, University of
http://orac.sunderland.ac.uk/

SuperJANET Information Server
http://gala.jnt.ac.uk/

SUSI
http://web.nexor.co.uk/susi/susi.html

Sussex, University of
http://www.cogs.susx.ac.uk/COGS

Trojan Room Coffee Machine
http://www.cl.cam.ac.uk/coffee/coffee.html

UCL MICE Home Page
http://www.cs.ucl.ac.uk/mice/mice.html

UK FACTS Center
http://www.uky.edu/ComputingCenter/Welcome.html

UK Guide
http://www.cs.ucl.ac.uk/misc/uk/intro.html

UNIXhelp for users
http://www.ucs.ed.ac.uk/Unixhelp/TOP_.html

Virtual Reality

    `http://www.cms.dmu.ac.uk:9999/People/cph/vrstuff.html`

Visualisation 2: Resource list

    `http://info.mcc.ac.uk/CGU/ITTI/Vis2/reslist.html`

Wales

    `http://www.cm.cf.ac.uk/Places/wales.html`

Warwick, University of

    `http://www.csv.warwick.ac.uk/default.html`

Web-Elements

    `http://www2.shef.ac.uk/chemistry/web-elements/web-elements-home.html`

Welcome to the Computing Service

    `http://www.ucs.ed.ac.uk/`

WWW Servers in UK

    `http://www.ucs.ed.ac.uk/General/uk.html`

X-Ray Group Public Page

    `http://cast0.ast.cam.ac.uk/Xray_www/xray_pubpage.html`

Z notation

    `http://www.comlab.ox.ac.uk/archive/z.html`

Zforum archive

    `http://ricis.cl.uh.edu/virt-lib/zed.html`

WWW information sources

There is an introduction to the World Wide Web project, describing the concepts, software and access methods at

    `ftp://rtfm.mit.edu in/pub/usenet/news.answers/www/faq`

It is aimed at people who know a little about navigating the Internet, but want to know more about the World Wide Web specifically.

    It is also posted to the Usenet groups

    `news.answers, comp.infosystems.www.users,`
    `comp.infosystems.www.providers, comp.infosystems.www.misc,`
    `comp.infosystems.gopher, comp.infosystems.wais and`
    `alt.hypertext every four days.`

The latest version is always available on the Web as

    `http://siva.cshl.org/~boutell/www_faq.html`

Thomas Boutell maintains this document. Feedback about it to

    `boutell@netcom.com.`

What's new on the Web?
http://www.ncsa.uiuc.edu/SDG/Software/Mosaic/Docs/whats-new.html

WWW robots, wanderers and spiders
http://web.nexor.co.uk/mak/doc/robots/robots.html

Common gateway interface specifications
http://hoohoo.ncsa.uiuc.edu/cgi/overview.html

WWW FAQ
http://siva.cshl.org/~boutell/www_faq.html

A list of Telnet accessible browsers
http://info.cern.ch/hypertext/WWW/FAQ/Bootstrap.html

A list of browsers, and locations
http://info.cern.ch/hypertext/WWW/Clients.html

A list of Amiga browsers, and their locations
http://insti.physics.sunysb.edu/AMosaic/home.html

Viola for X information
http://xcf.berkeley.edu/ht/projects/viola/README

Batch mode browsers
http://wwwhost.cc.utexas.edu/test/zippy/url_get.html

Information on writing servers and gateways
http://info.cern.ch/hypertext/WWW/Daemon/Overview.html

NCSA HTTPD server information
ftp://ftp.ncsa.uiuc.edu/pub/web/

GN Gopher/HTTP server information
http://hopf.math.nwu.edu/

Perl server information
http://bsdi.com/server/doc/plexus.html

Macintosh, MacHTTP server information
http://www.uth.tmc.edu/mac_info/machttp_info.html

HTTPS (Windows NT)
ftp://emwac.ed.ac.uk/pub/https

NCSA HTTPD for Windows
ftp://ftp.ncsa.uiuc.edu/Web/ncsa_httpd/contrib/whtp11a6.zip

CERN HTTP for VMS information
http://delonline.cern.ch/disk$user/duns/doc/vms/distribution.html

WWW help

A beginner's guide to HTML

> http://www.ncsa.uiuc.edu/General/Internet/WWW/HTMLPrimer.html

HTML documentation

> http://www.ucc.ie/info/net/htmldoc.html

HTML primer

> http://www.vuw.ac.nz/who/Nathan.Torkington/ideas/www-html.html

NCSA imagemap documents

> http://wintermute.ncsa.uiuc.edu/map-tutorial/image-maps.html

World Wide Web worm

> http://www.cs.colorado.edu/home/mcbryan/WWWW.html

IRC

What is IRC?

IRC stands for Internet Relay Chat. It was written by Jarkko Oikarinen in 1988 in Finland.

It was designed as a replacement for the 'talk' program but has become much more than that. IRC is a multi-user chat system, where people convene on 'channels', a virtual place, usually with a topic of conversation, to talk in groups, or privately. IRC gained international fame during the Gulf War, where updates from around the world came across the wire and most people on IRC gathered on a single channel to hear these reports. The user runs a 'client' program which connects to the IRC network via an IRC server. Servers exist to pass messages from user to user over the IRC network. IRC is like CB radio, with all that that implies, with channels ranging from mad, bad and dangerous to know through to useful, sensible or downright stupid. Addicts hang out here for days, refusing to sleep in case they miss something. It is a bit like an arcane society with its own codes and language but when you work it out, it is not that bad.

UK IRC servers

Demon Internet Services run an IRC server at

> irc.demon.co.uk

You can read more about this at

> ftp://ftp.demon.co.uk/pub/doc/irc

Contact is

> irc-admin@demon.net

Other IRC sites

EUROPE (most of these run on port 7000)

University of Lausanne, Institute of Anatomy, Lausanne, Switzerland
Lausanne.CH.EU.undernet.org 6667
`anatsg1.unil.ch`

University of Crete, Computer Science Department, Greece
`Crete.GR.EU.undernet.org 6666`

Observatoire de Paris, Meudon, France
Paris.FR.EU.undernet.org 6666
`hplyot.obspm.circe.fr`

École Nationale Superieure d'Ingénieurs de Caen, France
Caen.FR.EU.undernet.org 6667
`ismra.ismra.fr`

University of Paderborn, Paderborn, Germany
Paderborn.DE.EU.undernet.org 6667
`pbhrzx.uni-paderborn.de`

Netherlands
Delft.NL.EU.undernet.org 6667
`sg.tn.tudelft.nl`

Vienna, Austria
Vienna.AT.EU.undernet.org 6667
`olymp.wu-wien.ac.at`

Ljubljana, Slovenia
Ljubljana.Si.Eu.undernet.org 6668
`cmir.arnes.si 193.2.1.67`

NKI Ingenioerhoegskolen, Oslo, Norway
Oslo.No.EU.undernet.org 6667
`eros.nki.no`

Chalmers Tekniska Lekskola, Gothenburg, Sweden
Gothenburg.Se.EU.undernet.org 6667
`alcazar.cd.chalmers.se`

Krakow, Poland
Krakow.PL.EU.undernet.org
`galaxy.uci.agh.edu.pl`

North America

Montreal, Quebec, Canada
Montreal.QU.CA.undernet.org 6667
`aiken.info.polymtl.ca`

California Institute of Technology, Pasadena, CA, USA
Pasadena.CA.US.undernet.org 6667
`cancun.caltech.edu`

University of Oklahoma, Oklahoma, USA
Norman.OK.US.undernet.org 6667
`vinson.ecn.uoknor.edu`

University of Pittsburgh, PA, USA
Pittsburgh.PA.US.undernet.org 6667
`macaw.labs.cis.pitt.edu`

Northeastern University, Boston, MA, USA
Boston.MA.US.undernet.org 6667
`iota.coe.neu.edu`

Rensselaer Polytechnic Institute, Troy, New York, USA
Albany.NY.US.undernet.org 6667
`hermes.acm.rpi.edu`

Kansas State University, Manhattan, Kansas, USA
Manhattan.KS.US.undernet.org 6667
`piaget.phys.ksu.edu`

Carroll College, Wokesha, WI, USA
Milwaukee.WI.US.undernet.org 6667
`rush.cc.edu`

Iowa State University, Ames, IA, USA
Ames.IA.US.undernet.org 6667
`pv1648.vincent.iastate.edu`

Dixie College, St. George, Utah, USA
StGeorge.UT.US.undernet.org 6667
`sci.dixie.edu`

University of South Florida, Tampa, FL, USA
Tampa.FL.US.undernet.org 6667
`nosferatu.cas.usf.edu`

Vicksburg, MS, USA
Vicksburg.MS.US.undernet.org 6667
`ford.wes.army.mil`

Davis, CA, USA
Davis.CA.US.undernet.org 6667
`zen.ucdavis.edu`

Mexico

Universidad de las Americas, Puebla, Mexico
Puebla.MX.undernet.org 6666
`cca.pue.udlap.mx`

Asia

Yuan-Ze Institute of Technology, Chung-Li, Taiwan
Chung-Li.tw.undernet.org 6667
`neptune.yzit.edu.tw`

Australia

University of Wollongong, Department of Computer Science, Wollongong, Australia
Wollongong.NSW.AU.undernet.org 6667
`gorgon.cs.uow.edu.au`

Useful IRC newsgroups
news.unb.ca alt.irc
alt.irc.ircii
alt.irc.questions
alt.answers
news.answers

Telnet IRC

You can Telnet to a client at

```
telnet://tiger.itc.univie.ac:6668
telnet://telnet sci.dixie.edu:6677
telnet://telnet exuokmax.ecn.uoknor.edu:6677
telnet://telnet exuokmax.ecn.uoknor.edu:7766
telnet://telnet caen.fr.eu.undernet.org:6677
telnet://telnet obelix.wu-wien.ac.at:6996
telnet://telnet obelix.wu-wien.ac.at:6969
```

This resource is quite limited so use these when you have no other way of reaching IRC.

Other information

A good place to start are the IRC tutorials. They are available via FTP from

```
ftp://cs.bu.edu/irc/support/tutorial.1
ftp://cs.bu.edu/irc/support/tutorial.2
ftp://cs.bu.edu/irc/support/tutorial.3
```

IRChat mailing list

You can also join various IRC related mailing lists.
   You can join the irchat mailing list by mailing

```
irchat-request@cc.tut.fi
```

and asking to be added.

Technical information

Those looking for more technical information can get the IRC RFC (rfc1459) available at

```
ftp://cs.bu.edu/irc/support/rfc1459.txt
```

Commercial Internet

Cityscape's Web server

```
http://www.cityscape.co.uk
```

This aims to be the most comprehensive commercial Web information site in the UK. With over a quarter of a million accesses in the last two months, it certainly is busy. Cityscape offer a free auto registration Web page to anyone who fills in a form online. They also provide commercial Web services.

Demon

Demon Internet provides World Wide Web services for Internet users and companies that want to make information available via this medium. You can check the Demon Web server at

```
http://www.demon.co.uk/
```

Apollo

Apollo Advertising runs a commercial Web server at

```
http://apollo.co.uk/home.html
```

For more information contact Gordon Wilson on

apollo@cix.compulink.co.uk

Commercial use of the net

An excellent set of references to commercial use of the Internet is available on the Web at

http://pass.wayne.edu/business.html

Internet Advertising/Marketing Agencies Directory

This document is a directory of multimedia Internet advertising and marketing agencies that can be found on WWW and are accessible via Mosaic. This information is extracted from the forthcoming book, *How to Advertise on the Internet.*
For ordering information contact

at380@freenet.carleton.ca

or

Mstrange@Fonorola.Net

Commercial contacts

Apollo Advertising
http://apollo.co.uk/home.html

BEDROCK Information Solutions, Inc.
http://end2.bedrock.com/

Branch Information Services
http://branch.com/

Catalog of Home Pages (c) 1994 Internet Business Directory
http://ibd.ar.com/Catalogs/Catalog.HomePages.html

Clarknet Lighthouse Pages
http://www.clark.net/html/it.html

CommerceNet
http://www.commerce.net/

Commercial Servers on the Web
http://tns-www.lcs.mit.edu/commerce/servers.html

Commercial Sites on the Web
http://tns-www.lcs.mit.edu/commerce.html

CTSNET Marketplace
http://www.cts.com/market/

Digital's Electronic Shopping Mall
http://www.service.digital.com/html/emall.html

Electric Press, Inc.
http://www.elpress.com/homepage.html

Electronic Billboards on the Digital Superhighway
http://ibd.ar.com:80/Advertising.Info/Inet.Advertising.html

Entrepreneurs on the Web
http://sashimi.wwa.com/~notime/eotw/EOTW.html

EnviroLink Network
http://envirolink.org:/start_web.html

Global Electronic Marketing Service
http://www.gems.com/

Home Page Authoring Service
file://netcom2.netcom.com/pub/iceman/VC/hpa.html

How Does the Internet Differ from Current Advertising Methods?
http://ibd.ar.com:80/Info/About.Electrons.vs.Paper.html

Internet Ad Emporium
http://mmink.cts.com/mmink/mmi.html

Internet Advertising FAQ
http://ibd.ar.com:80/Advertising.Info/StrangeLove.html

Internet Business Directory
http://ibd.ar.com/

Internet Distribution Services
http://www.service.com/

Internet Marketing Inc.
http://venus.mcs.com/~advertiz/html/IntMarket.html

Internet Media Services
http://netmedia.com/

Internet Presence & Publishing Corporation
http://www.ip.net/

Internet Shopping Network
http://www.internet.net/

InterNex Information Services
http://www.internex.net/overview.html

Kaleidoscope Communications (The Global City)
http://kaleidoscope.bga.com/kald/KALD_top.html

Kaleidospace
http://kspace.com/

Marketing Hotlist (Ad agencies)
http://www.shore.net:/~adfx/3.html

MarketPlace.com (Cyberspace Development Inc.)
http://marketplace.com/

NetMarket
http://www.netmarket.com/

NSTN CyberMall
http://www.nstn.ns.ca/cybermall/cybermall.html

O'Reilly & Associates, Inc.
http://nearnet.gnn.com/

Oneworld Information Services
http://oneworld.wa.com/

Open Market Info
http://www.human.com/gateinfo.html

Oslonett Marketplace
http://www.oslonett.no/html/adv/ON-market.html

Quadralay MarketPlace
http://www.quadralay.com/home.html

Stanford Shopping Center
http://netmedia.com/ims/ssc/ssc.html

Stelcom Inc.
http://stelcom.com/

Studio X
http://www.nets.com/

TAG Online Mall
http://www.tagsys.com/

The Global On-Line Directory
http://www.gold.net/gold/

The Internet StoreFront
http://storefront.xor.com/

The Marketing Hotlist
http://www.shore.net:/~adfx/3.html

The Mother-of-all BBS
> http://www.cs.colorado.edu/homes/mcbryan/public_html/bb/summary
> .html

UWI Shopping Maul
> http://zapruder.pds.med.umich.edu/uwi/maul.html

Virtual Advertising – adfx
> http://www.halcyon.com/zz/top.html

Virtual Consultant
> file://netcom2.netcom.com/pub/iceman/VC/VC.html

Wimsey Information Services
> http://www.wimsey.com/

World Real Estate Listing Service
> http://interchange.idc.uvic.ca/wrels/index.html

WorldWide Marketplace
> http://www.cygnus.nb.ca/

Cityscape's Internet site registry

Cityscape's Web server offers a free self-registration Web page to all comers. This is a popular feature that many companies and services have used since its startup. This is a list of all the sites that have registered. This list is added to on a daily basis and it is worth a regular return trip to check out new arrivals.

CityScape Internet Services
Internet IP and UUCP provider, Internet consultancy and publishers of Global On-Line
> http://www.cityscape.co.uk/

University of Southampton Interactive Learning Centre
The Interactive Learning Centre gives support and advice to University staff who are creating/managing multimedia projects
> http://ilc.ecs.soton.ac.uk/welcome.html

University of Warwick
Higher Education Establishment
> http://www.warwick.ac.uk

INS (Iowa Network Services, Inc.)
Telecommunications Company offering: voice, video and Internet services
> http://www.infonet.net/

CRIST
Centre for Research in Information Storage Technology, University of Plymouth, UK
>   http://crist1.ee.plymouth.ac.uk

Sheffield Hallam University
Higher education
>   http://pine.shu.ac.uk/homepage.html

Information Technology Training Initiative
Information technology R&D for UK higher education
>   http://www.hull.ac.uk/Hull/ITTI/itti.html

MishMash
Online Infolodex/query
>   http://nyx10.cs.du.edu:8001/~sstaetz/home.html

PreCom Strategic Planning
Global Strategic Planning, Systems and Management Consulting Services
>   http://fender.onramp.net/~atw_dhw/precom.html

Dainamic Consulting
Marketing consultants
>   http://www.netpart.com/dai/home.html

InterPsych: The Internet Mental Health Research Charity
An international mental health research organization
>   http://www2.shef.ac.uk/default.html

Bath University Bulletin Board for Libraries
Resource for research scientists and library information specialists
>   http://www.bubl.bath.ac.uk/BUBL/home.html

Myers Equity Express
Home loans, mortgages, fill out quote form with live response
>   http://www.internet-is.com/myers/

System Management ARTS (SMARTS)
Sells computer products via Internet
>   http://mits.mdata.fi/~dreamer

Technical University of Ilmenau
Study and research in engineering, informatics, mathematics, business
>   http://www.tu-ilmenau.de/

Raven Systems Ltd
Custom software solutions for everyday problems
>   http://eskinews.eskimo.com/~ravensys/

EVG Consulting
Computer sales, services and consulting
       http://www.rpi.edu/~larsoe

Centre for Social Anthropology and Computing (CSAC)
Support for research in anthropology and ethnography
       http://lucy.ukc.ac.uk

Electronics & Networking Services
ENS offers circuit card repair and systems integration services
       http://tcp.ip.net/ENS/home.html

NAUTICUS
NAUTICUS: The National (USA) Maritime Center
       http://www.nauticus.org/Nauticus/home.html

Internet Presence & Publishing
ISDN-based Internet connectivity and WWW publishing
       http://tcp.ip.net/

The Linux Organization
Central archive of Linux-related information
       http://www.linux.org/

Microcentre
Microcentre University of Dundee
       http://alpha.mic.dundee.ac.uk/microcentre.html

University of Washington, Health Sciences Center for Educational Resources
The Center promotes and supports quality education through design, production,
evaluation and presentation of traditional and state-of-the-art learning materials
       http://newman.hs.washington.edu/cer-main.html

University of Kansas Office of Information Systems
Systems and programming, technical services, user services
       http://kufacts.cc.ukans.edu/cwis/kufacts_start.html

Department of Earth Sciences, University of Oxford
Research into many geological, mineralogical, geophysical and geodetic disciplines
       http://www.earth.ox.ac.uk/

De Montfort University
A centre for excellence which is the fastest growing University in Europe
       http://www.dmu.ac.uk/0h/www/home.html

VentureNET
Internet service and consulting
       http://www.venture.net/

Dundee University Library
The University of Dundee's Library and Information Service
```
http://gotwo.dundee.ac.uk/uldhome.html
```

SAIC Wateridge
Computer security with Unix/CMW emphasis
```
http://mls.saic.com
```

Professional Student
I am a Student at Edinburgh University doing a Bsc(Hons) in Artificial Intelligence and Computer Science
```
http://www.dcs.ed.ac.uk/students/cs2/mxm/index.html
```

3W Magazine
The Internet with attitude
```
http://www.3w.com/3W/
```

Lance Sloan
Lance Sloan – Unix Sysadmin for hire!
```
http://www.umcc.umich.edu/~lsloan/homepage.html
```

The Void
Come visit BlueDog, the smartest animal on the Web
```
http://hp8.ini.cmu.edu:5550/
```

NetPartners
Independent Internet consulting
```
http://www.netpart.com/
```

Canadian Himalayan Expeditions
International adventure travel
```
http://www.netpart.com/che/brochure.html
```

BEDROCK Information Solutions, Inc.
BEDROCK provides training, systems integration and internet solutions
```
http://end2.bedrock.com/start.html
```

Algorithmics Ltd
Services for MIPS developers
```
http://www.algor.co.uk/welcome.html
```

Beauty for Ashes
Ethereal poetry and photography
```
http://enuxsa.eas.asu.edu:8080/public/fetters/ashes.html
```

UC Berkeley CAD Group
design CAD tools and free softwares are available
```
http://www-cad.eecs.berkeley.edu
```

University of California, Davis
Department of Land, Air, Water Resources, Atmospheric Science group
`http://atm21.ucdavis.edu/`

Powerbase, Inc.
Franchiser for National Consultant Referrals, Inc. A 'No Charge' referral service for all types of experts and consultants
`http://www.cts.com`

T4 Computer Security
Network and information security consulting
`http://www.nuance.com/~fcp/html_index.html`

Lajos Kossuth University Main Library
The second national library of Hungary
`http://www.lib.klte.hu`

Ministry of Education (Singapore)
Education in Singapore, advancement of education
`http://www.moe.ac.sg/`

Interactive Systems Centre, University of Ulster
Interactive Multimedia Research Centre
`http://www.iscm.ulst.ac.uk/`

California Software, Inc.
We produce PC Internet software called InterAp
`http://www.calsoft.com`

Leavitt Publications, On-Line
Online 'zines, WWW page, Gnosis Archive, other...
`http://www.armory.com/~leavitt`

University of Kaiserslautern
University of Kaiserslautern, Kaiserslautern, Germany
`http://www.uni-kl.de/`

Grace College and Seminary
Christian college and seminary in Indiana
`http://www.grace.edu`

Internet Marketing Inc.
We provide cutting edge marketing and advertising services on all areas of the Internet; we're young, hip and in-the-know
`http://venus.mcs.com/~advertiz/html/prices.html`

WebWorld
A Web-based cyberworld you can travel in, build in and visually link to other parts of the World Wide Web
```
http://sailfish.peregrine.com/WebWorld/welcome.html
```

Centre for Atmospheric Science
Chemistry Department, Cambridge University
```
http://www.atm.ch.cam.ac.uk/
```

InterData
Distributor for TEAMUP INTERNATIONAL
```
http:/www.interdata.com/teamup.html
```

Intuitive Software
Developers of information management software
```
http://www.cityscape.co.uk/recall/
```

Digitalis Television Productions
InfoVid Outlet: the educational and how-to video warehouse
```
http://branch.com:1080/infovid/c100.html
```

Branch Information Services
An electronic shopping mall – many products!
```
http://branch.com:1080
```

Colorburst Studios
Eye-dazzling Niobium jewelry
```
http://www.teleport.com/~paulec/
```

University of Montana
Main information hub
```
http://ftp.cs.umt.edu
```

ACM
Association for Computing Machinery
```
http://info.acm.org/
```

National Consultant Referrals, Inc.
A no charge referrals service for experts internationally
```
http://crash.cts.com:80/~kline/
```

Canadian Airlines
One of Canada's major airlines
```
http://www.CdnAir.CA/
```

Northern New Jersey OS/2 User's Group
e-mail to nnjos2@intac.com for further information
```
http://www.intac.com/nnjos2ug.html
```

DeLorme Mapping
Street Atlas USA and Global Explorer CD-ROMs. Publishers of paper and CD-ROM maps and datasets
> `http://www.delorme.com/`

University of Aberdeen Students' Representative Council
Welfare and services provider run by students for students
> `http://sysb.abdn.ac.uk/`

Erasmus Business Support Centre
University to business link
> `http://www.fbk.eur.nl/`

Tangofolies
Any/all aspects of tango, Argentina, dance, notation
> `http://litsun35.epfl.ch:8001/tango/`

Lehrstuhl für Informatik II; RWTH AAchen
> `http://www-i2.informatik.rwth-aachen.de/`

HungerWeb
Hunger-related multimedia education and infoserver
> `http://www.hunger.brown.edu/oxfam/`

Venable, Baetjer, Howard & Civiletti
A US/international law firm based in the Washington/Baltimore metropolitan area
> `http://venable.com/vbh.htm`

SurfNet
Providing live views of the ocean, surf and tide reports and a gallery of surfing photographs
> `http://sailfish.peregrine.com/surf/surf.html`

Frontline Distribution Ltd
Computer hardware, software and services, trade only distributor
> `http://www.frontline.co.uk`

Thomas I. M. Ho
World Wide Web enthusiast
> `http://solomon.technet.sg:8000/bin/tho.html`

Imperial College Theoretical Physics Group
Theoretical Physics and Cosmology Research
> `http://euclid.tp.ph.ic.ac.uk`

U.Va. Recycling Office
On the surface, a mild-mannered recycling office...
> `http://ecosys.drdr.virginia.edu`
rec.arts.comics archives

Multimedia archives for the rec, arts, comics newgroups
```
http://student.dhhalden.no/studenter/jonal/Comics/rac.home.html
```

PC Week Labs
An unofficial server set up by some analysts at PC Week, a weekly newspaper serving the needs of large networked environments and the people who support them
```
http://linux.pcweek.ziff.com:8001/
```

The Writers Alliance, Inc.
Internet training onsite worldwide
```
http://www.clark.net/pub/journalism/brochure.html
```

Stanford University
```
http://www.stanford.edu/
```

Network Computing Devices, Inc.
International vendor of X Terminals, PC X servers, electronic mail software
```
http://www.ncd.com
```

TQM Communications
London-based information services company
```
http://www.tecc.co.uk/tqm/
```

UT Dallas
The University of Texas of Dallas
```
http://www.utdallas.edu/
```

XOR Network Engineering, Inc.
Provides a full range of network engineering and system support services
```
http://storefront.xor.com/
```

Paradise League Council
Oversees development of the multi-player graphical network-based game Paradise Netrek
```
http://www.cis.ufl.edu/~thoth/paradise
```

The University of Kent at Canterbury, UKC
```
http://swan.ukc.ac.uk/
```

Clemson University
A leading land-grant University located in South Carolina, a state in the southeastern US
```
http://www.clemson.edu/home.html
```

US Geological Survey
Earth science in the public service
```
http://info.er.usgs.gov/
```

X-Ray Cafe
World famous music club in Portland, USA
    http://www.ee.pdx.edu/xray.html

Portland State University
School events, local-music, Beavis & Butthead and more!
    http://www.ee.pdx.edu/

HyperTEXT Services
Editing and writing for hypertext docs
    http://www.cityscape.co.uk/deemer/

Virtual MeetMarket
The easiest way to meet someone new on the World Wide Web
    http://wwa.com:1111/

Dogwood Blossoms
Online Journal of Haiku
    http://199.20.16.10/dbindex.htm

Crynwr Software
We sell packet driver support for MS-DOS machines
    http://199.20.16.10/dbindex.htm

HK-R
The university of Ronneby/Karlskrona Sweden
    http://www.hk-r.se/

Education Online Sources
Education information, created for and by the K12 community.
    http://garnet.geo.brown.edu/eos1/

Fang's Frog Records
An Internet record label!
    http://www.cityscape.co.uk:81/bar/voiced.html

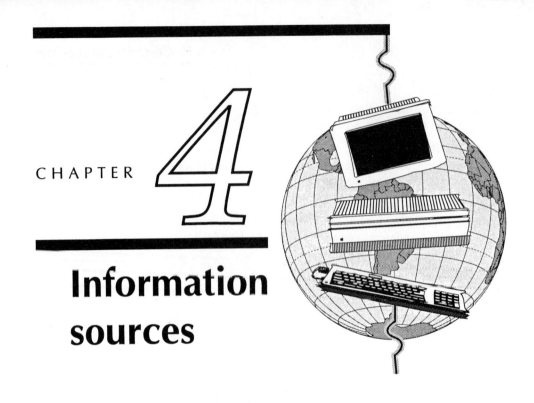

CHAPTER

Information sources

The Internet is an information source. Some of the following documents are available on the Internet in one form or another. I have tidied up or re-arranged most of them to make them more readable, but I have not attempted to correct any errors within them. The Mailbase User Card will give you an overview of the Mailbase system including how to get further information using e-mail commands. The IETF/RARE catalogue of network training materials lists a huge variety of training and help resources available from the Internet. Kevin Savetz's unofficial Internet booklist offers an overview of the huge range of general and specific purpose books about the Internet published to date. You can get an up to date version of this list from ftp://rtfm.mit.edu/pub/ usenet/news.answers/internet-services/book-list. If you are interested in which commercial organisations in the UK have registered domain names, the UK Commercial Domains list will be useful. The Commercial Internet Exchange (CIX) is the providers 'club', a non-profit trade association of service providers globally. The document here briefly covers CIX and lists the membership. A final document is the JANET Acceptable Use guidelines, these give an indication of how the academic network in the UK relates to the world.

Mailbase User Reference Card

```
User Commands Reference Card    March 1994
***************************
```

```
Copyright Mailbase 1994
The Computing Service, University of Newcastle upon Tyne.
```

```
This is the on-line version of the reference card - a formatted
copy may be obtained from Mailbase: send your e-mail request to
mailbase-helpline@mailbase.ac.uk
```

```
Please remember to include your postal address!
```

```
If you are not the type of person to plough through a lengthy
document and just want to get started, this card may provide
you with all the information you need. If you require a
comprehensive introduction to Mailbase you may retrieve the
User's Guide by sending the following command in an e-mail
message to mailbase@mailbase.ac.uk
```

```
send mailbase user-guide
```

```
Welcome to Mailbase (TM)
******************
```

```
Mailbase is...
```

```
the UK's major electronic mailing list service which enables
groups to manage their own discussion topics (Mailbase lists)
and associated files. The service is run by a dedicated team
based at Newcastle University, and is funded by the Joint
Information Systems Committee (JISC) of the Higher Education
Funding Councils for England, Scotland and Wales.
```

```
If you are new to Mailbase you may find it useful to read
through some other Mailbase documents - particularly the
User's Guide.
```

Other documents

For a list of on-line documentation about Mailbase, send the following command in an e-mail message to: mailbase@mailbase.ac.uk

index mailbase

You can then use the "send" command to retrieve those documents which interest you.

Support from Mailbase

"help" returns a summary of the Mailbase commands. If the "command" option is used then a more detailed description of a particular command is given.

Example: help review
Will return information on the command review.

If you have problems with Mailbase first look at the file of "frequently asked questions". To retrieve this file send the following command to mailbase@mailbase.ac.uk

send mailbase user-faq

If you still have a problem contact your List Owner, the address is:

listname-request@mailbase.ac.uk
where listname is the name of your chosen list.

For example to contact the List Owner for the list mac-dtp, the address would be:
mac-dtp-request@mailbase.ac.uk

If you are still need help send an e-mail message to:
mailbase-helpline@mailbase.ac.uk

explaining the problem - we will do our best to help.

Sending Mailbase Commands
****

Commands should be sent as an electronic mail message to:
mailbase@mailbase.ac.uk

More than one command may appear in a message to Mailbase; They
may be in any order, in UPPER, lower, or MiXeD case. If you
normally terminate your e-mail messages with a signature,
please use "stop" after the final command sent to Mailbase. As
an example, if you wish to join an open list, then depending
upon the type of mail system your mail message should look
similar to the following.

To:	mailbase@mailbase.ac.uk
Subject:	test (you may leave this blank)
Text of message:	join eng-lit Cliff Spencer

To check if there are any files associated with a particular
list send an index command.

To:	mailbase@mailbase.ac.uk
Subject:	test (you may leave this blank)
Text of message:	index eng-lit

Contributing to List Discussions

For example to the English Literature (eng-lit) list.

To:	eng-lit@mailbase.ac.uk
Subject:	romantic poetry
Text of message:	A recent study has shown that...

Quick Reference
****
Notation

Braces { and } enclose alternative items, one of which must be
given. Square brackets [and] enclose optional items. A
vertical bar | means or.

Items in angle brackets <> are to be replaced appropriately.

Please note that lists quoted in the examples on this card are fictitious.

COMMANDS
****

find lists <word>

help [command]

index [listname]

join <listname> <firstname> <lastname>

leave {<listname> | all}

line limit <number>

list me

lists [full]

resume mail {<listname> | all }

review <listname>

send <listname> <filename>

statistics [commands | lists | <listname>]

stop

suspend mail {<listname> | all }

REMEMBER ALL COMMANDS ARE SENT TO
mailbase@mailbase.ac.uk

USER COMMANDS

****
Joining and leaving a list

Use the "join" command to add your name to a Mailbase list

Example: join fluid-dynamics George Stevens
Synonym: subscribe

You will begin to receive messages from the list(s) you have
joined - if you wish to make a contribution send your
message(s) to the list address. You can see an example in the
section Contributing to List Discussions.

"Leave" will remove your name from a specified Mailbase list,
or, if the all option is used, from all those lists where your
membership address corresponds to your current mail address.

Example: leave read-digest
Synonym: unsubscribe

Use "suspend mail" to temporarily suspend mail from a specified
list, or from every list if the all option is used.

Example: suspend mail cti-humgrad

"resume mail" will restore mail from a chosen list, or from all
(joined) lists if the all option is used.

Example: resume mail cti-humgrad

Checking your membership

"list me" shows which lists you are member of, and whether you
are a List Owner or Moderator.

Synonym: listme

Mailbase statistics

Use "statistics" to obtain data on a specific Mailbase list if
the listname option is given, or on all lists if the lists
option is chosen. With the commands option, statistics on

Mailbase commands are shown. If no options are given, statistics on both commands and lists are returned.

Example: statistics eng-lit

Retrieving files

Use "index listname" to obtain the names of files associated with a specific list.

Example: index romantic-poets

"send" retrieves files via electronic mail (see index command). Large files are automatically broken down into several messages each 1000 lines long.

Example: send mac-users dtp-review
Synonym: get, send me

You may set your own file size, up to a maximum of 5,000 lines, by using the "line limit" command. If required it should precede a send command. The minimum line limit value is 1000.

Example: line limit 2000
Synonym: line-limit

List information

"lists" returns a list of all the current Mailbase lists. The full option adds short descriptions provided by List Owners.

Example: lists full

Use "find lists" to search Mailbase for lists which have descriptions matching your subject area.

Example: find lists medical

Use "review" to obtain details of the members of a Mailbase list, and a brief description of the purpose of that list.
Example: review lib-cdroms

```
Other Mailbase services

In addition to the e-mail service described above, there are
other Mailbase facilities which enable access to most of the
publicly available information.

*                   Anonymous FTP Service (File retrieval).
*                   The Mailbase On-Line Service (Read only).
*                   The Mailbase Gopher Service.
*                   The Mailbase World Wide Web Server.
Please refer to the Mailbase User's Guide for more details.


================================================================
(cs March 1994)

END
```

IETF/RARE catalog of network training materials

This catalog is an ongoing collaborative venture by the Network Training Task
Force, working under the umbrella of the user services working groups of RARE
(the Association of European Networks) and IETF (Internet Engineering Task
Force). The Task Force is chaired by Jill Foster.

Entry contributors:	Jennifer Sellers
	Verity Brack
	Mark Prior
	Margaret Isaacs

Compiler:	Margaret Isaacs

28th October 1993

ENTRY
Classification: Documentation – Network services
Country: US
Title: New User's Guide to Unique and Interesting
Resources on the Internet
Author: Perry, Andrew
Organization: NYSERNet

Location: NYSERNet Inc.
          111 College Place, Rm. 3-211
          Syracuse, NY 13244-4100
Language: English
Keyword/s: OPACS; databases; Internet; CWIS;
directories; New York
Abstract: Lists some 50 Internet resources and
services, mostly available via telnet or ftp.
Describes services and provides step-by-step
instructions for accessing each service.
Contact name:
Contact address:
Contact phone number: 315-443-4120
Contact e-mail: info@nysernet.org
Latest revision date: April, 1992
Cost: charge made

Type: ftp file
URL: ftp: //nysernet.org/pub/guides/Guide.V.2.2.text
LoginID
Password
Filesize: 307 K
Fileformat: ascii text
System requirements:

Type: printed guide
Publisher: NYSERNet
Size: 145 pp.
Reference:

Notes:
Last revision date: April, 1992
Last Validated: October, 1993
Date of update of this record: October, 1993
Record maintainer Name: Jennifer Sellers
Record maintainer E-mail: sellers@quest.arc.nasa.gov

ENTRY
Classification: Documentation – Network Services
Country: US
Title: NorthWestNet User Services Internet Resource
Guide
Author: Kochmer, Jonathan

Organization: NorthWestNet
Location: 15400 SE 30th Place, Suite 202
     Bellevue, WA 98007
Language: English
Keyword/s: Internet; Network services; supercomputers;
databases; Usenet
Abstract: Guide to the Internet, covering electronic
mail, file
transfer, remote login, discussion groups, online
library catalogues and supercomputer access.
Contact name:
Contact address:
Contact phone number: 206-562-3000
Contact e-mail: nusirg-orders@nwnet.net
Latest revision date: March, 1992
Cost: charge made

Type: file
Electronic mail address:
Filename: user-guide
Path: ftphost.nwnet.net/nic/nwnet
Filesize:
E-mail command:

Type: ftp file
URL: ftp: //ftp.nwnet.net/user-
docs/nusirg/nusirg,whole-guide.ps.Z
Filesize: 451 K
Fileformat: compressed PostScript text
System requirements:

Type: printed guide
Publisher: NorthWestNet Academic Computing Consortium,
Inc.
Size: 300 pp.
Reference:

Notes:
Last Validated: October, 1993
Date of update of this record: October, 1993
Record maintainer Name: Jennifer Sellers
Record maintainer E-mail: sellers@quest.arc.nasa.gov

ENTRY
Classification: Documentation – Network Services
Country: US
Title: Internet Resource Guide
Author:
Organization: NSF Network Service Center (NNSC)
Location:
Language: English
Keyword/s:
Abstract: Covers various types of Internet resources,
including listings describing networks, supercomputer
conters, library catalogs, archives, directory
services, networks and network information
centers.
Contact name:
Contact address:
Contact phone number:
Contact e-mail:
Latest revision date: November, 1992
Cost: free
Type: ftp file
URL: ftp: //ds.internic.net/resource-
guide/wholeguide.txt
Filesize: 215 K
Fileformat: ascii text

Notes:
Last Validated: October, 1993
Date of update of this record: October, 1993
Record maintainer Name: Jennifer Sellers
Record maintainer E-mail: sellers@quest.arc.nasa.gov

ENTRY
Classification: Documentation – Network Services
Country: US
Title: Internet Explorer's Toolkit
Author: Perez, Ernest
Organization:
Location:
Language: English
Keyword/s: librarian
Abstract: Hypertext system containing text files about
using the Internet. For the professional librarian

user. Attempts to bring together useful source
information such as text files, e-mail messages, ftp
sites and sample directories collected by author over a
period.
Contact name: Ernest Perez, Ph.D.
Contact address: Access Information Associates
            2183 Buckingham, Suite 106
            Richardson, TX 75081
Contact phone number: 214-530-4800
Contact e-mail: eperez@utdallas.edu
Latest revision date: 1992
Cost: free

Type: ftp file
URL: ftp: //hydra.uwo.ca/LIBSOFT/EXPLORER.ZIP
Filesize: 245 K
Fileformat: compressed hypertext
System requirements: PC running MS-DOS

Notes:
Last Validated:
Date of update of this record: October, 1993
Record maintainer Name: Jennifer Sellers
Record maintainer E-mail: sellers@quest.arc.nasa.gov

ENTRY
Classification: Documentation – Network Services –
BITNET
Country: US
Title: Using BITNET: an Introduction
Author: Conklin, James B.
Organization: CREN
Location:
Language: English
Keyword/s: BITNET; listserv
Abstract: Covers basic electronic mail, using Listserv
e-mail
discussion lists, getting documents and other files
from Listserv, Netserv as a source of documents and
other information, with instructions and plenty of
examples.
Contact name:
Contact address:

Contact phone number:
Contact e-mail:
Latest revision date: 1991
Cost: free

Type: e-mail file
Electronic mail address: listserv@bitnic.educom.edu
Filesize:
E-mail command: SENDME BITNET INTRO

Notes:
Last Validated:
Date of update of this record: October, 1993
Record maintainer Name: Jennifer Sellers
Record maintainer E-mail: sellers@quest.arc.nasa.gov

ENTRY
Classification: Guides – Network Etiquette
Country: US
Title: The Net: User Guidelines and Netiquette
Author: Rinaldi, Arlene H.
Organization: Computer User Services, Florida Atlantic
University
Location:
Language: English
Keyword/s: netiquette; network applications; Usenet;
ethics
Abstract: Guide to responsible practice in making use
of network services. Gives guidelines in areas of
telnet, ftp, e-mail, Listserv groups, mailing lists,
Usenet, plus "The Ten Commandments for Computer
Ethics."
Contact name: Arlene Rinaldi
Contact address:
Contact phone number:
Contact e-mail: RINALDI@ACC.FAU.EDU
Latest revision date: September, 1992
Cost: free

Type: ftp file
URL: ftp:
//ftp.sura.net/pub/nic/internet.literature/netiquette.t
xt

Filesize: 16 K
Fileformat: ascii text

Notes:
Last Validated:
Date of update of this record: October, 1993
Record maintainer Name: Jennifer Sellers
Record maintainer E-mail: sellers@quest.arc.nasa.gov

ENTRY
Classification: Guides – Network Etiquette
Country: US
Title: Emily Postnews Answers Your Questions on
Netiquette
Author: Templeton, Brad
Organization:
Location:
Language: English
Keyword/s:
Abstract: Lessons about network etiquette through
advice on good practice, heavily laden with irony.
Contact name:
Contact address: brad@looking.on.ca
Contact phone number:
Contact e-mail:
Latest revision date: 1992
Cost: free

Type: ftp file
URL: ftp: //pit-manager.mit.edu [NOTE: COULD NOT
FIND!]
Filesize:
Fileformat: text
System requirements:

Notes:
Last Validated:
Date of update of this record:
Record maintainer Name: Jennifer Sellers
Record maintainer E-mail: sellers@quest.arc.nasa.gov

ENTRY
Classification: Guides – Network Services
Country: US
Title: Ecolinking
Author: Rittner, Don
Organization:
Location:
Language: English
Keyword/s: Internet; telecommunications; environment; databases
Abstract: Introduction to telecommunications in general, including commercial services like GEnie, America Online, DIALOG, MEAD, etc. Chapters on how to use the Internet. Focus is on using communications to further the cause of the environment.
Contact name:
Contact address:
Contact phone number:
Contact e-mail:
Latest revision date: 1992
Cost: charge made
Type: book
Publisher: PeachPit Press
Size:
Reference:

Notes:
Date of update of this record:
Record maintainer Name: Jennifer Sellers
Record maintainer E-mail: sellers@quest.arc.nasa.gov

ENTRY
Classification: Guides – Network Services
Country: US
Title: Surfing the Internet
Author: Polly, Jean
Organization: NYSERNet, Inc.
Location:
Language: English
Keyword/s:
Abstract: Overview of the Internet with somewhat of a focus on education. Includes projects underway and various kinds of services, including bulletin board

systems, databases, OPACS, listservs, and muses. Gives contacts for getting connected and discusses common Internet tools.
Magazine article, which is included in the ftp file, is a non-technical introduction to the Internet without the specific information given in the ftp file.
Contact name: Jean Armour Polly
Contact address: NYSERNet, Inc.
         200 Elwood Davis Rd., Suite 103
         Liverpool, NY 13088-6147
Contact phone number: 315-453-2912 x224
Contact e-mail: jpolly@nysernet.org
Latest revision date: May, 1993
Cost: ftp file free

Type: ftp file
URL: ftp:
//nysernet.org/pub/resources/guides/surfing.2.0.3.txt
Filesize: 60 K
Fileformat: ascii text
System requirements:
Type: journal article
Publisher: Wilson Library Bulletin
Size: 2 pp.
Reference: v. 66 no. 10, pp. 38-39

Notes:
Last Validated:
Date of update of this record: October, 1993
Record maintainer Name: Jennifer Sellers
Record maintainer E-mail: sellers@quest.arc.nasa.gov

ENTRY
Classification: Guides – Network Services
Country: US
Title: Hitchhiker's Guide to the Internet
Author: Krol, E.
Organization: University of Illinois Urbana
Location:
Language: English
Keyword/s: Internet; RFC; NIC; mail reflector; addressing; routing protocols
Abstract:

Contact name: Ed Krol
Contact address: University of Illinois
        195 DCL
        1304 West Springfield Avenue
        Urbana, IL 61801-4399
Contact phone number: 217-333-7886
Contact e-mail: Krol@uxc.cso.uiuc.edu
Latest revision date: September, 1989
Cost:

Type: ftp file
URL: ftp:
//nic.cerf.net/internet/readings/hitchhikers-guide-to-
internet.txt
Filesize: 61 K
Fileformat: ascii text

Publisher: (IETF)
Size: 24 pp.
Reference: RFC 1118

Notes:
Last Validated:
Date of update of this record: October, 1993
Record maintainer Name: Jennifer Sellers
Record maintainer E-mail: sellers@quest.arc.nasa.gov

ENTRY
Classification:=CADocumentation – Network services – Janet
Country:=CAUK
Title:=CAThe JANET Network
Author:=CAVerity Brack
Organization:=CAAcademic Computing Services Dept, University
of Sheffield
Location:=CASheffield S10 2TN, UK
Language:=CAEnglish
Keyword/s:=CAJanet; gateways; services; e-mail; access
Abstract: =CABrief description of Janet , including e-mail,
gateways, file transfer and remote access, JIPS and
services available on Janet. Some site-specific
information.
Contact name:=CAVerity Brack
Contact address:=CAAcademic Computing Services, University of

Sheffield, Sheffield S10 2TN
Contact phone number:=CA(0742) 824423
Contact e-mail:=CAV.Brack@sheffield.ac.uk
Latest revision date:=CASeptember 1993
Cost:=CAfree

Type: e-mail file
Electronic mail address:=CAV.Brack@sheffield.ac.uk
Filename:=CAc-comms1.doc
Path:=CA\appnotes\cards
Filesize:=CA25,775 bytes
E-mail command:=CAsend a message to Verity Brack

Type: Printed leaflet
Publisher=CAACS, University of Sheffield
Size:=CAA4 card, folded into 3
Reference: =CAC-Comms1

Notes:
Last Validated:
Date of update of this record: Oct.93
Record maintainer Name: Verity Brack
Record maintainer E-mail: V.Brack@sheffield.ac.uk

ENTRY
Classification: =CADocumentation – Networking tools – E-mail
Country:=CAUK
Title:=CAE-mail Abroad: Summary of Information
Author:=CAVerity Brack
Organization:=CAAcademic Computing Services Dept, University
of Sheffield
Location:=CASheffield, S10 2TN, UK
Language:=CAEnglish
Keyword/s:=CAe-mail; gateways, Janet; addresses
Abstract: =CAA brief summary of e-mail addressing for Janet
and for other networks worldwide. Instructions on sending
e-mail messages via gateways on Janet.
Contact name:=CAVerity Brack
Contact address:=CAAcademic Computing Services, University of
Sheffield, Sheffield S10 2TN
Contact phone number:=CA(0742) 824423
Contact e-mail:=CAV.Brack@sheffield.ac.uk

Latest revision date:=CASeptember 1993
Cost:=CAfree

Type: e-mail file
Electronic mail address:=CAV.Brack@sheffield.ac.uk
Filename:=CAqn-mail3.doc
Filetype:
Path:=CA\appnotes
Filesize:=CA21,654 bytes
E-mail command:=CAsend a message to Verity Brack

Type: printed leaflet
Publisher=CAACS, University of Sheffield
Size:=CA4 page A5 leaflet
Reference: =CAQN-Mail3

Notes:
Last validated:
Date of update of this record: Oct.93
Record maintainer Name: Verity Brack
Record maintainer E-mail: V.Brack@sheffield.ac.uk

ENTRY
Classification:=CAGuides – Networking tools – E-mail
Country:=CAUK
Title:=CAElectronic Mail and Related Services to Janet and
Beyond
Author:=CAVerity Brack
Organization:=CAAcademic Computing Services Dept, University
of Sheffield
Location:=CASheffield S10 2TN, UK
Language:=CAEnglish
Keyword/s:=CAe-mail; Janet; gateways; login; file transfer;
networks
Abstract: =CADetails of using e-mail, file transfer and
remote login from Sheffield to other sites and networks.
Large section on use of gateways. Some site-specific
information.
Contact name:=CAVerity Brack
Contact address:=CAAcademic Computing Services, University of
Sheffield, Sheffield S10 2TN
Contact phone number:=CA(0742) 824423
Contact e-mail:=CAV.Brack@sheffield.ac.uk

Latest revision date:=CASeptember 1992
Cost:=CAfree

Type: e-mail file
Electronic mail address:=CAV.Brack@sheffield.ac.uk
Filename:=CAap-mail2
Fileformat:=CAWord for Windows
Path:=CA\appnotes
Filesize:=CA203,628 bytes
E-mail command:=CAsend a message to Verity Brack

Type: printed booklet
Publisher=CAACS, University of Sheffield
Size:=CA31 pages, A4
Reference: =CAAP-Mail2

Notes:
Last Validated:
Date of update of this record: Oct.93
Record maintainer Name: Verity Brack
Record maintainer E-mail: V.Brack@sheffield.ac.uk

ENTRY
Classification: =CAGuides – Network services – Janet
Country:=CAUK
Title:=CANetwork Services Available Over Janet
Author:=CAVerity Brack
Organization:=CAAcademic Computing Services Dept, University
of Sheffield
Location:=CASheffield S10 2TN, UK
Language:=CAEnglish
Keyword/s:=CAJanet; services; information; resources
Abstract: =CAA detailed guide to the main types of
information service available via Janet, with specific
examples. Covers on-line interactive services, library and
catalogue services, software archives, mailing lists, and
directory services.
Contact name:=CAVerity Brack
Contact address:=CAAcademic Computing Services, University of
Sheffield, Sheffield S10 2TN
Contact phone number:=CA(0742) 824423
Contact e-mail:=CAV.Brack@sheffield.ac.uk

Latest revision date:=CAJuly 1992
Cost:=CAfree

Type: e-mail file
Electronic mail address:=CAV.Brack@sheffield.ac.uk
Filename:=CAap-coms3.doc
Fileformat:=CAWord for Windows
Path:=CA\appnotes
Filesize:=CA172,514 bytes
E-mail command:=CAsend a message to Verity Brack

Type: printed booklet
Publisher=CAACS, University of Sheffield
Size:=CA18 pages, A4
Reference: (e.g. ISBN)=CAAP-Comms3

Alternative access:=CABUBL section BH1D
Notes:
Last Validated:
Date of update of this record: Oct.93
Record maintainer Name:=CAVerity Brack
Record maintainer E-mail:=CAV.Brack@sheffield.ac.uk

ENTRY
Classification:=CATraining – Network services – JANET
Country:=CAUK
Title:=CACourse Notes and Exercises: Network Services on
Janet
Author:=CAVerity Brack
Organization:=CAAcademic Computing Services Dept, University
of Sheffield
Location:=CASheffield S10 2TN, UK
Language:=CAEnglish
Keyword/s:=CAJanet; use; bulletin boards; information
services
Abstract: =CANotes and exercises covering the use of
information services on Janet. Includes using the NISS
gateway, the NISS and BUBL bulletin boards, Janet News,
OPACs and the Paradise directory service.
Contact name:=CAVerity Brack
Contact address:=CAAcademic Computing services, University of
Sheffield, Sheffield S10 2TN

Contact phone number:=CA(0742) 824423
Contact e-mail:=CAV.Brack@sheffield.ac.uk
Latest revision date:=CAOctober 1993
Cost:=CAfree

Type: e-mail file
Electronic mail address:=CAV.Brack@sheffield.ac.uk
Filename:=CAcn-coms1.doc
Fileformat:=CAWord for Windows
Path:=CA\courses
Filesize:=CA141,657 bytes
E-mail command:=CAsend a message to Verity Brack

Type: printed booklet
Publisher=CAACS, University of Sheffield
Size:=CA8 pages, A4
Reference: (e.g. ISBN)=CACN-Comms1

Notes:
Last Validated:
Date of update of this record: Oct.93
Record maintainer Name: Verity Brack
Record maintainer E-mail: V.Brack@sheffield.ac.uk

ENTRY
Classification:=CAGuides – Network services – Databases
Country:=CAUK
Title:=CABIDS User Guide
Author:=CA?Terry Morrow
Organization:=CABath Information and Data Services,
University of Bath
Location:=CAClaverton Down, Bath BA2 7AY, UK
Language:=CAEnglish
Keyword/s:=CABIDS; ISI; citation indexes; ISTP; references
Abstract: =CAShort user guide on searching the BIDS ISI
bibliographic citation database. Details of the service
and on using the various menu options.
Contact name:=CABath Information and Data Services (BIDS)
Contact address:=CAUniversity of Bath, Claverton Downs, Bath
BA2 7AY
Contact phone number:=CA(0225) 460371
Contact e-mail:=CAbidshelp@bath.ac.uk

Latest revision date:=CAOctober 1992
Cost:=CAcharge

Type: =CAprinted leaflet
Publisher=CABath University Computing Services
Size:=CAA4 + one third folded into 4
Reference: (e.g. ISBN)=CAA0001

Notes:
Last Validated:
Date of update of this record: Oct.93
Record maintainer Name: Verity Brack
Record maintainer E-mail: V.Brack@sheffield.ac.uk

ENTRY
Classification:=CATraining – Network services – Databases
Country:=CAUK
Title:=CABIDS Self-Help Guide
Author:=CATerry Morrow
Organization:=CABath Information and Data Services,
University of Bath
Location:=CAClaverton Down, Bath BA2 7AY
Language:=CAEnglish
Keyword/s:=CABIDS; ISI; use; searching; references
Abstract: =CADetails on using BIDS ISI. Large section of
sample searches.
Contact name:=CABath Information and Data Services (BIDS)
Contact address:=CAUniversity of Bath, Claverton Downs, Bath
BA2 7AY
Contact phone number:=CA(0225) 460371
Contact e-mail:=CAbidshelp@bath.ac.uk
Latest revision date:=CAMay 1992
Cost:=CAcharge

Type: =CAprinted booklet
Publisher=CABath University Computing Services
Size:=CA42 pages of A5
Reference: (e.g. ISBN)=CAA0007

Notes:
Last Validated:
Date of update of this record: Oct.93
Record maintainer Name: Verity Brack
Record maintainer E-mail: V.Brack@sheffield.ac.uk

ENTRY
Classification: =CADocumentation – Networks – Janet
Country:=CAUK
Title:=CAJanet Starter Card
Author:=CACaroline Leary
Organization:=CAComputing Service, University of Sussex
Location:=CABrighton, Sussex
Language:=CAEnglish
Keyword/s:=CAJanet; e-mail; gateways; file transfer; access;
services
Abstract: =CAA brief description of the Janet network,
including using e-mail, file transfer, interactive access,
JIPS and national services available on Janet. Short
descriptions of Janet gateway services.
Contact name:=CAJanet Liaison Desk, Joint Network Team
Contact address:=CARutherford Appleton Laboratory, Chilton,
Didcot, OX11 0QX, UK
Contact phone number:=CA(0235) 445517
Contact e-mail:=CAjanet-liaison-desk@jnt.ac.uk
Latest revision date:=CAAugust 1993
Cost:=CAfree

Type: =CAprinted leaflet
Publisher=CAJNT
Size:=CAA4 + two thirds, folded into 5
Reference: (e.g. ISBN)=CA

Notes:
Last Validated:
Date of update of this record: Oct.93
Record maintainer Name: Verity Brack
Record maintainer E-mail: V.Brack@sheffield.ac.uk

ENTRY
Classification:=CADocumentation – Networks – Janet
Country:=CAUK
Title:=CAJanet Starter Pack
Author:=CACaroline Leary
Organization:=CAComputing Service, University of Sussex
Location:=CABrighton, Sussex
Language:=CAEnglish
Keyword/s:=CAJanet; organisation; services; e-mail; gateways;
protocols

Abstract: =CATechnical and organisational details of Janet
intended for computing services personnel.
Contact name:=CAJanet Liaison Desk, Joint Network Team
Contact address:=CARutherford Appleton Laboratory, Chilton,
Didcot, OX11 0QX
Contact phone number:=CA(0235) 445517
Contact e-mail:=CAjanet-liaison-desk@jnt.ac.uk
Latest revision date:=CAJuly 1992
Cost:=CAfree

Type: =CAprinted book
Publisher=CAJNT
Size:=CA110 pages, A4
Reference: (e.g. ISBN)

Notes:
Last Validated:
Date of update of this record: Oct.93
Record maintainer Name: Verity Brack
Record maintainer E-mail: V.Brack@sheffield.ac.uk

ENTRY
Classification:=CAGuides – Network services – Databases
Country:=CAUK
Title:=CABIRON User Guide
Author:=CAPublication Development Associates
Organization:=CAPublication Development Associates
Location:=CAColchester, Essex
Language:=CAEnglish
Keyword/s:=CABIRON; data archive; study descriptions;
catalogue; ESRC
Abstract: =CADetailed instructions for using the BIRON system
to obtain information about study and statistical datasets
held by the ESRC.
Contact name:=CAESRC Data Archive, University of Essex
Contact address:=CAWivenhoe Park, Colchester, Essex CO4 3SQ
Contact phone number:=CA(0206) 872001
Contact e-mail:=CAarchive@essex.ac.uk
Latest revision date:=CAJuly 1991
Cost:=CA?

Type: =CAprinted book
Publisher=CAESRC Data Archive, University of Essex

Size:=CA42 pages, A4
Reference: (e.g. ISBN)

Notes:
Last Validated:
Date of update of this record: Oct.93
Record maintainer Name: Verity Brack
Record maintainer E-mail: V.Brack@sheffield.ac.uk

ENTRY
Classification:=CAGuides – Network security
Country:=CAUK
Title:=CA?
Author:=CAPaul Leyland
Organization:=CAComputing Service, University of Oxford
Location:=CA13, Banbury Road, Oxford OX2 6NN, UK
Language:=CAEnglish
Keyword/s:=CApasswords; security; misuse
Abstract:
Contact name:=CAPaul Leyland
Contact address:=CAComputing Service, University of Oxford
OX2 6NN
Contact phone number:=CA(0865) 273200
Contact e-mail:=CApcl@oxford.ac.uk
Latest revision date:=CAFebruary 1992
Cost:

Type: e-mail file
Electronic mail address:=CApcl@oxford.ac.uk
Filename:=CApasswd.tex
Fileformat:=CATeX
Filesize:
E-mail command:=CAsend a message to Paul Leyland

Type: printed newsletter article
Publisher=CAOxford University Computing Service
Size:=CA2 pages, A4
Reference: (e.g. ISBN)

Notes:
Last Validated:
Date of update of this record: Oct.93

Record maintainer Name: Verity Brack
Record maintainer E-mail: V.Brack@sheffield.ac.uk

ENTRY
Classification: Documentation – Network facilities – AARNet
Country: Australia
Title: Getting the most out of AARNet (Unix version)
Author: Cecil Goldstein, Ron Heard
Organization: Computing Services, Queensland University of
Technology
Location: Brisbane
Language: english
Keywords:
Abstract: Guide to AARNet and its services – e-mail, file
transfer and archives, interactive connection, news, etc.
Gives example dialogues. Also deals with net etiquette,
strategies for resource location, protocols, addressing,
and the DNS.
Contact name:
Contact address:
Contact phone number:
Contact e-mail
Latest revision date: November 1991
Cost:

Type: ftp file
URL: ftp://ftp.qut.edu.au/user-
guide/aarnet_user_guide_unix_v1.ps
Filesize: 472k
Fileformat: postscript

Type: ftp file
URL: ftp://ftp.qut.edu.au/user-
guide/aarnet_user_guide_unix_v1.txt
Filesize: 163k
Fileformat: text

Type: ftp file
URL: ftp://ftp.qut.edu.au/user-
guide/aarnet_user_guide_unix_v1.wp
Filesize: 235k
Fileformat: wordperfect

Type: printed guide
Publisher: Queensland University of Technology
Size: 52pp.
Reference: ISBN 0-86856-806-6

Notes:
Last Validated:
Date of update of this record: Oct.93
Record maintainer Name: Mark Prior
Record maintainer E-mail: mrp@itd.adelaide.edu.au

ENTRY
Classification: Documentation – Network facilities – AARNet
Country: Australia
Title: Getting the most out of AARNet (VAX/VMS version)
Author: Cecil Goldstein, Ron Heard
Organization: Computing Services, Queensland University of
Technology
Location: Brisbane
Language: english
Keywords:
Abstract: Abstract: Guide to AARNet and its services –
e-mail, file transfer and archives, interactive connection,
News, etc. Gives example dialogues. Also deals with net
etiquette, strategies for resource location, protocols,
addressing, and the DNS.
Contact name:
Contact address:
Contact phone number:
Contact e-mail
Latest revision date: November 1991
Cost:

Type: ftp file
URL: ftp://ftp.qut.edu.au/user-
guide/aarnet_user_guide_vms_v1.ps
Filesize: 466k
Fileformat: postscript

Type: ftp file
URL: ftp://ftp.qut.edu.au/user-
guide/aarnet_user_guide_vms_v1.txt

Filesize: 160k
Fileformat: text

Type: ftp file
URL: ftp://ftp.qut.edu.au/user-
guide/aarnet_user_guide_vms_v1.wp
Filesize: 216k
Fileformat: wordperfect

Type: printed guide
Publisher: Queensland University of Technology
Size:
Reference:

Notes:
Last Validated:
Date of update of this record: Oct.93
Record maintainer Name: Mark Prior
Record maintainer E-mail: mrp@itd.adelaide.edu.au

ENTRY
Classification: Resource guides – Social sciences
Country: Australia
Title: Internet Voyager: Social Scientist's Guidebook to
AARNet/Internet Online Information Sources
Author: Dr T. Matthew Ciolek
Organization: Coombs Computing Unit, RSPacS/RSSS,
Australian National University
Location:
Language: english
Keyword/s: ftp archives; bulletin boards; dbases; e-
journals; research centers
Abstract: The 90+ online services listed in the Internet
Voyager have been electronically accessed, explored and
verified by its compiler. In other words, the document is
based on first-hand experience, not on the network hearsay.
Services found by the compiler to be too difficult to
access/use are NOT listed in this guide. Pointers and
bibliographic references to other relevant guidebooks and
electronic lists are given by the end of the document.
Contact name: Dr T. Matthew Ciolek
Contact address: Coombs Computing Unit, RSPacS/RSSS,
Australian National University, Canberra ACT 0200,

AUSTRALIA
Contact phone number: +61 6 249 0110
Contact e-mail: tmciolek@coombs.anu.edu.au
Latest revision date: 20 July 1993
Cost: free

Type: ftp file
URL:
file://coombs.anu.edu.au/coombspapers/coombsarchives/coombs
-computing/internet-voyager-inf/internet-voyager-1-2.txt
Filesize: 59Kb
Fileformat: low ASCII

Type: ftp file
URL:
file://coombs.anu.edu.au/coombspapers/coombsarchives/coombs
-computing/internet-voyager-inf/internet-voyager-2-2.txt
Filesize: 49Kb
Fileformat: low ASCII

Notes: The Internet Voyager document (created Oct 1991)
has ceased to be maintained. Since Jul 1993 it's role is
now largely taken over by the gopher-based COOMBSQUEST Soc.
Sci and Humanities Information Facility (ANU) running on
the coombs.anu.edu.au and on the cheops.anu.edu.au
machines.
Last Validated:
Date of update of this record: 27 October 1993
Record maintainer Name: Dr T. Matthew Ciolek
Record maintainer E-mail: tmciolek@coombs.anu.edu.au

ENTRY
Classification: Training – Network Services – AARNet
Country: Australia
Title: Utilising AARNet
Author: Linda Heron, Chris Walker, Griffith University
Division of Information Services
Language: english
Keywords: AARNet; network services; e-mail; ftp; news;
telnet; gopher
Abstract: This guide is used during training sessions
conducted by Information Technology Services at Griffith
University for clients of the University. The guide relates

to use of the network via a unix account; and does not at this stage attempt to cover platform specific client software.
Contact name: Linda Heron
Contact address: Division of Information Services, Griffith University, Nathan, Queensland, 4111, Australia
Contact Phone: +61 7 875 6457
Contact e-mail: L.Heron@gu.edu.au
Latest revision date: April 1993
Cost: free

Type: gopher file
URL: gopher://gopher.gu.edu.au/Administration/Division of Information Services/ITS training Courses

Last Validated:
Date of update of this record: Oct.93
Record maintainer Name: Mark Prior
Record maintainer E-mail: mrp@itd.adelaide.edu.au

ENTRY
Classification: Resource Guides – Education
Country: Australia
Title: AARNet Information Sources for Education
Author: Pam Epe, Library/ Karen Scott, Computing User Support
Organization: University of Wollongong
Location:
Language: English
Keyword/s:
Abstract: This guide was produced for use in a introductory session on AARNet and other networks for the Faculty of Education.
Contact name: Pam Epe, Research Services Librarian
Contact address: University of Wollongong Library, Northfields Avenue, Wollongong NSW 2522, Australia
Contact phone number: +61 42 214176
Contact e-mail: pamepe@uow.edu.au
Latest revision date: March 1993
Cost: Free

Type: word document

Notes: To be available on the University of Wollongong
gopher or by sending e-mail message to contact name.
Last Validated:
Date of update of this record: Oct.93
Record maintainer Name: Mark Prior
Record maintainer E-mail: mrp@itd.adelaide.edu.au

ENTRY
Classification: Resource Guides – Geography
Country: Australia
Title: AARNet Information Sources for Geography
Author: Pam Epe, Library/ Karen Scott, Computing User
Support
Organization: University of Wollongong
Language: English
Keyword/s:
Abstract: This guide was produced for use in a
introductory session on the use of AARNet and other
networks for Department of Geography
Contact name: Pam Epe, Research Services Librarian
Contact address: University of Wollongong Library,
Northfields Avenue, Wollongong NSW 2522, Australia
Contact phone number: +61 42 214176
Contact e-mail: pamepe@uow.edu.au
Latest revision date: March 1993
Cost: Free

Type: file
File format: word document

Notes: To be available on University of Wollongong gopher
or by sending e-mail message to contact name.
Last Validated:
Date of update of this record: Oct.93
Record maintainer Name: Mark Prior
Record maintainer E-mail: mrp@itd.adelaide.edu.au

ENTRY
Classification: Resource Guides
Country: Australia
Title: AARNet Information Sources for Health and
Behavioral Sciences

Author: Pam Epe, Library/ Karen Scott, Computing User
Support
Organization: University of Wollongong
Language: English
Keyword/s:
Abstract: This guide was produced for use in conjunction
with an introductory session on AARNet and other networks
for the Faculty of Health and Behavioral Sciences.
Contact name: Pam Epe, Research Services Librarian
Contact address: University of Wollongong Library,
Northfields Avenue, Wollongong NSW 2522, Australia
Contact phone number: +61 42 214176
Contact e-mail: pamepe@uow.edu.au
Latest revision date: March 1993
Cost: Free

Type: file
File format: word document

Notes: To be available on the University of Wollongong
gopher or by sending e-mail message to contact name.
Last Validated:
Date of update of this record: Oct.93
Record maintainer Name: Mark Prior
Record maintainer E-mail: mrp@itd.adelaide.edu.au

ENTRY
Classification: Resource Guides – Languages
Country: Australia
Title: AARNet Information Sources for Languages
Author: Pam Epe – Library/ Karen Scott – Computing User
Support
Organization: University of Wollongong
Language: English
Keyword/s:
Abstract: This guide was produced for use in an
introductory session on AARNet and other networks for the
Department of Languages.
Contact name: Pam Epe, Research Services Librarian
Contact address: University of Wollongong Library,
Northfields Avenue, Wollongong NSW 2522, Australia
Contact phone number: +61 42 214176
Contact e-mail: pamepe@uow.edu.au

Latest revision date: November 1992
Cost: Free

Type: file
File format: word document

Notes: To be available on the University of Wollongong
gopher or by sending e-mail message to contact name.
Last Validated:
Date of update of this record: Oct.93
Record maintainer Name: Mark Prior
Record maintainer E-mail: mrp@itd.adelaide.edu.au

ENTRY
Classification: Resource Guides – Law
Country: Australia
Title: AARNet Information Sources for Law
Author: Pam Epe – Library/ Karen Scott – Computing User
Support
Organization: University of Wollongong
Language: English
Keyword/s:
Abstract: This document was produced for use in an
introductory session on AARNet and other networks for the
Faculty of Law.
Contact name: Pam Epe, Research Services Librarian
Contact address: University of Wollongong Library,
Northfields Avenue, Wollongong NSW 2522, Australia
Contact phone number: +61 42 214176
Contact e-mail: pamepe@uow.edu.au
Latest revision date: February 1993
Cost: Free

Type: file
File format: word document

Notes: To be available on the University of Wollongong
gopher or by sending e-mail message to contact name.
Last Validated:
Date of update of this record: Oct.93
Record maintainer Name: Mark Prior
Record maintainer E-mail: mrp@itd.adelaide.edu.au

Information sources

ENTRY
Classification: Resource Guides – AARNet
Title: AARNet Sources for Library Staff
Author: Pam Epe, Library
Organization: University of Wollongong
Language: English
Keyword/s:
Abstract: This document was produced for use of Library staff in finding particular Library oriented resources.
Contact name: Pam Epe, Research Services Librarian
Contact address: University of Wollongong Library, Northfields Avenue, Wollongong NSW 2522, Australia
Contact phone number: +61 42 214176
Contact e-mail: pamepe@uow.edu.au
Latest revision date: May 1993
Cost: Free

Type: file
File format: word document

Notes: To be available on the University of Wollongong gopher or by sending e-mail message to contact name.
Last Validated:
Date of update of this record: Oct.93
Record maintainer Name: Mark Prior
Record maintainer E-mail: mrp@itd.adelaide.edu.au

ENTRY
Classification: Resource Guides – AARNet
Country: Australia
Title: Introduction to AARNet
Author: Pam Epe – Library/ Karen Scott – Computing User Support
Organization: University of Wollongong
Language: English
Keyword/s:
Abstract: This guide was produced for use in general introductory sessions on AARNet and other networks held on campus.
Contact name: Pam Epe, Research Services Librarian
Contact address: University of Wollongong Library, Northfields Avenue, Wollongong NSW 2522, Australia
Contact phone number: +61 42 214176

Contact e-mail: pamepe@uow.edu.au
Latest revision date: June 1993
Cost: Free

Type: file
File format: word document

Notes: To be available on the University of Wollongong
gopher or by sending e-mail message to contact name.
Last Validated:
Date of update of this record: Oct.93
Record maintainer Name: Mark Prior
Record maintainer E-mail: mrp@itd.adelaide.edu.au

ENTRY
Classification: Resource Guides – Health
Country: Australia
Title: AARNet Information Sources for Health and
Behavioral Sciences
Author: Pam Epe, Library/ Karen Scott, Computing User
Support
Organization: University of Wollongong
Language: English
Keyword/s:
Abstract: This guide was produced for use in conjunction
with an introductory session on AARNet and other networks
for the Faculty of Health and Behavioral Sciences.
Contact name: Pam Epe, Research Services Librarian
Contact address: University of Wollongong Library,
Northfields Avenue, Wollongong NSW 2522, Australia
Contact phone number: +61 42 214176
Contact e-mail: pamepe@uow.edu.au
Latest revision date: March 1993
Cost: Free

Type: file
File format: word document

Notes: To be available on the University of Wollongong
gopher or by sending e-mail message to contact name.
Last Validated:
Date of update of this record: Oct.93

Record maintainer Name: Mark Prior
Record maintainer E-mail: mrp@itd.adelaide.edu.au

ENTRY
Classification: Resource Guides – Librarians
Country: Australia
Title: AARNet Sources for Library Staff
Author: Pam Epe, Library
Organization: University of Wollongong
Language: English
Keyword/s:
Abstract: This document was produced for use of Library
staff in finding particular Library oriented resources.
Contact name: Pam Epe, Research Services Librarian
Contact address: University of Wollongong Library,
Northfields Avenue, Wollongong NSW 2522, Australia
Contact phone number: +61 42 214176
Contact e-mail: pamepe@uow.edu.au
Latest revision date: May 1993
Cost: Free

Type: file
File format: word document
Notes: To be available on the University of Wollongong
gopher or by sending e-mail message to contact name.
Last Validated:
Date of update of this record: Oct.93
Record maintainer Name: Mark Prior
Record maintainer E-mail: mrp@itd.adelaide.edu.au

ENTRY
Classification: Training – Network Services – Business
Country: Australia
Title: Telnet for Leisure and tourism
Author:
Organization: University of Technology, Sydney
Location:
Language: english
Keyword/s:
Abstract:
Contact name: Peter Warning
Contact address: Faculty Liaison Librarian (Business),

University of Technology, Sydney, P.O.Box 123, Broadway,
NSW, Australia 2007
Contact phone number:
Contact e-mail: P.Warning@uts.edu.au
Latest revision date:
Cost: free

Type: gopher file
URL:
gopher://infolib.murdoch.edu.au:70/11/.ftp/pub/train/oz/uts
/business/Telnet_for_Leisure_&_Tourism.hqx
Filesize:
Fileformat:
System requirements:

Date of update of this record: Oct.93
Record maintainer Name: Mark Prior
Record maintainer E-mail: mrp@itd.adelaide.edu.au

ENTRY
Classification: Training – Network Services – Engineering
Country: Australia
Title: Bitnet List for Mechanical Engineering
Author:
Organization: University of Technology, Sydney
Location:
Language: english
Keyword/s:
Abstract:
Contact name: Anne Newton
Contact address: Faculty Liaison Librarian (Engineering),
University of Technology, Sydney, P.O.Box 123, Broadway,
NSW, Australia 2007
Contact phone number:
Contact e-mail: A.Newton@uts.edu.au
Latest revision date:
Cost: free

Type: gopher file
URL:
gopher://infolib.murdoch.edu.au:70/11/.ftp/pub/train/oz/uts
/engineering/Bitnet_Lists_for_Mech_Eng_ftp.hqx
Filesize:

Fileformat:
System requirements:

Date of update of this record: Oct.93
Record maintainer Name: Mark Prior
Record maintainer E-mail: mrp@itd.adelaide.edu.au

ENTRY
Classification: Training – Network services – Engineering
Country: Australia
Title: Gopher and WAIS handout
Author:
Organization: University of Technology, Sydney
Location:
Language: english
Keyword/s:
Abstract:
Contact name: Anne Newton
Contact address: Faculty Liaison Librarian (Engineering),
University of Technology, Sydney, P.O.Box 123, Broadway,
NSW, Australia 2007
Contact phone number:
Contact e-mail: A.Newton@uts.edu.au
Latest revision date:
Cost: free

type: gopher file
URL:
gopher://infolib.murdoch.edu.au:70/11/.ftp/pub/train/oz/uts
/engineering/gopher_&_wais_handout.hqx
Filesize:
Fileformat:
System requirements:

Date of update of this record: Oct.93
Record maintainer Name: Mark Prior
Record maintainer E-mail: mrp@itd.adelaide.edu.au

ENTRY
Classification: Training – Network Services – Engineering
Country: Australia
Title: Mechanical Engineering – Telnet

Author:
Organization: University of Technology, Sydney
Location:
Language: english
Keyword/s:
Abstract:
Contact name: Anne Newton
Contact address: Faculty Liaison Librarian (Engineering),
University of Technology, Sydney, P.O.Box 123, Broadway,
NSW, Australia 2007
Contact phone number:
Contact e-mail: A.Newton@uts.edu.au
Latest revision date:
Cost: free

type: gopher file
URL:
gopher://infolib.murdoch.edu.au:70/11/.ftp/pub/train/oz/uts
/engineering/Mech_Eng_handout-telnet_ftp.hqx
Filesize:
Fileformat:
System requirements:

Date of update of this record: Oct.93
Record maintainer Name: Mark Prior
Record maintainer E-mail: mrp@itd.adelaide.edu.au

ENTRY
Classification: Training – Network Services – Engineering
Country: Australia
Title: Trumpet – ftp
Author:
Organization: University of Technology
Location:Sydney
Language: english
Keyword/s:
Abstract:
Contact name: Anne Newton
Contact address: Faculty Liaison Librarian (Engineering),
University of Technology, Sydney, P.O.Box 123, Broadway,
NSW, Australia 2007
Contact phone number:
Contact e-mail: A.Newton@uts.edu.au

Latest revision date:
Cost: free

type: gopher file
URL:
gopher://infolib.murdoch.edu.au:70/11/.ftp/pub/train/oz/uts
/engineering/Trumpet_ftp.hqx
Filesize:
Fileformat:
System requirements:

Date of update of this record: Oct.93
Record maintainer Name: Mark Prior
Record maintainer E-mail: mrp@itd.adelaide.edu.au

ENTRY
Classification: Training – Network Services – Maths and
Computer Science
Country: Australia
Title: MACS handout – ftp
Author:
Organization: University of Technology
Location: Sydney
Language: english
Keyword/s:
Abstract:
Contact name: Elizabeth Sietsma
Contact address: Faculty Liaison Librarian (Maths &
Computing Science), University of Technology, Sydney,
P.O.Box 123, Broadway, NSW, Australia 2007
Contact phone number:
Contact e-mail: E.Sietsma@uts.edu.au
Latest revision date:
Cost: free

type: gopher file
URL:
gopher://infolib.murdoch.edu.au:70/11/.ftp/pub/train/oz/uts
/maths/MACS_AARNet_handout-_ftp.hqx
Filesize:
Fileformat:
System requirements:

Date of update of this record: Oct.93
Record maintainer Name: Mark Prior
Record maintainer E-mail: mrp@itd.adelaide.edu.au

ENTRY
Classification: Training – Network Service – Maths and
Computer Science
Country: Australia
Title: MACS handout – news
Author:
Organization: University of Technology, Sydney
Location:
Language: english
Keyword/s:
Abstract:
Contact name: Elizabeth Sietsma
Contact address: Faculty Liaison Librarian (Maths &
Computing Science), University of Technology, Sydney,
P.O.Box 123, Broadway, NSW, Australia 2007
Contact phone number:
Contact e-mail: E.Sietsma@uts.edu.au
Latest revision date:
Cost: free
type: gopher file
URL:
gopher://infolib.murdoch.edu.au:70/11/.ftp/pub/train/oz/uts
/maths/MACS_AARNethandout-_news.hqx
Filesize:
Fileformat:
System requirements:

Date of update of this record: Oct.93
Record maintainer Name: Mark Prior
Record maintainer E-mail: mrp@itd.adelaide.edu.au

ENTRY
Classification: Training – Network Service – Maths and
Computer Science
Country: Australia
Title: MACS handout – gopher & WAIS
Author:
Organization: University of Technology

Location: Sydney
Language: english
Keyword/s:
Abstract:
Contact name: Elizabeth Sietsma
Contact address: Faculty Liaison Librarian (Maths &
Computing Science), University of Technology, Sydney,
P.O.Box 123, Broadway, NSW, Australia 2007
Contact phone number:
Contact e-mail: E.Sietsma@uts.edu.au
Latest revision date:
Cost: free

type: gopher file
URL:
gopher://infolib.murdoch.edu.au:70/11/.ftp/pub/train/oz/uts
/maths/MACS_AARNet_handout-gopher_wais.hqx
Filesize:
Fileformat:
System requirements:

Date of update of this record: Oct.93
Record maintainer Name: Mark Prior
Record maintainer E-mail: mrp@itd.adelaide.edu.au
ENTRY
Classification: Training – Network Services – Maths and
Computer Science
Country: Australia
Title: MACS handout – telnet
Author:
Organization: University of Technology, Sydney
Location:
Language: english
Keyword/s:
Abstract:
Contact name: Elizabeth Sietsma
Contact address: Faculty Liaison Librarian (Maths &
Computing Science), University of Technology, Sydney,
P.O.Box 123, Broadway, NSW, Australia 2007
Contact phone number:
Contact e-mail: E.Sietsma@uts.edu.au
Latest revision date:
Cost: free

type: gopher file
URL:
gopher://infolib.murdoch.edu.au:70/11/.ftp/pub/train/oz/uts
/maths/MACS_AARNet_handout-telnet.hqx
Filesize:
Fileformat:
System requirements:

Date of update of this record: Oct.93
Record maintainer Name: Mark Prior
Record maintainer E-mail: mrp@itd.adelaide.edu.au

ENTRY
Classification: Training – Network Services – Maths and
Computer Science
Country: Australia
Title: MACS handout – X500
Author:
Organization: University of Technology, Sydney
Location:
Language: english
Keyword/s:
Abstract:
Contact name: Elizabeth Sietsma
Contact address: Faculty Liaison Librarian (Maths &
Computing Science), University of Technology, Sydney,
P.O.Box 123, Broadway, NSW, Australia 2007
Contact phone number:
Contact e-mail: E.Sietsma@uts.edu.au
Latest revision date:
Cost: free

type: gopher file
URL:
gopher://infolib.murdoch.edu.au:70/11/.ftp/pub/train/oz/uts
/maths/MACS_AARNEThandout-X-500.hqx
Filesize:
Fileformat:
System requirements:

Date of update of this record: Oct.93
Record maintainer Name: Mark Prior
Record maintainer E-mail: mrp@itd.adelaide.edu.au

ENTRY
Classification: Training – Network Services – Nursing
Country: Australia
Title: ANU gopher – how to...
Author:
Organization: University of Technology, Sydney
Location:
Language: english
Keyword/s:
Abstract:
Contact name: Paul Adams
Contact address: Faculty Liaison Librarian (Nursing),
University of Technology, Sydney, P.O.Box 123, Broadway,
NSW, Australia 2007
Contact phone number:
Contact e-mail: P.Adams@uts.edu.au
Latest revision date:
Cost: free

type: gopher file
URL:
gopher://infolib.murdoch.edu.au:70/11/.ftp/pub/train/oz/uts
/nursing/ANU_gopher_howto.hqx
Filesize:
Fileformat:
System requirements:

Date of update of this record: Oct.93
Record maintainer Name: Mark Prior
Record maintainer E-mail: mrp@itd.adelaide.edu.au

ENTRY
Classification: Training – Network Services – Nursing
Country: Australia
Title: Health interest groups
Author:
Organization: University of Technology, Sydney
Location:
Language: english
Keyword/s:
Abstract:

Contact name: Paul Adams
Contact address: Faculty Liaison Librarian (Nursing),
University of Technology, Sydney, P.O.Box 123, Broadway,
NSW, Australia 2007
Contact phone number:
Contact e-mail: P.Adams@uts.edu.au
Latest revision date:
Cost: free

type: gopher file
URL:
gopher://infolib.murdoch.edu.au:70/11/.ftp/pub/train/oz/uts
/nursing/Health_Interest_Groups.hqx
Filesize:
Fileformat:
System requirements:

Date of update of this record: Oct.93
Record maintainer Name: Mark Prior
Record maintainer E-mail: mrp@itd.adelaide.edu.au

ENTRY
Classification: Training – Network Services – Nursing
Country: Australia
Title: Health lists (training)
Author:
Organization: University of Technology, Sydney
Location:
Language: english
Keyword/s:
Abstract:
Contact name: Paul Adams
Contact address: Faculty Liaison Librarian (Nursing),
University of Technology, Sydney, P.O.Box 123, Broadway,
NSW, Australia 2007
Contact phone number:
Contact e-mail: P.Adams@uts.edu.au
Latest revision date:
Cost: free

type: gopher file
URL:
gopher://infolib.murdoch.edu.au:70/11/.ftp/pub/train/oz/uts

/nursing/Health_lists_(training).hqx
Filesize:
Fileformat:
System requirements:

Date of update of this record: Oct.93
Record maintainer Name: Mark Prior
Record maintainer E-mail: mrp@itd.adelaide.edu.au

ENTRY
Classification: Training – Network Services – Nursing
Country: Australia
Title: Telnet – Health (Training)
Author:
Organization: University of Technology, Sydney
Location:
Language: english
Keyword/s:
Abstract:
Contact name: Paul Adams
Contact address: Faculty Liaison Librarian (Nursing),
University of Technology, Sydney, P.O.Box 123, Broadway,
NSW, Australia 2007
Contact phone number:
Contact e-mail: P.Adams@uts.edu.au
Latest revision date:
Cost: free

type: gopher file
URL:
gopher://infolib.murdoch.edu.au:70/11/.ftp/pub/train/oz/uts
/nursing/Telnet_Health_(training).hqx
Filesize:
Fileformat:
System requirements:

Date of update of this record: Oct.93
Record maintainer Name: Mark Prior
Record maintainer E-mail: mrp@itd.adelaide.edu.au

ENTRY
Classification: Training – Network Services – Education

Country: Australia
Title: Adult Education – e-conferences
Author:
Organization: University of Technology, Sydney
Location:
Language: english
Keyword/s:
Abstract:
Contact name: Christian Langeveldt
Contact address: Faculty Liaison Librarian (Education),
University of Technology, Sydney, P.O.Box 123, Broadway,
NSW, Australia 2007
Contact phone number: +61 2 330 3312
Contact e-mail: C.Langeveldt@uts.edu.au
Latest revision date:
Cost: free

type: gopher file
URL:
gopher://infolib.murdoch.edu.au:70/11/.ftp/pub/train/oz/uts
/educ/Adult_Educ_E-Conferences_.hqx
Filesize:
Fileformat:
System requirements:

Date of update of this record: Oct.93
Record maintainer Name: Mark Prior
Record maintainer E-mail: mrp@itd.adelaide.edu.au

ENTRY
Classification: Training – Network Services – Education
Country: Australia
Title: Adult Education – ftp guide
Author:
Organization: University of Technology, Sydney
Location:
Language: english
Keyword/s:
Abstract:
Contact name: Christian Langeveldt
Contact address: Faculty Liaison Librarian (Education),
University of Technology, Sydney, P.O.Box 123, Broadway,
NSW, Australia 2007

Contact phone number: +61 2 330 3312
Contact e-mail: C.Langeveldt@uts.edu.au
Latest revision date:
Cost: free

type: gopher file
URL:
gopher://infolib.murdoch.edu.au:70/11/.ftp/pub/train/oz/uts
/educ/Adult_Educ_ftp_guide_.hqx
Filesize:
Fileformat:
System requirements:

Date of update of this record: Oct.93
Record maintainer Name: Mark Prior
Record maintainer E-mail: mrp@itd.adelaide.edu.au

ENTRY
Classification: Training – Network Services – Education
Country: Australia
Title: Adult Education – Telnet
Author:
Organization: University of Technology, Sydney
Location:
Language: english
Keyword/s:
Abstract:
Contact name: Christian Langeveldt
Contact address: Faculty Liaison Librarian (Education),
University of Technology, Sydney, P.O.Box 123, Broadway,
NSW, Australia 2007
Contact phone number: +61 2 330 3312
Contact e-mail: C.Langeveldt@uts.edu.au
Latest revision date:
Cost: free

type: gopher file
URL:
gopher://infolib.murdoch.edu.au:70/11/.ftp/pub/train/oz/uts
/educ/Adult_Educ_Telnet_93_.hqx
Filesize:
Fileformat:
System requirements:

Date of update of this record: Oct.93
Record maintainer Name: Mark Prior
Record maintainer E-mail: mrp@itd.adelaide.edu.au

ENTRY
Classification: Training – Network Services – Education
Country: Australia
Title: Teacher Education – Telnet
Author:
Organization: University of Technology, Sydney
Location:
Language: english
Keyword/s:
Abstract:
Contact name: Christian Langeveldt
Contact address: Faculty Liaison Librarian (Education),
University of Technology, Sydney, P.O.Box 123, Broadway,
NSW, Australia 2007
Contact phone number: +61 2 330 3312
Contact e-mail: C.Langeveldt@uts.edu.au
Latest revision date:
Cost: free
type: gopher file
URL:
gopher://infolib.murdoch.edu.au:70/11/.ftp/pub/train/oz/uts
/educ/Teacher_Educ_(Telnet).hqx
Filesize:
Fileformat:
System requirements:

Date of update of this record: Oct.93
Record maintainer Name: Mark Prior
Record maintainer E-mail: mrp@itd.adelaide.edu.au

ENTRY
Classification: Training – Network Services – Education
Country: Australia
Title: Teacher Education – e-conferences
Author:
Organization: University of Technology, Sydney
Location:

Language: english
Keyword/s:
Abstract:
Contact name: Christian Langeveldt
Contact address: Faculty Liaison Librarian (Education),
University of Technology, Sydney, P.O.Box 123, Broadway,
NSW, Australia 2007
Contact phone number: +61 2 330 3312
Contact e-mail: C.Langeveldt@uts.edu.au
Latest revision date:
Cost: free

type: gopher file
URL:
gopher://infolib.murdoch.edu.au:70/11/.ftp/pub/train/oz/uts
/educ/Teacher_Educ_e-conferences.hqx
Filesize:
Fileformat:
System requirements:

Date of update of this record: Oct.93
Record maintainer Name: Mark Prior
Record maintainer E-mail: mrp@itd.adelaide.edu.au

ENTRY
Classification: Training – Network Services – Science
Country: Australia
Title: Physical Science Lists
Author:
Organization: University of Technology, Sydney
Location:
Language: english
Keyword/s:
Abstract:
Contact name: Sally Scholfield
Contact address: Faculty Liaison Librarian (Science),
University of Technology, Sydney, P.O.Box 123, Broadway,
NSW, Australia 2007
Contact phone number:
Contact e-mail: S.Scholfield@uts.edu.au
Latest revision date:
Cost: free

type: gopher file

URL:
gopher://infolib.murdoch.edu.au:70/11/.ftp/pub/train/oz/uts
/science/Physical_Science_lists.hqx
Filesize:
Fileformat:
System requirements:

Date of update of this record: Oct.93
Record maintainer Name: Mark Prior
Record maintainer E-mail: mrp@itd.adelaide.edu.au

ENTRY
Classification: Training – Network Services – Science
Country: Australia
Title: Physical Science – news
Author:
Organization: University of Technology, Sydney
Location:
Language: english
Keyword/s:
Abstract:
Contact name: Sally Scholfield
Contact address: Faculty Liaison Librarian (Science),
University of Technology, Sydney, P.O.Box 123, Broadway,
NSW, Australia 2007
Contact phone number:
Contact e-mail: S.Scholfield@uts.edu.au
Latest revision date:
Cost: free

type: gopher file
URL:
gopher://infolib.murdoch.edu.au:70/11/.ftp/pub/train/oz/uts
/science/Physical_Science_news.hqx
Filesize:
Fileformat:
System requirements:

Date of update of this record: Oct.93
Record maintainer Name: Mark Prior
Record maintainer E-mail: mrp@itd.adelaide.edu.au

ENTRY
Classification: Training – Network Services – Science
Country: Australia
Title: Physical Science – telnet
Author:
Organization: University of Technology, Sydney
Location:
Language: english
Keyword/s:
Abstract:
Contact name: Sally Scholfield
Contact address: Faculty Liaison Librarian (Science),
University of Technology, Sydney, P.O.Box 123, Broadway,
NSW, Australia 2007
Contact phone number:
Contact e-mail: S.Scholfield@uts.edu.au
Latest revision date:
Cost: free

type: gopher file
URL:
gopher://infolib.murdoch.edu.au:70/11/.ftp/pub/train/oz/uts
/science/Physical_Science_telnet.hqx
Filesize:
Fileformat:
System requirements:

Date of update of this record: Oct.93
Record maintainer Name: Mark Prior
Record maintainer E-mail: mrp@itd.adelaide.edu.au

ENTRY
Classification: Training – Network services
Country: UK
Title: Network Training Pack – Unit 1
Author: NISP/ITTI Network Training Materials Project
Organization: University of Newcastle upon Tyne
Location: Newcastle upon Tyne
Language: English
Keyword/s: Networks; e-mail; remote login; ftp; NIR tools
Abstract: Introductory overview of networking, consisting
of presentation, notes on online demonstrations, user
handout, workshop exercises

Contact name: Margaret Isaacs
Contact address: Computing Service, University of Newcastle
upon Tyne, Newcastle upon Tyne NE1 7RU
Contact phone number: +44 91 222 8069
Contact e-mail: margaret.isaacs@ncl.ac.uk
Latest revision date: August 1993
Cost: free

Type: ftp directory
URL: directory://tuda.ncl.ac.uk/pub/network-
training/trainpack/unit1
Filesize: 3 Mb (total)
Fileformat: multi-format
System requirements: PowerPoint presentation file requires
PowerPoint or PowerPoint viewer (in /pub/network-
training/software) – runs on PC with Windows or Apple Mac.

Notes: The first unit of the Network Training Pack.
Last Validated: September 1993
Date of update of this record: 27/10/1993
Record maintainer Name: Margaret Isaacs
Record maintainer E-mail: margaret.isaacs@ncl.ac.uk

ENTRY
Classification: Documentation – Network services – Social
Science
Country: UK
Title: JANET for social scientists
Author: Nicky Ferguson
Organization: Economic and Social Research Council
Location: Swindon
Language: English
Keyword/s: JANET; NISS
Abstract: Guide to the basics of using JANET – explains
e-mail, libraries and bulletin boards, file transfer,
distribution lists and remote login. Lists a number of
addresses for remote login likely to be useful to social
scientists.
Contact name: nicky.ferguson@uk.ac.esrc.prime.a
Contact address:
Contact phone number:
Contact e-mail:
Latest revision date: 7/12/1992

Cost: free

Type: e-mail file
Electronic mail address: mailbase@mailbase.ac.uk
Fileformat: text
E-mail command: get itti-networks esrc-refcard.*

Type: ftp file
URL: file://mailbase.ac.uk/pub/lists/itti-
networks/files/esrc-refcard.txt
Filesize: 11K
Fileformat: text

Type: ftp file
URL: file://mailbase.ac.uk/pub/lists/itti-
networks/files/esrc-refcard.RTF
Filesize: 232K
Fileformat: RTF

Type: ftp file
URL: file://mailbase.ac.uk/pub/lists/itti-
networks/files/esrc-refcard.W4W
Filesize: 121K
Fileformat: Word for Windows

Type: printed card
Publisher: ESRC
Size: 6 pp.
Reference:

Notes: Basic introductory document
Last Validated:
Date of update of this record: 27/10/1993
Record maintainer Name: Margaret Isaacs
Record maintainer E-mail: margaret.isaacs@ncl.ac.uk

ENTRY
Classification: Documentation – Networks – JANET
Country: UK
Title: JANET: an overview for libraries
Author: Peter Stone
Organization: JANET User Group for Libraries
Location:

Language: English
Keyword/s: JANET; Libraries
Abstract: Basics about the network and its organisation.
Lists access details of some useful services for the
library community
Contact name: Dr Richard Heseltine, Secretary – JUGL
Contact address: Brynmor Jones Library, University of Hull,
Hull, HU6 7RX
Contact phone number: 0 482 465436
Contact e-mail: R.G.Heseltine@uk.ac.hull.seq
Latest revision date: June 1993
Cost:

Type: Reference card
Publisher: JUGL
Size: 6 pp.
Last Validated:
Date of update of this record: October 1993
Record maintainer Name: Margaret Isaacs
Record maintainer E-mail: margaret.isaacs@ncl.ac.uk

ENTRY
Classification: Documentation – Network services
Country: UK
Title: Mailbase User's Guide
Author:
Organization: UK Networked Information Services Project
Location: Newcastle upon Tyne
Language: English
Keyword/s: Mailbase; Discussion lists; Listservers
Abstract: Details on how to use the Mailbase service via
electronic mail. Mailbase is an electronic mailing list
service for list distribution and archiving.
Contact name: Jill Foster
Contact address: NISP, Computing Service, University of
Newcastle upon Tyne NE1 7RU
Contact phone number: +44 91 222 8080
Contact e-mail: mailbase-helpline@uk.ac.mailbase
Latest revision date: January 1993
Cost: free

Type: e-mail file
E-mail server address: mailbase@mailbase.ac.uk

Filesize: 24K
File format: text
E-mail command: send mailbase user-guide

Type: ftp file
URL: file://mailbase.ac.uk/pub/mailbase/user-guide
Filesize: 24K
Fileformat: text

Type: ftp file
URL: file://mailbase.ac.uk/pub/mailbase/user-guide.RTF
Filesize: 44K
Fileformat: RTF

Type: Printed guide
Publisher: NISP
Size: 11 pp., A4

Notes:
Last Validated:
Date of update of this record: Oct.1993
Record maintainer Name: Margaret Isaacs
Record maintainer E-mail: margaret.isaacs@ncl.ac.uk

ENTRY
Classification: Documentation – Networks – SURFnet
Country: Netherlands
Title: SURFnet Guide1993
Author:
Organization: SURFnet BV
Location: Utrecht
Language: English and Dutch
Keyword/s:
Abstract: Comprehensive guide to services accessible via
SURFnet complete with access details. Explains in non-
technical language about networks, e-mail, remote login,
file transfer, bulletin boards, remote job entry,
electronic conferencing, etc.
Contact name:
Contact address: SURFnet BV, PO Box 19035,
3501 DA Utrecht, The Netherlandsecht, The Netherlands
Contact phone number:
Contact e-mail: info@SURFnet.nl
Latest revision date: 1993

Cost: free

Type: e-mail file,
E-mail server mail address: mailserv@file.nic.SURFnet.nl
Filesize:
E-mail command: send user-support/gids/READ.ME

Type: ftp file
URL: file://ftp.nic.SURFnet.nl/publications/guide/ascii-format/guide.txt
Filesize: 322 K
Fileformat: text

Type: ftp file
URL: file://ftp.nic.SURFnet.nl/publications/guide/wp-format/guide93.wp
Filesize: 379 K
Fileformat: Word Perfect 5.1

Type: ftp file
URL: file://ftp.nic.SURFnet.nl/publications/guide/ps-format/guide93.ps
Filesize: 1649 K
Fileformat: postscript
Type: printed guide
Publisher: SURFnet bv
Size: 265 pp.
Reference: ISBN 90-737749-02-6

Last Validated:
Date of update of this record: October 1993
Record maintainer Name: Margaret Isaacs
Record maintainer E-mail: margaret.isaacs@ncl.ac.uk

Kevin Savetz's booklist

This booklist is reproduced with the kind permission of Kevin Savetz.

The Unofficial Internet Book List

The most complete bibliography of books about the Internet

Version 0.5 – 19 June 1994 – featuring LOTS of new book information. This
is an interim release – I still have a towering stack of new books to review or add
to the list.

Send comments and updates to Kevin Savetz <savetz@rahul.net>.

This document is copyright 1994 by Kevin M. Savetz. All rights reserved.
More legal stuff is near the end of this file. This document is brand new
and in transition. If you notice that an Internet-related book is
missing, or information herein needs updating, please send e-mail to
"savetz@rahul.net".

*** Table of Contents
Vital Statistics
This Month's Featured Book
Alphabetical List of Internet Books
Upcoming titles
Publisher/Ordering Information
Internet Book Information & Updates Online
Legal, Ethical and Moral Stuff
Where to Find this Document

*** Vital Statistics
Number of books in this list: 106
Least expensive book: free (Guide for Accessing California Legislative
Info, NetPages)
Most expensive book: $70 (OPAC Directory 1994)
Thickest book: 1380 pages (The Internet Unleashed)
Thinnest book: 10 pages (The Internet at a Glance)
[These stats based on information I have on hand, not guaranteed.]

*** This Month's Featured Book [updated 19 June 1994]
Title: Netiquette
Author: Virginia Shea
Publisher: Albion Books
ISBN: 0-9637025-1-3
Price: $19.95
Pages: 154
Published: 1994
For more information: info@albion.com
This slim book does an excellent job of helping those new to Cyberspace
learn the basic tenants of Netiquette – or "network etiquette". I can't
imagine how much trouble and how many mumbled apologies would be averted
if everyone read this book before posting that first message. Netiquette

is easy to read and loaded with interesting real-life examples. Chapters cover the etiquette of e-mail and of discussion groups as well as providing excellent netiquette guidelines for business, home and school use. Particularly useful sections cover "electronic style" and the "core rules" of the online world. One chapter covers copyright issues and another the etiquette of e-mail privacy. There's even a tiny chapter on "Love & Sex in Cyberspace".

This book is filled with good advice for living your life online and off. Useful tidbits include: "Don't cheat on your spouse (and if you do, don't do it on company time)", "Don't CC: Steve Jobs on your analysis of the war in Bosnia" and the vague but truest rule, "Don't do stupid things." All very good advice. This book should be required reading for anyone collecting their Internet Learner's Permit. Highly recommended. You can retrieve a brief excerpt from Netiquette: "The Core Rules of Netiquette" by sending e-mail to netiquette-request@albion.com with the words "archive send core" in the subject line.

*** Alphabetical List of Internet Books
Title: All About Internet FTP: Learning and Teaching to Transfer Files on the Internet
Author: David Robison
Publisher: Library Solutions Press
ISBN: 1-882208-04-8 (book alone) or 1-882208-06-4 (book with diskettes)
Price: $30 ($45 with disk)
Pages: 90
Published: 1994
For more information: (510) 841-2636, or alipow@library.berkeley.edu
Notes: For use by Internet trainers or for self-study.

Title: Everybody's Guide to the Internet
Author: Adam Gaffin
Publisher: M.I.T. Press
ISBN: 0-262-57105-6
Price: $14.95
Pages: about 260
Published: July, 1994
For more information: ?
Thanks for the info: Adam Gaffin (adamg@world.std.com)
Notes: This is basically a printed version of version 2.2 of the EFF's online guide "The Big Dummy's Guide to the Internet", plus an index. Litigious lawyers from another publishing house prevented the printed version from sharing the same name.

Title: Canadian Internet Handbook
Author: Jim Carroll and Rick Broadhead
Publisher: Prentice Hall Canada
ISBN: 0-13-304395-9
Price: $16.95
Pages: 414
Published: 1994
For more information: handbook@uunet.ca. For orders: Toll-free in Canada:
1-800-567-3800. U.S. and Overseas: +1 (416) 293-3621
Notes: If you live in Canada, get this book. It contains sections about
getting Internet access in Canada, growth of 'net use there, short basic
sections about how to use of some of the most popular Internet tools, a
huge directory of Canadian Internet service providers, and even more huge
list of gopher servers and campus-wide information systems in Canada and
to top it off, lists of Canadian-based Usenet groups, WWW, Archie, IRC
servers and online catalogs. I wish I lived in Canada just so I could
make more use of this book.

Title: The Complete Idiot's Guide to the Internet
Author: Peter Kent
Publisher: Alpha Books
ISBN: 1-56761-414-0
Price: $19.95
Pages: 386
Goodies: DOS disk
Published: 1994
For more information: 800-428-5331 or 317-581-3500
Notes:

Title: The Complete Internet Directory
Author: Eric Braun
Publisher: Fawcett
ISBN: ?
Price: $25
Pages: 325
Published: 1993
For more information:
Notes: A directory of newsgroups, discussion lists, FTP sites and so on,
with just a few pages on how to use these resources.

Title: Computers Under Attack: Intruders, Worms, and Viruses
Author: Peter Denning
Publisher: ACM Press/Addison-Wesley
ISBN: 0-201-53067-8

Price: $23.95
Pages: 574
Published: 1990
For more information: ?
Thanks for the info: John Quarterman in RFC 1432
Notes: Details of celebrated network security cases. Includes Stoll's
original article about the Wiley Hacker, and responses and articles by
others on the same subject. Has extensive coverage of the 1988 Internet
Worm. Also includes information on viruses. Has quite a bit of material
on the cultures of the networks, and on social, legal, and ethical
matters. Starts with the standard historical network papers, including
"Notable Computer Networks" by Quarterman and Hoskins.

Title: Connecting to the Internet
Author: Susan Estrada
Publisher: O'Reilly & Associates
ISBN: 1-56592-061-9
Price: $15.95
Pages: 170
Published: 1993.
Notes: This small book focuses on choosing the best type of network
connection for your personal, school or business needs, and how to get
the best price for the type of access you require. Explains the
differences between SLIP, PPP, ISDN, X.25 and other options. Includes an
extensive list of Internet service providers. This is a single-purpose
book, telling how to choose a connection and get online. It doesn't try
to teach you how to use the net once you're there. That is graceful in
its simplicity.

Title: Crossing the Internet Threshold: an Instructional Handbook
Author: Roy Tennant, John Ober and Anne Lipow
Publisher: Library Solutions Press
ISBN: 1-883308-01-3
Price: $45
Pages: 134
Published: 1993
For more information: (510) 841-2636. FTP for info:
simsc.si.edu:/networks/crossing.ad
Thanks for the info: Robert Slade <ROBERTS@decus.ca>
Notes: An instructional package for librarians teaching Internet basics.
This book is useful for newcomers to the Internet. This book is useful
for trainers. This book is useful for librarians. Ultimately, this book
is most useful for those training librarians who are new to the Internet.
A newcomer to the Internet might find this material a bit disorganized,

but very definitely helpful and useful. It is heartening to see the very strong emphasis on Internet etiquette and culture which all too often gets short shrift, even in introductory guides. The grouping of discussion lists and electronic journals with e-mail is a logical extension which is not always made. The work is not limited to the novice, though; many Internet users would find the fact sheets to be a handy quick reference.

Title: The Cuckoo's Egg: Tracking a Spy Through the Maze of Computer Espionage
Author: Clifford Stoll
Publisher: Doubleday
ISBN: 0-385-24946-2
Price: $5.95
Pages: 332
Published: 1989
For more information: ?
Notes: A spy novel, except it's true: a first person account by a down-on-his-luck Berkeley astronomer who with others tracked down a KGB network spy. Contains a very good recipe for chocolate chip cookies, too!

Title: Cyberpunk
Author: Katie Hafner and John Markoff
Publisher: Simon & Schuster
ISBN: 0-671-68322-5
Price: $22.95
Pages: 368
Published: 1991
Thanks for the info: John Quarterman in RFC 1432
Notes: Interviews with some of the crackers who have appeared conspicuously in the press in the past few years. One of the co-authors is the New York Times reporter who broke the Morris story to the public. Very readable.

Title: DFUe – Ein Handbuch. Recherchen in weltweiten Netzen
Language: German
Authors: Martin Rost & Michael Schack
Publisher: Heise-Verlag, Hannover
ISBN: 3-88229-026-9
Price: 58 DM
Pages: 389
Published: 1993
Fore more information: maro@toppoint.de
It's an introduction to Internet (e-mail, FTP, telnet, IRC, archie,

gopher, hytelnet, wais, WWW), uucp-Net, Bitnet (Netserver, Listservs, Trickle-Server, Bitftp, Astra), WIN, FidoNet, MausNet and Z-Net with many examples for each.

Title: Directory of Directories on the Internet: A Guide to Information Sources
Author: Gregory B. Newby
Publisher: Meckler
ISBN: 0-88736-768-2
Price: $29.50
Pages: 153
Published: 1993
For more information: gbnewby@uiuc.edu
Notes: Intended for those who need to identify Internet information resources that point to other resources.

Title: Doing Business on the Internet
Author: Mary Cronin
Publisher: Van Nostrand Reinhold
ISBN: 0-442-01770-7
Price: $29.95
Pages: 308
Published: 1994
For more information: ?
Thanks for the info: matisse@well.sf.ca.us (J Matisse Enzer)
Notes: Promotional info says: One view of how the Internet has changed the way some companies are doing business. Must reading for anyone looking at the impact of the Internet on commerce and why Internet access is becoming critical for businesses. Matisse Enzer says: Excellent overview and detailed discussion of the Internet from a business users' perspective. An entirely non-technical book, Doing Business discusses the commercial aspects and issues of the Internet: advertising, research, customer contact, etc. Highly recommended.

Title: DOS User's Guide to the Internet
Author: James Gardner
Publisher: Prentice Hall
ISBN: 0-13-106873-3
Price: $34.95
Pages: 308
Goodies: DOS disk
Published: 1993
For more information: (515) 284-6751 or phyllis@prenhall.com
Thanks for the info: Robert Slade <ROBERTS@decus.ca>

Notes: A minimalist software package and manual for setting up a UUCP connection for mail and news. This title is almost completely misleading. This book is not for DOS users, except that you must be running DOS to run the MKS UUCP for DOS programs for which this book is a manual. This book is also not about the Internet, as such. Both the specifics and the concepts refer to UUCP rather than the Internet. The text of the book does point out that there are differences, but the examples given relate to UUCP. That said, for those who are interested in making their first move to a direct Internet connection, this could be an excellent choice. UUCP was designed to be quite comfortable with dialup connections, and this book and associated programs, help to automate a number of the connection functions while freeing the user from much of the technical detail that TCP/IP requires.

Title: The Easy Internet Handbook
Author: Javed Mostafa, Thomas Newell, Richard Trenthem
Publisher: Hi Willow Research and Publishing
ISBN: 0-931510-50-3
Price: $20
Pages: 150
Published: 1994
For more information: tnewell@fiat.gslis.utexas.edu or 800-237-6124
Notes:

Title: Electronic Style: A Guide to Citing Electronic Information
Author: Xia Li and Nancy Crane
Publisher: Meckler
ISBN: 0-88736-909-X
Price: $15
Pages: 80
Published: 1993
For more information: ?
Notes: Here is where to find out how to cite in your bibliographies references found von the Internet, on CD-ROMs and online database searches.

Title: The Electronic Traveler: Directory Of Tourism Information Sources
Author: M. L. Endicott
Publisher: ?
ISBN: ?
Price: $50.00
Pages: ?
Published: May 1994
For more information: Marcus L. Endicott <mendicott@igc.apc.org>

Notes: From the publisher's info: As the title of this new book says, The Electronic Traveler is a directory of tourism information available to everyone with a computer and a telephone: it is a guidebook to online travel information sources. It explains in plain English exactly what travel and tourism information is available on the information highway and how to access it. It covers the Internet, popular proprietary interactive systems, Computer Reservation Systems (CRSs), independent bulletin board systems (BBSs), and commercial fulltext databases.

Title: The Electronic Traveller: Exploring Alternative Online Systems
Author: Elizabeth Powell Crowe
Publisher: Windcrest/McGraw-Hill
ISBN: 0-8306-4498-9
Price: $16.95
Pages: ?
Published: ?
For more information: ?
Notes:

Title: The Elements of E-Mail Style
Author: David Angell & Brent Heslop
Publisher: Addison-Wesley
ISBN: 0-201-62709-4
Price: $12.95
Pages: 157
Published: March 1994
For more information: dangell@shell.portal.com
Thanks for the info: David F. Angell (dangell@shell.portal.com)
Notes: How to write effective e-mail. It simplifies and summarizes essential writing techniques so users can upgrade their writing skills and see their e-mail make maximum impact in minimal time.

Title: EcoLinking: Everyone's Guide to Online Environmental Information
Author: Don Rittner
Publisher: Peachpit Press
ISBN: 0-938151-35-5
Price: $18 95
Pages: 368
Published: 1992
For more information: (800) 283-9444
Notes: Directed at concerned citizens, environmentalists and scientists interested in sharing ideas and research on environmental issues. Covers resources on FIDONET, BITNET, INTERNET, USENET, local bulletin boards, America Online, CompuServe, EcoNet, GENIE, WELL.

Title: Exploring the Internet: a Technical Travelogue
Author: Carl Malamud
Publisher: Prentice-Hall
ISBN: 0-13-296898-3
Price: $26.95
Pages: 379
Published: 1992
For more information: (515) 284-6751
Thanks for the info: Robert Slade <ROBERTS@decus.ca>
Notes: A look at the Internet and the emerging global village in 21
countries and 56 cities. Not technical, but lots of fun stories about
travelling around the world (physically).

Title: Firewalls and Internet Security
Author: Cheswick/Bellovin
Publisher: Addison-Wesley
ISBN: 0-201-63357-4
Price: $26.95
Pages: ?
Published: 1994
For more information: firewall-book@research.att.com
Thanks for the info:
Notes: Practical suggestions for firewall construction and other aspects
of Internet security.

Title: From A to Z39.50: a network primer
Author: James Michael and Mark Hinnebusch
Publisher: Meckler
ISBN: 0-88736-766-6
Price: $25
Pages: 225
Published: March 1994
For more information: ?
Notes: Introduction and discussion about the issues and standards
involves in electronic telecommunications.

Title: A Guide for Accessing California Legislative Information over
Internet
Author: Legislative Counsel Bureau, State of California
Publisher: State of California
ISBN: none listed
Price: free to California residents
Pages: 30
Published: 1994

For more information: comments@leginfo.public.ca.gov
Thanks for the info: Mike Quinn
Notes: This pamphlet tells how you can find California legislative
information online. Explains what legislation info is available, what
assistance is available and how the information is organized. The
majority of the book is spent explaining the Internet, how to get access,
how to use electronic mail and where to go for more detailed information.
There's also a simple glossary of legislative terms. This pamphlet is
also available online, in PostScript format. Send e-mail:
  To: ftpmail@leginfo.public.ca.gov
  Body: connect leginfo.public.ca.gov
    get README_public_access_guide_ps
    quit

Title: The Hacker Crackdown: Law and Disorder on the Electronic Frontier
Author: Bruce Sterling
Publisher: Bantam
ISBN: 0-553-08058-X
Price: $23
Pages: 352
Published: 1992
For more information: ?
Thanks for the info: John Quarterman in RFC 1432
Notes: An in-depth examination of the forces of law who try to deal with
computer crime, and of the issues involved, written by one of the science
fiction writers who invented cyberpunk. The real story behind Operation
Sundevil and the Legion of Doom. Readable, informative, amusing, and
necessary.

Title: Hackers: Heroes of the Computer Revolution
Author: Steven Levy
Publisher: Anchor Press/Doubleday
ISBN: 0-385-19195-2 (hard) 0-440-13405-6 (paper)
Price: $17.95 / $4.95
Pages: 458
Published: 1984
For more information: ?
Notes: Describes the early culture and ethos of hackers and computer
homebrewers and that ultimately resulted in the Internet and Usenet.

Title: Hands-On Internet: A Beginning Guide for PC Users
Author: David Sachs & Henry Stair
Publisher: Prentice Hall
ISBN: 0-13-056392-7

Price: $29.95
Pages: 274
Goodies: DOS disk
Published: 1994
For more information: ?
Notes:

Title: How The Internet Works
Author: Joshua Eddings
Publisher: Ziff-Davis Press
ISBN: 1-56276-192-7
Price: $US 24.95, $CAN 34.95, UK 22.99
Pages: 218
Published: 1994
For more information: ab136@freenet.carleton.ca or 800/688-0448
Thanks for the info: Dick Lee <ab136@freenet.carleton.ca>
Notes: Very good primer on the Internet and how it works. There are many
rich illustrations which serve to explain the concepts very effectively.
Contents include the protocols, telnet, downloading files, archie, e-
mail, mailing lists, Usenet, gophers, WAIS, WWW as well as a look into
audio/video, virtual reality, security issues and the future. Of
necessity, many of these are treated very briefly but as an overall
introductory manual, I found it very readable and informative.

Title: In acht Sekunden um die Welt (In eight seconds around the world)
Language: German
Author: Gunther Maier/Andreas Wildberger
Publisher: Addison Wesley
ISBN: 3-89319-701-X
Price: DM 39.90 / oeS 311,00
Pages: 160
Published: released 1994 (Second edition)
For more information: wildberg@nestroy.wu.wien.ac.at
Thanks for the info: pcsaal15@fub46.zedat.fu-berlin.de (Lutz Lademann)
Notes: It's a quite comprehensive introduction to the Internet, its
history and the services available (Mail, News, Gopher, FTP, Telnet, WWW
and more). For more information about the book mail one of the authors:
wildberg@nestroy.wu.wien.ac.at (Andreas Wildberger.) Three chapters of
this book are available via WWW:
  URL: http://rektorat.wu-wien.ac.at/stuff/netzbuch.html

Title: The Instant Internet Guide
Author: Brent Heslop & David Angell
Publisher: Addison-Wesley

ISBN: 0-201-62707-8
Price: $14.95
Pages: 209
Published: 3rd printing.
For more information: dangell@shell.portal.com
Thanks for the info: matisse@well.sf.ca.us (J Matisse Enzer)
Notes: Good quick intro to Internet and quick reference sections on using
e-mail, usenet, gopher, telnet, file transfers, very basic UNIX etc. Nice
check-list of questions to ask when shopping for Internet access.
Oriented entirely towards a dial-up terminal user on a unix system.

Title: Internet Access Providers: An International Resource Directory
Author: Greg Notess
Publisher: Meckler
ISBN: 0-88736-933-2
Price: $30
Pages: 330
Published: May 1994
For more information: meckler@tigger.jvnc.net (publisher) or
align@montana.edu (author)
Notes: This directory provides descriptive information on over 300
companies and networks that offer dial-in Internet access. Aimed at those
without current access, looking for personal access.

Title: The Internet and Special Librarians: Use, Training and the Future
Author: Sharyn Lander Hope Tillman
Publisher: Special Libraries Association
ISBN: 0-87111-413-5
Price: $34.95
Pages: 187
Published: 1993
For more information: tillman@babson.edu or sla1@capcon.net
Notes: Implications of a study of special librarians' use of the Internet
and the future of librarianship. Includes a glossary, primer on Internet
basics, resources and how to get connected.

Title: The Internet at a Glance
Author: Susan E. Feldman
Publisher: Datasearch
ISBN: None listed
Price: $7
Pages: 10
Published: 1994
For more information: Susan Feldman <suef@TC.Cornell.EDU>

Thanks for the info: Susan Feldman <suef@TC.Cornell.EDU>
Notes: A collection of "cheatsheets" for the net. It's very short (only
10 thin pages) but it covers the very basics for using the Internet and
UNIX. Topics include Finding Resources on the Internet, Tools, electronic
mail, anonymous FTP, telnet, mailing lists and newsgroups, basic UNIX
commands and the vi editor.

Title: Internet Basics
Author: Steve Lambert & Walt Howe
Publisher: Random House
ISBN: 0-679-75023-1
Price: $27.00
Pages: 495
Published: 1993
For more information: ?
Thanks for the info: Gayle Keresey (aflgayle@aol.com)
Notes: General book on the Internet with a slight slant towards Delphi.
(Howe is Delphi's Internet SIG Manager.)

Title: The Internet Companion, A Beginner's Guide To Global Networking
Author: Tracy LaQuey with Jeanne C. Ryer
Publisher: Addison-Wesley Publishing
ISBN: 0-201-62224-6
Price: $10.95
Pages: 196
Published: 1993
For more information: internet-companion@world.std.com
Thanks for the info: Robert Slade <ROBERTS@decus.ca>
Notes: The Companion includes a detailed history of the Internet, a
discussion on "netiquette" (network etiquette), and how to find resources
on the net. It is difficult to know what is supposed to be
"companionable" about this volume. Physically, it would be easy to carry
it along with you. You probably wouldn't want to, though. This is not a
guide for explorations, either. It does give one some background on the
Internet, but it is not in a step-by-step fashion. (How to access the
Internet is the *last* topic to be covered.) The newcomer to the
Internet will more likely want to read it all (possibly at one sitting;
it's small enough) and look at the network gestalt. This work is somewhat
less technical than the UNIX biased "Whole Internet Guide". However, it
goes too far in the opposite direction. The authors boast that it was
finished in less than two months. It shows. Companies which are getting
into the Internet in a big way might make this the introductory volume
for new users: it is generally upbeat and non-threatening. However, help
should be on hand when people actually start using the net.

222

Title: The Internet Companion Plus
Author: Tracy LaQuey & Jeanne Ryer
Publisher: Addison Wesley
ISBN: 0-201-62719-1
Price: $19.95
Pages: ?
Goodies: DOS disk
Published: 1993
For more information: $19.95
Notes:

Title: The Internet Complete Reference
Author: Harley Hahn & Rick Stout
Publisher: Osborne McGraw-Hill
ISBN: 0-07-881980-6
Price: $29.95
Pages: 818
Published: ?
For more information: ?
Notes:

Title: The Internet Connection: System Connectivity and Configuration
Author: by John S. Quarterman and Smoot Carl-Mitchell
Publisher: Addison-Wesley
ISBN: 0-201-54237-4
Price: $32.25
Pages: 271
Published: 1994
For more information: awbook@aw.com
Notes: According to the publisher, this book gives step-by-step
instruction on connection to the Internet for system designers, system
administrators and their managers, offers assistance in setting up
naming, mail and news systems and explains the use of common Internet
services such as archie, WAIS, and Gopher.

Title: Internet Connections: A Librarian's Guide to Dial-Up Access and
Use
Author: Engle, Mary E., et al.
Publisher: American Library Association
ISBN: 0-8389-7677-8
Price: $22.00
Pages: 166
Published: 1993
For more information: ?

Notes:

Title: The Internet Directory
Author: Eric Braun
Publisher: Fawcett Columbine
ISBN: 0-449-90898-4
Price: $25.00
Pages: 704
Published: 1994
For more information: ?
Thanks for the info: Gayle Keresey (aflgayle@aol.com)
Notes: Each chapter in this book covers a particular information service
or resource type, including mailing lists, newsgroups, FTP archives,
Gophers, WAIS, WWW, etc. All sources have been verified. Extensive index.
A must have for Internet surfers.

Title: Internet Essentials
Author: ?
Publisher: Que College
ISBN: ?
Price: ?
Pages: ?
Published: Feb 1994
For more information: ?
Thanks for the info: Connie Marijs <otsgroup@pop.knoware.nl>
Notes: {Unsure if this actually exists.} A Jump-Start to Getting on the
Internet. This guide will help you to learn what the Internet is and how
it works; get connected to this worldwide network; understand the basics
of how to navigate the Internet; take advantage of newsgroups, electronic
conferencing, and electronic journals; expand your access to information
and data through FTP and Telnet. Readers follow concise, 10-minute
lessons to learn about everything from hardware to E-mail, from
downloading files to participating newsgroups. Contains mini-tutorials,
specific directions, how-to information.

Title: The Internet for Dummies
Author: John Levine & Carol Baroudi
Publisher: IDG Books
ISBN: 1-56884-024-1
Price: $19.95
Pages: 355
Published: 1993
For more information: (415) 312-0650 or dummies@iecc.com
Thanks for the info: Graham Keith Rogers <scgkr@mucc.mahidol.ac.th>

Notes: Intended as a beginners guide to the Internet, includes useful sections on mail, gopher, news, ftp, etc. All in a fairly light-hearted style intended to set novices at ease. At over 350 pages, there is much information and the book is well indexed. For those who have a direct connection, i.e. SLIP or PPP.

Title: Internet: Getting Started
Author: April Marine, Susan Kirkpatrick, Vivian Neou & Carol Ward
Publisher: Prentice Hall
ISBN: 0-13-327933-2
Price: $28.00
Pages: 360
Published: 1993
For more information: (515) 284-6751
Notes: Explains how to join the Internet, the various types of Internet access, and procedures for obtaining a unique IP address and domain name. An extensive list of Internet access providers of all types is provided, including access outside of the United States. The guide explains many concepts essential to the Internet, such as the Domain Name System, IP addressing, protocols, and electronic mail. Doesn't tell you how to use the 'net, just how to get connected.

Title: The Internet Guide for New Users
Author: Daniel P Dern
Publisher: McGraw-Hill
ISBN: Paperback 0-07-016511, Hardcover 0-07-016510-6
Price: Paperback $27.95, Hardcover $40.00
Pages: 570
Published: 1993
For more information: ddern@world.std.com
Notes: A very complete introduction to the world of the Internet. Along with the obligatory topics such as telnet, FTP and Archie, the book suggests how to get an Internet account and teaches enough UNIX to survive on the net. This book is more complete and in-depth than many other Internet books: Dern's deep knowledge of all things Internet shines through, although sometimes the book is a bit too formal. The book, like Dern, is laced with dry humor and is UNIX-centric. Highly recommended.

Title: Internet Instant Reference
Author: Paul E. Hoffman
Publisher: Sybex
ISBN: 0-7821-1512-8
Price: $12.99
Pages: 317

Published: 1994
For more information: ?
Notes: This book is part quick reference, part lexicon and part Internet tutorial. Arranged in dictionary format, it defines Internet jargon (like shareware and hypertext) gives brief descriptions of tools (like Knowbot and Listserv), includes short command summaries for using popular programs (like FTP, emacs and elm), and describes various net organizations, policies and legislation. Nice design and layout. This book contains a wide variety of information, but is sort of unevenly edited and contains some factual errors that might not be clear to newbies (for instance, in one section it confuses the terms upload and download).

Title: The Internet Library: Case Studies of Library Internet Management and Use
Author: Julie Still, ed.
Publisher: Meckler
ISBN: 0-88736-965-0
Price: $37.50
Pages: 200
Published: June 1994
For more information: ?
Notes: The case studies in this volume focus on how electronic resources have changed relationships with the library and on the way libraries relate to the larger world.

Title: Internet: Mailing Lists
Author: Edward Hardie & Vivian Neou
Publisher: Prentice Hall
ISBN: 0-13-289661-3
Price: $26.00
Pages: 356
Published: 1993
For more information: ?
Notes: A list of Internet mailing list. Note that a current "list of lists" is available online for free, both via Usenet and FTP.

Title: The Internet Message: Closing the Book with Electronic Mail
Author: Marshall Rose
Publisher: Prentice Hall
ISBN: 0-13-092941-7
Price: $44.00
Pages: ?
Published: 1993

For more information: ?
Notes: Technical discussion of mail agent and system design

Title: The Internet Navigator
Author: Paul Gilster
Publisher: John Wiley & Sons, Inc.
ISBN: 0-471-59782-1
Price: $24.95
Pages: 470
Published: Aug. 1993
For more information: (800) 263-1590 or gilster@rock.concert.net
Thanks for the info: Gayle Keresey (aflgayle@aol.com)
Notes: Information for the dial-up Internet user. Includes Internet
history, signing on to the net, UNIX commands, getting files, telnet,
electronic mail, BITNET, electronic journals, Usenet, gophers and
Internet resources. Useful for those who want step-by-step instructions
for dial-up terminal access. Somewhat academic in tone.

Title: The Internet Passport: NorthWestNet's Guide to Our World Online
Author: Jonathan Kochmer
Publisher: NorthWestNet and the Northwest Academic Computing Consortium
ISBN: 0-9635281-0-6
Price: $29.95
Pages: 516
Published: 4th ed.
For more information: (206) 562-3000 or e-mail passport@nwnet.net. Order
forms can be obtained via FTP as: ftp.nwnet.net/user-
docs/passport/nonmem-order-form.txt
Thanks for the info: Robert Slade <ROBERTS@decus.ca>
Notes: Covers everything from net etiquette to supercomputers; very
comprehensive. This work is a fairly bare bones and no nonsense guide to
the Internet. The book is orderly, and the explanations and illustrations
are clear. Each chapter covers a single topic and ends with additional
references, most often online materials or sources. The work is well
researched and highly competent in most cases. There is, in the early
chapters, a gracelessness to it which lacks any kind of appeal.
Nevertheless, it is a thoroughly researched and valuable reference for
those interested in using the resources of the Internet. It costs $39.95
but schools and not-for-profit organizations can buy it for $19.95 plus
shipping.

Title: Internet Primer for Information Professionals: A Basic Guide to
Internet Networking Technology
Author: Elizabeth Lane and Craig Summerhill

Publisher: Meckler
ISBN: 0-88736-831-X
Price: $37.50
Pages: 175
Published: 1993
For more information: ?
Notes: Description of the current state of the Internet, as well as the proposed NREN, as well as basic information on network usage and concepts.

Title: Internet Public Access Guide
Author: Phil Hughes
Publisher: SSC Publications
ISBN: 0-916151-70-0
Price: $2.95
Pages: 64
Published: 1994
For more information: sales@ssc.com or (206) 527-3385.
Thanks for the info: Graham Keith Rogers <scgkr@mucc.mahidol.ac.th>
Notes: Graham Rogers says: "64-page guide to Internet basics. Very easy to follow instructions, clearly set out. With the small size not everything can be included but the price represents good value. The paper cover deteriorates with use." I say: A whole lot of information for the money. Well-presented, simple and above all, short. Covers "What is the Internet?", terms, UNIX basics, e-mail, Usenet, FTP, rlogin and telnet, finger, archie, gopher and veronica. Easy-to-follow examples. They'll sell you just one, but the book is primarily intended to be sold to service providers and distributed to their users.

Title: Internet Quickstart
Author: Mary Ann Pike and Tod G. Pike
Publisher: Que
ISBN: 1-56529-658-3
Price: $21.99
Pages: 387
Published: March 1994
For more information: 800-428-5331 or 317-581-3500
Thanks for the info: Connie Marijs <otsgroup@pop.knoware.nl>
Notes: A series of quick tutorials, this book explains Internet basics to absolute beginners. Lots of extras – like buzzword definitions, tips, and warnings – help users get more from this premier online service. Task oriented skill sessions cover topics such as log-on, E-Mail, database searches, Internet news and more.

Title: The Internet Resource Quick Reference
Author: William Tolhurst
Publisher: Que
ISBN: ?
Price: ?
Pages: ?
Published: 1994
For more information: ?
Notes: Contains a list of USENET news groups, a list of publicly accessible mailing lists, Scott Yanoff's list of online resources and the Inter-Network Mail Guide. All of this information is available online.

Title: The Internet Roadmap
Author: Bennett Falk
Publisher: Sybex
ISBN: 0-7821-1365-6
Price: $12.99
Pages: 263.
Published: 1994
Thanks for the info: David M. Stevenson <david@dms.muc.de>
Notes: David M. Stevenson says, "This book is written by someone who is concerned that the reader get a good grasp of the Internet system quickly. In my case he succeeded; and what he can do for me, he can do for you!" I say: This book is a winner. It explains the basics of the Internet in a clear and concise style. Covers the tools for reading Usenet news, doing e-mail, using FTP, gopher and WorldWideWeb. Doesn't get into the newer, funkier tools too much. It's an easy read and doesn't get bogged down in esoteric, dull stuff. I even like the cover.

Title: Internet shouyouka ni mukete (CIX) (Feasibility Reserch for Commercial Internet in Japan)
Language: Japanese
Author: SI Division
Publisher: Toppan
ISBN: 4-8101-8907-4
Price: 1600 Yen (Around $16)
Pages: 142
Published: November 1993
For more information: ?
Thanks for the info: Hideyuki Matsushima (hideyuki@apic.or.jp)
Notes: This is the first and only book on commercial Internet service in Japan. Published as reserch report, its purpose is to clarify Internet status in the United States and business feasibility study on CIX in Japan. Coverage includes: What is Internet and its historical story in

the US, Structure of commercial service in Internet, Image of commercial Internet in Japan. Report covers the feasibility of Internet withing various regulated Japanese environments. It is must-read book for companies in Japan wishing enter the Internet business.

Title: The Internet Starter Kit for Macintosh
Author: Adam Engst
Publisher: Hayden Books
ISBN: 1-56830-064-6
Price: $29.95
Pages: 640
Goodies: Mac floppy disk filled with great software
Published: 1993
For more information: ace@tidbits.com
Notes: This terrific book (with a floppy disk) gives Macintosh users the complete scoop on getting connected to the Internet using PPP, SLIP, etc. This is one of my very favorite Internet books because it's so readable. It's definitely the best one dedicated to Mac users.

Title: Internet System Handbook
Author: Danial Lynch and Marshall Rose
Publisher: Addison-Wesley
ISBN: 0-201-56741-5
Price: $54.95
Pages: ?
Published: 1993
For more information: ?
Thanks for the info: Robert Slade <ROBERTS@decus.ca>
Notes: Essays by people involved with the Internet. Strong on protocols, weak on direction. The book is divided into four parts. The first section deals with an historical and organizational background to the Internet. The second section, written by the people who built the Internet, deals with technical aspects of the major protocols and applications of the Internet. Part three, "Infrastructure," covers issues not centrally relevant to the operation of the Internet, but supporting its use: network performance and management, backbone and node tools, directory services and operational security. The bibliographic information contained in the book overall might be worth the price alone. Quarterman's contribution is carefully and fully researched and well organized. It includes not only texts, but periodicals and online sources as well.

Title: The Internet Unleashed
Author: Steve Bang, Martin Moore, Rick Gates, et al.

Publisher: Sams Publishing
ISBN: 0-672-30466-X
Price: $44.95
Pages: 1,380
Goodies: 1 PC-format HD disk. (Macintosh users can mail in an enclosed coupon to receive a disk with similar Mac software for a nominal shipping and handling fee.)
Published: April 1994
Notes: This book is a huge tome, weighing in with 62 chapters plus 7 appendices. It is co-written by a zillion authors, and falls in the "everything you could possibly ever want to know about the Internet" category, with blanket coverage of accessing the 'net from different types of home computers, networks and with high-speed connections. This book covers just about every Internet topic you can think of, from security to MUDs, from doing business on the 'net to copyright issues and problems.

Title: 1994 Internet White Pages
Author: Seth Godin & James S. McBride
Publisher: IDG Books
ISBN: 1-56884-300-3
Price: $29.95
Pages: ?
Published: 1994
For more information: ?
Notes: A thick book listing about 100,000 e-mail addresses. (Although that may seem like a lot, it's not very comprehensive.) Addresses are listed by last name and are also indexed by Internet domain name. This book may be useful for finding associates' e-mail addresses, but is probably no more useful than using one of the many 'net-based e-mail-address search utilities. The book is unevenly edited (I'm in there three times!) and was woefully out of date before the ink was dry.

Title: The Internet Yellow Pages
Author: Harley Hahn and Rick Stout
Publisher: Osborne Publishing (McGraw Hill)
ISBN: 0-07-882023-5
Price: $27.95
Pages: 447
Published: 1994
Thanks for the info: jeynes@adobe.com
Notes: This is a summary book that is laid out like the phone book yellow pages, and includes descriptions of various services available on the Internet. Most of these services are Usenet newsgroups,

established mailing lists, or ftp site/directory listings. It's an interesting, readable and unique way to present a catalog of stuff on the 'net.

Title: Mac Internet Tour Guide
Author: Michael Fraase
Publisher: Ventana Press
ISBN: 1-56604-062-0
Price: $27.95
Pages: 286
Goodies: Mac floppy disk with a bit useful software. Periodic updates via e-mail. One month of free online time from MRNet.
Published: 1993
For more information: dilennox@aol.com or FTP to ftp.farces.com
Notes: This book (with floppy disk) for Macintosh users helps newcomers get online and get acquainted with graphical Internet software "Fetch" and "Eudora".

Title: Introducing the Internet: A Trainer's Workshop
Author: Lee David Jaffe
Publisher: Library Solutions Press
ISBN: 1-882208-03-X (book alone) or 1-882208-05-6 (with diskettes)
Price: $30.00 ($45.00 with diskettes)
Pages: 92
Published: 1994
For more information: (510) 841-2636 or alipow@library.berkeley.edu
Thanks for the info:
Notes: The 2nd in a series of supplements to "Crossing the Internet Threshold". Based on trainer's handouts and script. A guide for trainers whose audience is made up of pre-Internet users.

Title: Libraries and the Internet/NREN: Perspectives, Issues and Challenges
Author: Charles McClure et al
Publisher: Meckler
ISBN: 0-88736-824-7
Price: $25
Pages: 500
Published: March 1994
For more information: ?
Notes: This major study identifies key factors within the library and larger environments that will affect libraries' involvement in national networking policies.

Title: Managing uucp and Usenet
Author: ?
Publisher: O'Reilly & Associates
ISBN: ?
Price: ?
Pages: ?
Published: ?
For more information: info@ora.com
Thanks for the info:
Notes: Intended for system administrators who need to set up and maintain
UUCP connections or access Usenet, the book realizes that in the UNIX
world many sysadmins are just plain folks. The necessary technical
details are here, but presented in a logical and non-threatening manner.

Title: The Matrix: Computer Networks and Conferencing Systems Worldwide
Author: John S. Quarterman
Publisher: Digital Press
ISBN: 0-13-565607-9
Price: $50.00
Pages: ?
Published: 1990
For more information: ?
Notes:
Title: Navigating the Internet
Author: Mark Gibbs & Richard Smith
Publisher: Sams
ISBN: 0-672-30362-0
Price: $24.95
Pages: 500
Published: 1993
For more information: 800-428-5331 or 317-581-3500
Notes: <<To be reviewed in next edition of the booklist>>

Title: Navigating the Internet, Deluxe Edition
Author: Richard Smith and Mark Gibbs
Publisher: Sams
ISBN: 0-672-30485-6
Price: $29.95
Pages: 640
Goodies: 1 PC-format HD disk. (Macintosh users can mail in an coupon to
receive a Mac disk with similar software for a nominal shipping and
handling fee) and one month free connect time
Published: April 1994
For more information: 800-428-5331 or 317-581-3500

Notes: Nearly identical to Navigating the Internet (above) except it includes a disk with Internet Software for Microsoft Windows and a few extra chapters: "A Better Window on the Web: Mosaic", "Using the Internet for Business", as well as versions of the online references Gopher Jewels and PDIAL. I suppose it's worth the extra five bucks for this book versus the vanilla Navigating the Internet, especially if you use Windows and need the software.

Title: Netiquette
Author: Virginia Shea
Publisher: Albion Books
ISBN: 0-9637025-1-3
Price: $19.95
Pages: 154
Published: 1994
For more information: info@albion.com
Notes: This slim book does an excellent job of helping those new to Cyberspace learn the basic tenants of network etiquette, or "netiquette". It's easy to read and loaded with interesting real-life examples. Chapters cover netiquette of e-mail and of discussion groups as well as providing excellent netiquette guidelines for business, home and school use. Particularly useful sections cover Electronic Style (looking good online, tone of voice and signature files) and the "core rules" of the online world. One chapter covers copyright issues and another the etiquette of e-mail privacy. There's even a tiny chapter on "Love & Sex in Cyberspace". This book should be required reading for anyone collecting their Internet Learner's Permit. (You can retrieve a brief excerpt from Netiquette: "The Core Rules of Netiquette" by sending e-mail to netiquette-request@albion.com with the words "archive send core" in the subject line.)

Title: Netguide
Author: Peter Rutten, Albert Bayers III & Kelly Moloni
Publisher: Random House
ISBN: 0-679-75106-8
Price: $19.00
Pages: ?
Published: 1994
For more information: ?
Thanks for the info: Educom newsletter
Notes: As the "TV Guide of Cyberspace," this book provides pointers by subjects to Internet sites, USENET newsgroups, and commercial resources (CompuServe, American Online, etc.). It proves that there's something for everyone somewhere out in the electronic world.

Title: NetPages
Publisher: Aldea Communications
ISBN: none listed
Price: Free
Pages: ~200
Published: 1994 (updated twice a year)
For more information: 619-943-0101 or e-mail to info@aldea.com
Notes: Of the various Internet White and Yellow pages books out there,
this one looks and acts the most like a "real" telephone book: personal
listings of your name and e-mail address are free, advertising space in
the yellow pages section is available for a fee, and the book itself it
distributed for free. With only a few thousand names in the first
edition, this listing is hardly the most complete, but it only contains
information about people who choose to be listed.

Title: NetPower: Resource Guide to Online Computer Services
Author: Persson, Eric
Publisher: Fox Chapel Publishing
ISBN: 1-56523-031-0
Price: $39.95 + $3.00 shipping
Pages: 774
Published: 1993
For more information: netpower1@aol.com, 1-800-457-9112
Notes: All I know is what their catalog says: The most exciting section
of this guide is devoted to the Internet. Netpower includes a primer and
tutorial on using the network, information on getting started and
navigating with Internet tools, and hundreds of Internet accessible
resources with contact information and descriptions. The guide will point
you in the direction of millions of megabytes of information all yours
free for the downloading around the Internet.

Title: The New Hacker's Dictionary
Author: edited by Eric Raymond and Guy L. Steele
Publisher: MIT press
ISBN: ISBN 0-262-18154-1
Price: $10.95
Pages: 453
Published: 2nd edition, 1994.
For more information: (800) 356-0343 or (617) 625-8481
Thanks for the info :Petrea Mitchell
<pravn@mvp.rain.com,@agora.rdrop.com>
Notes: The New Hacker's Dictionary is a great book for learning about the
various slang, jargon and customs and folklore of the net (as well as
other lairs of the hacker.) Very silly and highly recommended. An FTPable

version, called the Jargon File version 3.0, is available from
rtfm.mit.edu, but the bound book makes great bathroom reading and
contains silly cartoons and stuff.

Title: New Riders' Official Internet Yellow Pages
Author: Christine Maxwell and Czeslaw Jan Grycz
Publisher: New Riders Publishing
ISBN: 1-56205-306-X
Price: $29.95
Pages: 877
Published: 1994
For more information: ?
Notes: <<Review to be included in next edition of the Booklist>>

Title: On INTERNET 94: An International Title and Subject Guide to
Electronic Journals, Newsletters, Texts, Discussion Lists, and Other
Resources on the Internet
Author: Internet World Magazine
Publisher: Meckler
ISBN: 0-88736-929-4
Price: $45.00
Pages: 500
Published: 1994
For more information: ?
Notes: "Your guide to the full range of Internet-accessible data files –
from artificial intelligence to women's studies, from space exploration
to rock music, from environment studies to AIDS research." Nearly 6,000
mailing lists, electronic journals, archives, etc.

Title: The Online User's Encyclopedia: Bulletin Boards and Beyond.
Author: Bernard Aboba
Publisher: Addison-Wesley
ISBN: 0-201-62214-9
Price: $32.95
Pages: 806
Published: 1993
For more information: ?
Thanks for the info: Gayle Keresey (aflgayle@aol.com)
Notes: Comprehensive compendium of information and guide to bulletin
boards and the computer networks they are connected to. First edition of
this book was a manual for the BMUG BBS. Indispensable guide to
connecting your modem to the world.

Title: OPAC Directory 1994
Author: Mecklermedia
Publisher: Meckler
ISBN: 0-88736-962-6
Price: $70
Pages: 500
Published: May 1994
For more information: ?
Notes: A detailed listing of dial-in online public access catalogs and databases. Includes Accessing Online Bibliographic Databases, the annotated list of 700+ Internet-accessible OPACs.

Title: PC Internet Tour Guide
Author: Michael Fraase
Publisher: Ventana Press
ISBN: 1-56604-084-1
Price: $24.95
Pages: 284
Goodies: PC floppy disk with useful software. Two periodic updates via e-mail. One month of free online time from MRNet.
Published: 1994
For more information: dilennox@aol.com
Notes: This book (with floppy disk) for MS-DOS users helps newcomers get online and take their first steps on the net. Fraase first wrote the Mac Internet Tour Guide, and this book seems more like an afterthought than a follow-up. Chapters cover obligatory topics like What is the Internet, Getting Connected, Network News, Transferring Files, Using Gopher and Other Internet Resources. The book's organization leaves something to be desired: talk of telnet, FAQs and Netfind (hardly unimportant topics) are lumped together in the "Other Resources" chapter near the back of the book. The book includes some interesting real-life examples and ideas for things to do online, but too much (for my taste) focuses on how to set up and use the bundled software.

Title: Pocket Guides to the Internet: Volume 1 – Telnetting
Author: Mark Veljkov & George Hartnell
Publisher: Meckler
ISBN: 0-88736-943-X
Price: $9.95
Pages: 64
Published: 1994
For more information: ?
Notes:

Title: Pocket Guides to the Internet: Volume 2 – Transferring Files with File Transfer Protocol (FTP)
Author: Mark Veljkov & George Hartnell
Publisher: Meckler
ISBN: 0-88736-944-8
Price: $9.95
Pages: 64
Published: 1994
For more information: ?
Notes:

Title: Pocket Guides to the Internet: Volume 3 – Using and Navigating Usenet
Author: Mark Veljkov & George Hartnell
Publisher: Meckler
ISBN: 0-88736-945-6
Price: $9.95
Pages: 64
Published: 1994
For more information: ?
Notes:

Title: Pocket Guides to the Internet: Volume 4 – The Internet E-Mail System
Author: Mark Veljkov & George Hartnell
Publisher: Meckler
ISBN: 0-88736-946-4
Price: $9.95
Pages: 64
Published: 1994
For more information: ?
Notes:

Title: Pocket Guides to the Internet: Volume 5 – Basic Internet Utilities
Author: Mark Veljkov & George Hartnell
Publisher: Meckler
ISBN: 0-88736-947-2
Price: $9.95
Pages: 64
Published: 1994
For more information: ?
Notes: ?

Title: Pocket Guides to the Internet: Volume 6 – Terminal Connections
Author: Mark Veljkov & George Hartnell
Publisher: Meckler

ISBN: 0-88736-948-0
Price: $9.95
Pages: 64
Published: 1994
Notes:

Title: Practical Internetworking with TCP/IP and UNIX
Author: Carl-Mitchell/Quarterman
Publisher: Addison-Wesley
ISBN: tic@tic.com
Price: ?
Pages: ?
Published: ?
For more information: ?
Notes:

Title: Riding the Internet Highway
Author: Sharon Fisher
Publisher: New Riders Publishing
ISBN: 1-56205-192-X
Price: $16.95
Pages: 266
Published: 1993
For more information: phyllis@prenhall.com
Thanks for the info: Robert Slade <ROBERTS@decus.ca>
Notes: Fisher shows admirable restraint in limiting the scope of this
book. Where others try to produce "complete" documentation for the
"whole" Internet, Fisher flatly states (correctly) that this is
impossible. Where others try to take you "from the modem up", Fisher
suggests you get some basic experience with local bulletin boards. The
intent is to give desktop (PC and Mac) users some basic grounding in
Internet functions and tools. As such, the book is much less imposing
than most of the others of this ilk. (Cheaper, too.) For the majority of
new users, however, this is a good, basic introduction. What shortcomings
there are in specific information can be quickly filled in once a user
has gotten onto the net. The very personal style here probably more than
makes up for any other lacks – the Internet is primarily other people, not
technologies.

Title: SATURN: A Beginners Guide To Using the Internet
Author: Kyle Cassidy
Publisher: RCNJ Press
ISBN: ?
Price: $3
Pages: 110

Published: ?
For more information: cassidy@saturn.rowan.edu
Notes: This is the only Internet book that I know of that is specifically
for VAX/VMS users (you poor things.) The manual is somewhat specific for
our VAX 4000, but it can be used by anyone who is netting with VMS. It's
also available online for free, FTPable from
gboro.rowan.edu:/pub/Saturn_Guide

Title: sendmail
Author: Bryan Costales
Publisher: O'Reilly & Associates
ISBN: 1-56592-056-2
Price: $32.95
Pages: 830
Published: 1993
For more information: ?
Notes: While not strictly an Internet book, this tome focuses on one
thing: the UNIX program sendmail, which is a huge part of how electronic
mail moves around on the Internet. Mainly for system administrators, the
book shows how to use every function, mode and mood of sendmail to get
your e-mail where it's going. A great, if single-minded, book.
Title: The Simple Book
Notes: {I know nothing about this book. Do you?}

Title: The Smiley Dictionary
Author: Seth Godin
Publisher: ?
ISBN: ?
Price: ?
Pages: ?
Published: ?
For more information: ?
Notes:

Title: smileys
Author: Lesley Strother
Publisher: O'Reilly & Associates
ISBN: 1-56592-041-4
Price: 93
Pages: 595
Published: 1993
For more information: ?
Notes: A collection of 650 "smileys". While not an Internet book per se,
smileys are certainly used enough on the Internet to warrant an entry
here.

Title: TCP/IP Illustrated, Volume 1, The Protocols
Author: W. Richard Stevens
Publisher: Addison Wesley
ISBN: 0-201-63346-9
Price: ?
Pages: 576
Published: 1994
For more information:
Thanks for the info: Bob Stein <stein@gcomm.com> and Robert Slade
<ROBERTS@decus.ca>
Notes: Bob says: This textbook is the best way to understand the nuts and
bolts of TCP/IP the Internet's networking protocols. Great figures,
diagrams, tables, and other references. (No volume 2 yet.) Robert says:
Great text for the protocols of TCP/IP (illustrated by examples from a
real network.)

Title: TCP/IP Network Administration
Author: Hunt
Publisher: O'Reilly & Associates
ISBN: 0-937175-82-X
Price: ?
Pages: ?
Published: 1992
For more information: info@ora.com
Notes:

Title: Teach Yourself the Internet: Around the World in 21 Days
Author: Neil Randall
Publisher: Sams
ISBN: 0-672-30519-4
Price: $27.00
Pages: 700
Published: July 1994
For more information: 800-428-5331 or 317-581-3500
Thanks for the info: Connie Marijs <otsgroup@knoware.nl>
Notes: This well-organized tutorial can be used by individuals, in
seminars, training sessions, and classrooms. It takes readers on a global
learning expedition of the Internet in just 21 fun-filled lessons.

Title: Total SNMP
Author: Harnedy
Publisher: CBM Books
ISBN: 1-878956-33-7
Price: $45

Pages: ?
Published: 1994
For more information: books@propress.com
Notes:

Title: The Traveler's Guide to the Information Highway
Author: Dylan Tweney
Publisher: Ziff Davis Press
ISBN: 1-56276-206-0
Price: $24.95
Pages: 139
Published: June 1994
For more information: 72241.443@compuserve.com
Notes: A guide to the Internet, CompuServe, Prodigy, America Online,
Delphi, GEnie, and ZiffNet for CompuServe, this book is the first of its
kind to feature real maps of each service, making it exceptionally easy
to navigate the online world. There are also easy-to-follow instructions
for using each one, plus tips, shortcuts, and pointers to the best and
most interesting features. A comprehensive and easy-to-use introduction
to the Internet and the largest commerical online services.

Title: Using the Internet
Author: William A. Tolhurst, Mary Ann Pike & Keith A. Blanton
Publisher: Que
ISBN: 1-56529-353-3
Price: $39.95
Pages: 1188
Goodies: DOS disk
Published: Jan. 1994
For more information: tpike@pittslug.sug.org
Thanks for the info: Gayle Keresey (aflgayle@aol.com)
Notes: Introduction to, structure of, and history of the Internet.
Finding and using resources, legal considerations, features and services,
and tools and technology.

Title: Using UUCP and Usenet
Author: Grade Todino and Dale Dougherty
Publisher: O'Reilly & Associates
ISBN: ?
Price: ?
Pages: 194
Published: 1991
For more information: ?
Notes:

Title: WAIS and Gopher Servers: a guide for librarians and Internet end-users
Author: Eric Lease Morgan
Publisher: Meckler
ISBN: 0-88736-932-4
Price: $30.00
Pages: 150
Published: March 1994
For more information: ?
Notes: The first book-length treatment of WAIS and Gopher servers.

Title: Welcome to... Internet from Mystery to Mastery
Author: Tom Badgett & Corey Sandler
Publisher: MIS Press
ISBN: 1-55828-308-0
Price: $19.95
Pages: 324
Published: 1993
For more information: ?
Thanks for the info: Gayle Keresey (aflgayle@aol.com)
Notes: Introduction to the Internet and its resources and navigational tools. The strength of this book is the chapter entitled "Collecting souvenirs on the Internet" which details subjects and tells you exactly where and how to find information about those subjects on the net.

Title: The Whole Earth Online Almanac
Author: Don Rittner
Publisher: Brady
ISBN: 1-56686-090-3
Price: $32.95
Pages: 540
Published: 1993
Notes: Covers America Online, CompuServe, GEnie, The WELL, FidoNet, the Internet and CD-ROMs. Each subject area includes applicable forums and databases, network discussion lists and other online sources and CD-ROMs.

Title: The Whole Internet User's Guide and Catalog
Author: Ed Krol
Publisher: O'Reilly & Associates
ISBN: 1-56592-063-5
Price: $24.95
Pages: 572
Published: 2nd edition, April 1994
For more information: info@ora.com

Notes: This book covers the basic utilities used to access the network and then guides users through the Internet's "databases of databases" to access the millions of files and thousands of archives available. It includes a resource index that covers a broad selection of approximately 300 important resources available on the Internet. The 2nd edition has been completely updated to reflect the development of new Internet tools, including Mosaic, MIME, tin, pine, xarchie and a greatly expanded resource catalog. Highly recommended.

Title: Windows Internet Tour Guide
Author: Michael Frasse
Publisher: Ventana Press
ISBN: 1-56604-081-7
Price: $24.95
Pages: 344
Goodies: Windows disk. Two free electronic updates via e-mail. One month of free online time from MRNet.
Published: 1994
For more information: dilennox@aol.com
Notes: <<To be reviewed in next edition on the booklist>>
Title: Your Internet Consultant: The FAQs of Life Online
Author: Kevin M. Savetz
Publisher: Sams
ISBN: 0-672-30520-8
Price: $25.00
Pages: 600
Published: July 1994
For more information: 800-428-5331 or 317-581-3500
Notes:

Title: Zen & the Art of Internet
Author: Brendan Kehoe
Publisher: Prentice Hall
ISBN: 0-13-121492-6
Price: $23.95
Pages: 193
Published: 3rd ed., Jan. 1994
For more information: (515) 284-6751 or phyllis@prenhall.com
Thanks for the info: matisse@well.sf.ca.us (J. Matisse Enzer)
Notes: This guide should give you a reference to consult if you're curious about what can be done with the Internet. It also presents the fundamental topics that are all too often assumed and considered trivial by many network users. It covers the basic utilities and information reaching other networks. An earlier, much less comprehensive version is

available via FTP; see previous section. Matisse Enzer says: Very
friendly general overview book. Not really a how-to book, rather a
Cultural Companion that explain what each type of Internet resource is,
as well as the cultural and traditional uses and issues. Includes a
chapter on "Things you will hear about..." this chapter explains many
famous (and infamous) Internet events and entities.

Title: !%@:: A Directory of Electronic Mail Addressing and Networks
Author: Donnalyn Frey & Rick Adams
Publisher: O'Reilly & Associates
ISBN: 1-56592-031-7
Price: $24.95
Pages: 458
Published: 1993
For more information: 800-998-9938 or info@ora.com
Thanks for the info: Robert Slade <ROBERTS@decus.ca>
Notes: This book is a reference work. It details the various computer
networks with gateways to the Internet. It is common to cite such works
as "indispensable": in fact, most users, and even site managers, muddle
along quite happily without it. Quick reference "electronic" versions
exist of very similar documents, which provide the addressing schemes for
the more common network and commercial service gateways. Frey and Adams
have, however, put together a very complete and interesting reference,
and I do suggest it to anyone managing, or using, extensive e-mail
correspondence. As a user of electronic mail, or the manager of a small
Internet node or UUCP site, it would be hard to say that you "need" this
book. If, however, you are at all interested in the topic of e-mail, you
will find this fascinating and useful.

*** Upcoming titles {let me know if any of these are out yet!}
Internet CD – SRI International
Resource tool – Includes CD
ISBN 013-123852-3   04/94 NEW to be published

Internet: Domain Administration – Vivian Neou: SRI International
ISBN 013-511180-3   04/94 NEW to be published

Internet Technology Series: Domain Name System – Paul Mockapetris
ISBN 013-106865-2   05/94 NEW to be published

"The Internet Book: Everything You Need to Know About Computer
Networking and How the Internet Works", Comer – very good explanation of
what the Internet is, how it works and how it came about, all at a level
for the non-technical reader (coming in June)

Your Internet Consultant: The FAQs of Life Online – Kevin M. Savetz (the editor of this booklist). Sams publishing, ISBN: 0-672-30520-8. $25.00, 600 pages. to be published July 1994. For more information: 800-428-5331 or 317-581-3500

*** Publisher/Ordering Information
Addison-Wesley. E-mail: 74230.3622@compuserve.com. Orders: (800) 822-6339. "Have your credit card handy!"

Meckler Corporation. (203) 226-6967.Fax: (203) 545-5840. 11 Ferry Lane West, Westport, CT 06880.

Macmillan Computer Publishing (Sams, Hayden, New Ridors, Que, Alpha) orders: 800-428-5331 or 317-581-3500

O'Reilly & Associates: info@ora.com. 707-829-0515, Fax 707-829-0104. 103A Morris Street, Sebastopol CA 95472.

Prentice-Hall. E-mail: info@prenhall.com or gopher: gopher.prenhall.com. 515-284-6751. Fax: 515-284-2607. Route 9W, Englewood Cliffs, NJ 07632.

*** Internet Book Information & Updates Online
The Top Ten Internet Book List is a weekly list that lists the top ten Internet Books sold in Europe. The list represents the ten most popular titles of Prentice Hall, Sams, Que and other publishers, based on weekly sales. It also announces new Internet books to be released. To subscribe, send e-mail to: otsgroup@pop.knoware.nl

Addison-Wesley information server, for periodic updates on new titles from this publisher. Send e-mail

> To: awbook@aw.com
> Subject: information
> Body: send information

O'Reilly & Associates information server, for periodic updates on new titles from this publisher. Send e-mail

> To: listproc@online.ora.com
> Subject: <leave blank>
> Body: subscribe ora-news "Your name" of "Your Company"

{ Any additions for me?}

***Legal, Ethical and Moral Stuff

Permission for the following types of distribution is hereby granted,
provided that this file is distributed intact, including the above
copyright notice:
- – non-commercial distribution
- – posting to Internet archives, BBSs and online services
- – distribution by teachers, librarians and Internet trainers
- – inclusion on software/FAQ/Internet-oriented CD-ROMS

Permission for commercial distribution may be obtained from the editor.
SHARE THIS INFORMATION FREELY AND IN GOOD FAITH. DO NOT
DISTRIBUTE
MODIFIED VERSIONS OF THIS DOCUMENT.

This document is new and in transition. If you notice that an Internet-
related book is missing, or information herein needs updating, please
contact the editor.

The editor and contributors have developed this FAQ as a service to the
Internet community. We hope you find it useful. This FAQ is purely a
volunteer effort. Although every effort has been made to insure that
answers are as accurate as possible, no guarantee is implied or intended.
While the editor tries to keep this document current, remember that the
Internet and the publishing world are constantly changing, so don't be
surprised if you happen across statements which are obsolete. If you do,
please send corrections to the editor. Corrections, questions, and
comments should be sent to Kevin Savetz at "savetz@rahul.net" (Internet)
or "savetz" (America Online.) Please indicate what version of this
document to which you are referring.

All prices in US dollars unless otherwise indicated.

Thanks to Pieter M. Lechner, UCLA Microcomputer Support Office, for his
bibliography of 50 Internet books. Thanks to Connie Marijs
<otsgroup@pop.knoware.nl> for her continued assistance. Thanks to
matisse@well.sf.ca.us (J Matisse Enzer) for allowing me to pilfer bits of
book reviews. Many thanks to Robert Slade <ROBERTS@decus.ca> for his
copious book reviews.

*** Where to Find this Document
This file is posted twice monthly (on the 5th and 19th of each month) to
the Usenet newsgroups alt.internet.services, alt.online-service,

alt.books.technical, misc.books.technical, alt.bbs.internet, misc.answers, alt.answers and news.answers.

You can receive it via anonymous FTP
rtfm.mit.edu:/pub/usenet/news.answers/internet-services/book-list

You can receive it via electronic mail
    To: mail-server@rtfm.mit.edu
    Subject: <subject line is ignored>
    Body: send usenet/news.answers/internet-services/internet-booklist

You can receive each new edition of this document automatically via electronic mail, if you are so inclined. This is a low-volume list, with updates every few weeks. Note that the following address is my personal e-mail box, filtered by a very simple mail filter. Your request must go in the SUBJECT line EXACTLY as shown below. Anything else will find its way into my e-mail box rather than to the subscription program.
    To: savetz@rahul.net
    Subject: subscribe booklist
    Body: <ignored>

UK commercial domains

This is a full listing of registered UK commercial domains. It gives a useful overview of who is registering to use the Internet.

AEA Technology, Harwell Laboratory

CHCC.AEATECH.UK	CHCC.HARWELL.AEA-TECHNOLOGY.UK
HARINST.AEATECH.UK	HARINST.AEA-TECHNOLOGY.UK

The British Library Board

BL.UK	BRITISH-LIBRARY.UK
LONDON.BL.UK	LONDON.BRITISH-LIBRARY.UK

CCTA (Central Computer and Telecommunications Agency)

CCTA.UK	CCTA.UK
HP330.CCTA.UK	HP330.CCTA.UK
NEPTUNE.CCTA.UK	NEPTUNE.CCTA.UK
TRITON.CCTA.UK	TRITON.CCTA.UK

Abekas Video Systems Ltd

ABEKRD.CO.UK	ABEKAS-VIDEO-SYSTEMS.CO.UK

Abstract Hardware Ltd

AHL.CO.UK	ABSTRACT-HARDWARE-LTD.CO.UK

Acorn Computers Ltd

ACORN.CO.UK	ACORN.CO.UK

Knowledge Base Services Ltd
ACRONYM.CO.UK   ACRONYM.CO.UK
ACT Financial Services
ACTFS.CO.UK   ACT-FINANCIAL-SYSTEMS.CO.UK
Active Book Company Ltd
ABCL.CO.UK   ACTIVE-BOOK-CO.CO.UK
Adax Europe Ltd
ADAX.CO.UK   ADAX-EUROPE.CO.UK
Adept Scientific Micro Systems
ADEPTSCIENCE.CO.UK   ADEPT-SCIENTIFIC-MICRO-SYSTEMS-LIMIT
                                 ED.CO.UK
Admiral Plc (Admiral Corporate Services)
ADMIRAL.CO.UK   ADMIRAL.CO.UK
Advance Geophysical
ADVANCE.CO.UK   ADVANCE-GEOPHYSICAL.CO.UK
Advanced RISC Machines Ltd (Advanced RISC Machines Limited)
ARMLTD.CO.UK   ADVANCED-RISC-MACHINES.CO.UK
Advent Imaging Ltd
ADVENT.CO.UK   ADVENT-IMAGING-LTD.CO.UK
AFE (Displays) Ltd
AFE.CO.UK   AFE.CO.UK
DISPLAYS.AFE.CO.UK   DISPLAYS.AFE.CO.UK
Amersham International (old name)
AI.CO.UK   AI.CO.UK
Amersham International
AMERSHAM.CO.UK   AMERSHAM-INTERNATIONAL.CO.UK
Applied Imaging International Ltd
AII.CO.UK   AII.CO.UK
Airtech Systems Management
AIRTECHSMS.CO.UK   AIRTECH-SYSTEMS-MANAGEMENT-AND-
                                 SECURITY.CO.UK
Aleph One Limited
ALEPH1.CO.UK   ALEPH-ONE-LTD.CO.UK
Algorithmics Ltd (ALGORITHMICS LTD)
ALGOR.CO.UK   ALGORITHMICS.CO.UK
Almac Computer Services Ltd
ALMAC.CO.UK   ALMAC-LTD.CO.UK
ERNIE.ALMAC.CO.UK   ERNIE.ALMAC-LTD.CO.UK
Alsys Ltd
ALSYS.CO.UK   ALSYS.CO.UK
AMEC plc
AMEC.CO.UK   AMEC.CO.UK
Andersen Consulting UK

ANDERSEN.CO.UK   ANDERSEN.CO.UK

APM Ltd (ANSA Project)
ANSA.CO.UK   ANSA.CO.UK

Anvil Software Limited (Anvil Software Limited)
ANVIL.CO.UK   ANVIL.CO.UK

AIT Ltd
AIT.CO.UK   APPLIED-INTERACTIVE-TECHNOLOGY.CO.UK

Apricot Computers Ltd (R&D division)
APRICOT.CO.UK   APRICOT.CO.UK

Harcourt Brace & Co. Ltd
APUK.CO.UK   APUK.CO.UK

Artificial Intelligence International
AIIL.CO.UK   ARTIFICIAL-INTELLIGENCE-INTERNATIONAL.CO.UK

Applied Systems Engineering
ASE.CO.UK   ASE.CO.UK

Aspect Development Inc.
ASPECT.CO.UK   ASPECT.CO.UK

Aspen Tech UK Ltd
ASPENTEC.CO.UK   ASPENTEC.CO.UK

Astec Europe Ltd (Astec Europe Ltd)
ASTEC.CO.UK   ASTEC-EUROPE-LTD.CO.UK

Astra Clinical Research Unit (Astra Pharmaceuticals Ltd)
ACRUNM.CO.UK   ASTRA-CLINICAL.CO.UK

AstroMed Ltd (Astromed Ltd)
ASTROM.CO.UK   ASTROMED-LTD.CO.UK

Atex
ATEX.CO.UK   ATEX.CO.UK

ATM Limited
ATML.CO.UK   ATML.CO.UK

ELF Atochem UK Ltd
ATO.CO.UK   ATO.CO.UK

Atomwide Ltd
ATOMWIDE.CO.UK   ATOMWIDE.CO.UK

Auspex Limited
AUSPEX.CO.UK   AUSPEX.CO.UK

Azlan Ltd
AZLAN.CO.UK   AZLAN.CO.UK

Barclays Bank plc
BARC.CO.UK   BARCLAYS.CO.UK

Barclays Network Services
BNSUK.CO.UK   BARCLAYS-NETWORK-SERVICES.CO.UK

British Broadcasting Corporation
BRD.BBC.CO.UK   BRD.BBC.CO.UK

DD.ENG.BBC.CO.UK DD.ENG.BBC.CO.UK
RD.ENG.BBC.CO.UK RD.ENG.BBC.CO.UK
RADIO.BBC.CO.UK RADIO.BBC.CO.UK
SCOT.BBC.CO.UK SCOT.BBC.CO.UK

British Gas Oil Exploration & Production Ltd
BGEP.CO.UK BGEP.CO.UK

Reed Consumer Books
REL.BHEIN.CO.UK REL.BHEIN.CO.UK

BICC Hemel Hempstead Development Centre (BICC plc)
BICCDC.CO.UK BICC-DEVELOPMENT-CENTRE.CO.UK

SRL Data
BILPIN.CO.UK BILPIN.CO.UK

Biosis UK
BIOSIS.CO.UK BIOSIS.CO.UK
ADMIN.BIOSIS.CO.UK ADMIN.BIOSIS.CO.UK
ETIVE.BIOSIS.CO.UK ETIVE.BIOSIS.CO.UK
FYNE.BIOSIS.CO.UK FYNE.BIOSIS.CO.UK
LEVEN.BIOSIS.CO.UK LEVEN.BIOSIS.CO.UK
NESS.BIOSIS.CO.UK NESS.BIOSIS.CO.UK
TAY.BIOSIS.CO.UK TAY.BIOSIS.CO.UK
–No short form– ZOOREC.BIOSIS.CO.UK

BIS Information Systems (NI)
BIS.CO.UK BISIS-ANT.CO.UK

BISS Ltd
BISS.CO.UK BISS.CO.UK

B. H. Blackwell Ltd
BWELL.CO.UK BLACKWELL.CO.UK

British Maritime Technology Ltd
BMTECH.CO.UK BMTECH.CO.UK

BNR Europe Ltd (Northern Telecom Ltd)
BNR.CO.UK BNR.CO.UK

Boldon James Limited
BJ.CO.UK BOLDON-JAMES-LIMITED.CO.UK

BP Oil (UK) Limited (BP Oil UK Limited)
BPOILUK.CO.UK BPOILUK.CO.UK

Brazier Systems & Consultants Ltd
BSCDEV.CO.UK BRAZIER-SYSTEMS-AND-CONSULTANTS.
CO.UK

British Aerospace PLC
DEF.BAE.CO.UK DEFENCE.BRITISH-AEROSPACE.CO.UK
AWC.DEF.BAE.CO.UK AWC.DEF.BRITISH-AEROSPACE.CO.UK
STE.DYN.BAE.CO.UK STEVENAGE.DYNAMICS.BRITISH-AERO
SPACE.CO.UK

WA.MAL.BAE.CO.UK	WARTON.MAL.BRITISH-AEROSPACE.CO.UK
SRC.BAE.CO.UK	SOWERBY-RESEARCH-CENTRE.BRITISH-AERO SPACE.CO.UK

British GAS Engineering Research Station (British GAS plc)

BGERS.CO.UK	BRITISH-GAS-ERS.CO.UK

British Telecom PLC

AOM.BT.CO.UK	AOM.BRITISH-TELECOM.CO.UK
AXION.BT.CO.UK	AXION.BRITISH-TELECOM.CO.UK
AZIT.BT.CO.UK	AZIT.BRITISH-TELECOM.CO.UK
B29HP.BT.CO.UK	B29HP.BRITISH-TELECOM.CO.UK
B29NET.BT.CO.UK	B29NET.BRITISH-TELECOM.CO.UK
BFSEC.BT.CO.UK	BFSEC.BRITISH-TELECOM.CO.UK
BOAT.BT.CO.UK	BOAT.BRITISH-TELECOM.CO.UK
BT-SYS.BT.CO.UK	BT-SYS.BRITISH-TELECOM.CO.UK
BT-WEB.BT.CO.UK	BT-WEB.BRITISH-TELECOM.CO.UK
BTCASE.BT.CO.UK	BTCASE.BRITISH-TELECOM.CO.UK
BTCS.BT.CO.UK	BTCS.BRITISH-TELECOM.CO.UK
BTNS.BT.CO.UK	BTNS.BRITISH-TELECOM.CO.UK
BTRCOSMOS.BT.CO.UK	BTRCOSMOS.BRITISH-TELECOM.CO.UK
BTRLC7.BT.CO.UK	BTRLC7.BRITISH-TELECOM.CO.UK
BTTELEX.BT.CO.UK	BTTELEX.BRITISH-TELECOM.CO.UK
BUZZARD.BT.CO.UK	BUZZARD.BRITISH-TELECOM.CO.UK
CARTOON.BT.CO.UK	CARTOON.BRITISH-TELECOM.CO.UK
CHAPLIN.BT.CO.UK	CHAPLIN.BRITISH-TELECOM.CO.UK
CHILLI.BT.CO.UK	CHILLI.BRITISH-TELECOM.CO.UK
COOLWORLD.BT.CO.UK	COOLWORLD.BRITISH-TELECOM.CO.UK
CROWN.BT.CO.UK	CROWN.BRITISH-TELECOM.CO.UK
CSC.BT.CO.UK	CSC.BRITISH-TELECOM.CO.UK
CYBORG.BT.CO.UK	CYBORG.BRITISH-TELECOM.CO.UK
CYCLONE.BT.CO.UK	CYCLONE.BRITISH-TELECOM.CO.UK
DRAKE.BT.CO.UK	DRAKE.BRITISH-TELECOM.CO.UK
DWARF.BT.CO.UK	DWARF.BRITISH-TELECOM.CO.UK
FMG.BT.CO.UK	FMG.BRITISH-TELECOM.CO.UK
FULCRUM.BT.CO.UK	FULCRUM.BRITISH-TELECOM.CO.UK
GALADRIEL.BT.CO.UK	GALADRIEL.BRITISH-TELECOM.CO.UK
GAPOS.BT.CO.UK	GAPOS.BRITISH-TELECOM.CO.UK
GARLAND.BT.CO.UK	GARLAND.BRITISH-TELECOM.CO.UK
GEATLAND.BT.CO.UK	GEATLAND.BRITISH-TELECOM.CO.UK
GFMS.BT.CO.UK	GFMS.BRITISH-TELECOM.CO.UK
GSSEC.BT.CO.UK	GSSEC.BRITISH-TELECOM.CO.UK
HFNET.BT.CO.UK	HFNET.BRITISH-TELECOM.CO.UK
IMST.BT.CO.UK	IMST.BRITISH-TELECOM.CO.UK
ITS.BT.CO.UK	ITS.BRITISH-TELECOM.CO.UK
JUNGLE.BT.CO.UK	JUNGLE.BRITISH-TELECOM.CO.UK

KBSS.BT.CO.UK	KBSS.BRITISH-TELECOM.CO.UK
KYNS.BT.CO.UK	KYNS.BRITISH-TELECOM.CO.UK
LACANJA.BT.CO.UK	LACANJA.BRITISH-TELECOM.CO.UK
LIBRARY.BT.CO.UK	LIBRARY.BRITISH-TELECOM.CO.UK
LSSEC.BT.CO.UK	LSSEC.BRITISH-TELECOM.CO.UK
MRN.BT.CO.UK	MRN.BRITISH-TELECOM.CO.UK
MROUND.BT.CO.UK	MROUND.BRITISH-TELECOM.CO.UK
MS.BT.CO.UK	MOBILE-SYSTEMS.BRITISH-TELECOM.CO.UK
MSN.BT.CO.UK	MSN.BRITISH-TELECOM.CO.UK
MUPPET.BT.CO.UK	MUPPET.BRITISH-TELECOM.CO.UK
NETEST.BT.CO.UK	NETEST.BRITISH-TELECOM.CO.UK
NSA.BT.CO.UK	NSA.BRITISH-TELECOM.CO.UK
NSAGW.NSA.BT.CO.UK	NSAGW.NSA.BRITISH-TELECOM.CO.UK
PASS.BT.CO.UK	PASS.BRITISH-TELECOM.CO.UK
PERF.BT.CO.UK	PERF.BRITISH-TELECOM.CO.UK
PIA.BT.CO.UK	PIA.BRITISH-TELECOM.CO.UK
PLANET.BT.CO.UK	PLANET.BRITISH-TELECOM.CO.UK
PSD.BT.CO.UK	PSD.BRITISH-TELECOM.CO.UK
PST.BT.CO.UK	PST.BRITISH-TELECOM.CO.UK
PSTCGAM.BT.CO.UK	PSTCGAM.BRITISH-TELECOM.CO.UK
R15A.BT.CO.UK	R15A.BRITISH-TELECOM.CO.UK
R8D.BT.CO.UK	R8D.BRITISH-TELECOM.CO.UK
RADIONET.BT.CO.UK	RADIONET.BRITISH-TELECOM.CO.UK
RT21500.BT.CO.UK	RT21500.BRITISH-TELECOM.CO.UK
RT21800.BT.CO.UK	RT21800.BRITISH-TELECOM.CO.UK
RTF.BT.CO.UK	RTF.BRITISH-TELECOM.CO.UK
SALTFARM.BT.CO.UK	SALTFARM.BRITISH-TELECOM.CO.UK
SES6A.BT.CO.UK	SES6A.BRITISH-TELECOM.CO.UK
SRD.BT.CO.UK	SRD.BRITISH-TELECOM.CO.UK
STARFLEET.BT.CO.UK	STARFLEET.BRITISH-TELECOM.CO.UK
STOWICS.BT.CO.UK	STOWICS.BRITISH-TELECOM.CO.UK
STRAT-SYS.BT.CO.UK	STRAT-SYS.BRITISH-TELECOM.CO.UK
STRATARCH.BT.CO.UK	STRATARCH.BRITISH-TELECOM.CO.UK
SUMMER.BT.CO.UK	SUMMER.BRITISH-TELECOM.CO.UK
SUPPDB.BT.CO.UK	SUPPDB.BRITISH-TELECOM.CO.UK
TA7A.BT.CO.UK	TA7A.BRITISH-TELECOM.CO.UK
TE.BT.CO.UK	TE.BRITISH-TELECOM.CO.UK
R20C.TE.BT.CO.UK	R20C.TE.BRITISH-TELECOM.CO.UK
VINEYARD.BT.CO.UK	VINEYARD.BRITISH-TELECOM.CO.UK
ZOO.BT.CO.UK	ZOO.BRITISH-TELECOM.CO.UK

BSG

BSG.CO.UK	BSG.CO.UK

British Standards Institution, Quality Assurance (British Standards Institution)
BSIQA.CO.UK   BSIQA.CO.UK
BSL Ltd
BSL.CO.UK   BSL.CO.UK
Berkely Software Services Ltd
BSSL.CO.UK   BSSL.CO.UK
Business Telecomunications Services Ltd
BTS.CO.UK   BTS.CO.UK
Building Research Establishment
BRE.CO.UK   BUILDING-RESEARCH-ESTABLISHMENT.CO.UK
Bull HN Information Systems (Bull H.N. Information Systems)
BULL.CO.UK   BULL.CO.UK
BUSS Limited
BUSS.CO.UK   BUSS.CO.UK
CADCentre Ltd
CAD-CEN.CO.UK   CADCENTRE.CO.UK
Callhaven PLC
CALLHAVEN.CO.UK   CALLHAVEN.CO.UK
Olivetti Research Ltd
CAM-ORL.CO.UK   CAM-ORL.CO.UK
Cambridge Algorithmica Ltd
CAMALG.CO.UK   CAMBRIDGE-ALGORITHMICA-LIMITED.CO.UK
Cambridge Animation Systems Ltd
CAM-ANI.CO.UK   CAMBRIDGE-ANIMATION.CO.UK
Cambridge Consultants Ltd
CAMCON.CO.UK   CAMBRIDGE-CONSULTANTS.CO.UK
Cambustion Ltd
CAMBUSTION.CO.UK   CAMBUSTION.CO.UK
Cameron Markby Hewitt
PYRCMH.CO.UK   CAMERON-MARKBY-HEWITT.CO.UK
Cambridge Oceanographic
CAMOCEAN.CO.UK   CAMOCEAN.CO.UK
Campden Food and Drink Research Association
CAMPDEN.CO.UK   CAMPDEN.CO.UK
Cambridge Scanning Ltd
CAMSCAN.CO.UK   CAMSCAN.CO.UK
Canon Research Centre Europe Ltd
CANON.CO.UK   CANON.CO.UK
Careful Computing Ltd (Real Time Consultants plc)
CAREFUL.CO.UK   CAREFUL.CO.UK
Computacenter Ltd
CCENTER.CO.UK   CCENTER.CO.UK
Creative Computer Systems Ltd
CCS.CO.UK   CCS.CO.UK

Commonwealth Development corporation
CDC.CO.UK   CDC.CO.UK

CECOMM – Southampton Institute (Southampton Institute of Higher Education Corporation)
CECOMM.CO.UK   CECOMM.CO.UK

CEGELEC Projects Ltd
CEGELECPROJ.CO.UK   CEGELEC-PROJECTS-LTD.CO.UK

Chase Research plc
CHASER.CO.UK   CHASE-RESEARCH.CO.UK

CHELGRAPH Limited (Chelgraph Limited)
CHELGRAPH.CO.UK   CHELGRAPH.CO.UK

Chernikeeff Networks Ltd
CHERNIKEEFF.CO.UK   CHERNIKEEFF.CO.UK

Chronologic Simulation
CHRONOLOGIC.CO.UK   CHRONOLOGIC.CO.UK

Churchill Management Limited
CHURCHILL.CO.UK   CHURCHILL.CO.UK

Churchill Software Ltd
CHUSL.CO.UK   CHUSL.CO.UK

CIMIO Limited
CIMIO.CO.UK   CIMIO-LIMITED.CO.UK

Itochu Electronics Co. Ltd
CIE.CO.UK   CITOH-ELECTRONICS.CO.UK

CityScape
CITYSCAPE.CO.UK   CITYSCAPE.CO.UK

Clecom Ltd
CLECOM.CO.UK   CLECOM.CO.UK

Clifford Chance
CCHANCE.CO.UK   CLIFFORD-CHANCE.CO.UK

Capita Managed Services Ltd
CMSL.CO.UK   CMSL.CO.UK

Klaus Schallhorn
CNIX.CO.UK   CNIX.CO.UK

Computer Newspaper Services Ltd
COMPNEWS.CO.UK   CNS-HOWDEN.CO.UK

C N Software Ltd
CNSLTD.CO.UK   CNSLTD.CO.UK

Coherent Technology Limited
COH.CO.UK   COHTECH.CO.UK
COLLETTE.COH.CO.UK   COLLETTE.COHTECH.CO.UK
SALLY.COH.CO.UK   SALLY.COHTECH.CO.UK
SARAH.COH.CO.UK   SARAH.COHTECH.CO.UK

CoBuild Ltd
COLLINS.CO.UK   COLLINS.CO.UK

COB.COLLINS.CO.UK	COBUILD.COLLINS.CO.UK
REF.COLLINS.CO.UK	REFERENCE.COLLINS.CO.UK

Fleet Digital Solutions Limited

CQM.CO.UK	COLLOQUIUM.CO.UK

Coltonsoft Ltd

COLTON.CO.UK	COLTON-SOFTWARE.CO.UK

Communication Arts Ltd

COMARTS.CO.UK	COMMUNICATION-ARTS.CO.UK

Compass Design Automation

COMPASS.CO.UK	COMPASS.CO.UK

Computer College (UniPalm Limited)

COMPUCOL.CO.UK	COMPUCOL.CO.UK

CompuGraphics International

CGI.CO.UK	COMPUGRAPHICS-INTERNATIONAL.CO.UK

Compulink Information Exchange Ltd

CLINK.CO.UK	COMPULINK.CO.UK
CIX.CLINK.CO.UK	CIX.COMPULINK.CO.UK
LIX.CLINK.CO.UK	LIX.COMPULINK.CO.UK

Computer Concepts Ltd

CCONCEPTS.CO.UK	COMPUTER-CONCEPTS.CO.UK

Computer International Limited

CIL.CO.UK	COMPUTER-INTERNATIONAL-LTD.CO.UK

Computer Service Technology Ltd

CST.CO.UK	COMPUTER-SERVICE-TECHNOLOGY.CO.UK

Computervision Research and Development Divis (Computervision Limited)

EDG.CV.CO.UK	EDG.COMPUTERVISION.CO.UK

Computhoughts Software Solutions (UK) Ltd

CTSS.CO.UK	COMPUTHOUGHTS.CO.UK

Compuware Ltd

COMPUWARE.CO.UK	COMPUWARE-LTD.CO.UK

Connaught Air Services

CONAIR.CO.UK	CONAIR.CO.UK

Concurrent Computer Corp Ltd (Concurrent Computer Corp Ltd)

CCUR.CO.UK	CONCURRENT.CO.UK
SLOUGH.CCUR.CO.UK	SLOUGH.CONCURRENT.CO.UK

Cambridge Parallel Processing Ltd

CPPUK.CO.UK	CPPUK.CO.UK

Cray Communications Ltd

CASE.CO.UK	CRAY-COMMUNICATIONS.CO.UK
TAUNTON.CASE.CO.UK	TAUNTON.CRAY-COMMUNICATIONS.CO.UK

CRAY Research (UK) Ltd

CRAY.CO.UK	CRAY-RESEARCH.CO.UK

Crosfield Electronics Ltd

CROSFIELD.CO.UK	CROSFIELD.CO.UK

NF.CROSFIELD.CO.UK	NFIELD.CROSFIELD.CO.UK
PB.CROSFIELD.CO.UK	PBORO.CROSFIELD.CO.UK
TC.CROSFIELD.CO.UK	TCT.CROSFIELD.CO.UK

Crscot

CRSCOT.CO.UK	CRSCOT.CO.UK

Comdisco Systems

CSE.CO.UK	CSE.CO.UK

Credit Suisse Financial Products

CSFP.CO.UK	CSFP.CO.UK

Current Science Ltd

CURSCI.CO.UK	CURRENT-SCIENCE-LTD.CO.UK

D-Cubed Ltd

D-CUBED.CO.UK	D-CUBED.CO.UK

Dabhand Computing Ltd

DABHAND.CO.UK	DABHAND.CO.UK

Data Connection Limited (Data Connection Ltd)

DATCON.CO.UK	DATA-CONNECTION.CO.UK

Data Sciences UK Ltd (Data Sciences UK LTD)

DATASCI.CO.UK	DATA-SCIENCES.CO.UK

Database Solutions

DBSOLN.CO.UK	DATABASE-SOLUTIONS.CO.UK

Data Cell Ltd (DataCell Ltd)

DATACELL.CO.UK	DATACELL-LTD.CO.UK

Data Logic Ltd

DATLOG.CO.UK	DATALOGIC.CO.UK

Datapath Ltd

DATAPATH.CO.UK	DATAPATH.CO.UK

Datastream International (DATASTREAM)

DATASTREAM.CO.UK	DATASTREAM.CO.UK

Datazone Limited

DZONE.CO.UK	DATAZONE.CO.UK

Dawson UK Ltd

DAWSON.CO.UK	DAWSON-UK.CO.UK

Delcam International plc

DELCAM.CO.UK	DELCAM.CO.UK

DELL Computer Corporation Ltd (UK) (DELL Computer Corporation Ltd (UK))

DELL.CO.UK	DELL.CO.UK

DEMON Systems Limited

DEMON.CO.UK	DEMON.CO.UK
CHLS.DEMON.CO.UK	CHALLIS.DEMON.CO.UK
DEMON.DEMON.CO.UK	DEMON.DEMON.CO.UK
GATE.DEMON.CO.UK	GATE.DEMON.CO.UK
POST.DEMON.CO.UK	POST.DEMON.CO.UK

DePuy International Limited
DEPUY.CO.UK   DEPUY.CO.UK
Derwent Publications Ltd
DERWENT.CO.UK   DERWENT.CO.UK
–No short form–   CC-MAIL.DERWENT.CO.UK
Desktop Connection Limited
DTC.CO.UK   DESKTOP.CO.UK
deVerill PLC
DEVERILL.CO.UK   DEVERILL-PLC.CO.UK
DEVTEQ Ltd
DEVTEQ.CO.UK   DEVTEQ.CO.UK
DAVE.DEVTEQ.CO.UK   DAVE.DEVTEQ.CO.UK
David Goodenough & Associates Limited
DGA.CO.UK   DGA.CO.UK
Dialog Semiconductor Limited
DIASEMI.CO.UK   DIALOG-SEMICONDUCTOR.CO.UK
Digital Exploration Ltd
DIGICON-EGR.CO.UK   DIGICON-EGR.CO.UK
Digitus Limited
DIGITUS.CO.UK   DIGITUS.CO.UK
The Direct Connection (Shirecase Ltd)
DIRCON.CO.UK   DIRCON.CO.UK
Dial International Telecom Ltd
DITLTD.CO.UK   DITLTD.CO.UK
Dixons Stores Group
DIXONS.CO.UK   DIXONS.CO.UK
–No short form–   NETSERV.DIXONS.CO.UK
DKB Financial Services Inc
DKBFP.CO.UK   DKBFP.CO.UK
DLB Systems Ltd
DLBSYS.CO.UK   DLBSYS.CO.UK
Data Logic Communications Ltd (Data Logic Communications Systems)
DLCS.CO.UK   DLCS.CO.UK
Dorotech Limited
DORO.CO.UK   DOROTECH.CO.UK
Dragon Systems UK Ltd (Dragon Systems Ltd)
DRAGON.CO.UK   .   DRAGON.CO.UK
Dragonhill Systems Ltd
DSL.CO.UK   DRAGONHILL.CO.UK
Johnson Hunter Limited (Johnson Hunter Ltd)
DUNAAD.CO.UK   DUNAAD.CO.UK
Du Pont Pixel Systems
DPS.CO.UK   DUPONT-PIXEL-SYSTEMS.CO.UK
MACMAIL.DPS.CO.UK   MACMAIL.DUPONT-PIXEL-SYSTEMS.CO.UK

Dyadic Systems Ltd
DYADIC.CO.UK   DYADIC.CO.UK

Dynatech Communications Ltd
DYNACOMM.CO.UK   DYNACOMM.CO.UK

Dynamic Graphics Limited
DGL.CO.UK   DYNAMIC-GRAPHICS-LTD.CO.UK

Dynamic Software AB, Dynasoft (Dynamic Software AB)
DYNASUK.CO.UK   DYNAMIC-SOFTWARE.CO.UK

Dynix Library Systems (UK) Limited
DYNIX.CO.UK   DYNIX.CO.UK

EA Technology
EATL.CO.UK   EA-TECHNOLOGY.CO.UK

Eagle Star Insurance
EAGLESTAR.CO.UK   EAGLESTAR.CO.UK

Earth Resource Mapping
ERM.CO.UK   EARTH-RESOURCE-MAPPING.CO.UK

EDC Software Ltd
EDC.CO.UK   EDC.CO.UK

EIT Group plc
EIT.CO.UK   EIT.CO.UK

ElectricMail Ltd
ELMAIL.CO.UK   ELECTRIC-MAIL.CO.UK

ELF UK – Geoscience Research Centre (ELF UK Geoscience Research Centre)
ELFGRC.CO.UK   ELF-GEOSCIENCE-RESEARCH.CO.UK

Elsevier Science UK
ELSEVIER.CO.UK   ELSEVIER.CO.UK

Enterprise Oil Plc
ENTOIL.CO.UK   ENTOIL.CO.UK

EO Europe Ltd
EOE.CO.UK   EO-EUROPE.CO.UK

Earth Observation Sciences Ltd
EOS.CO.UK   EOS.CO.UK

Epic Interactive Media Co. Ltd
EPIC.CO.UK   EPIC.CO.UK

Ernst & Young
ERNSTY.CO.UK   ERNSTY.CO.UK

Engineering Software Ltd
ESOFT.CO.UK   ESOFT.CO.UK

European CAD Developments Ltd
EUCAD.CO.UK   EUCAD.CO.UK

Euro Brokers Services Ltd (Euro Brokers Services Limited)
EUROBROK.CO.UK   EUROBROK.CO.UK

Eurographics UK Chapter
EG-UK.CO.UK   EUROGRAPHICS-UK.CO.UK

European Silicon Structures

ES2.CO.UK   EUROPEAN-SILICON-STRUCTURES.CO.UK

European Centre for Medium Range Weather F

ECMWF.CO.UK   EUROPEAN-WEATHER-CENTRE.CO.UK

UNICOS.ECMWF.CO.UK   UNICOS.EUROPEAN-WEATHER-CENTRE.CO.UK

VAX.ECMWF.CO.UK   VAX.EUROPEAN-WEATHER-CENTRE.CO.UK

VE1.ECMWF.CO.UK   VE1.EUROPEAN-WEATHER-CENTRE.CO.UK

VE1-GW.ECMWF.CO.UK   VE1-GW.EUROPEAN-WEATHER-CENTRE.CO.UK

Eurotherm Limited

ETHERM.CO.UK   EUROTHERM.CO.UK

EPA.ETHERM.CO.UK   PROCESS-AUTOMATION.EUROTHERM.CO.UK

EuroWorld Designs Ltd

EWDL.CO.UK   EWDL.CO.UK

ExNet Systems Ltd

EXNET.CO.UK   EXNET.CO.UK

Electronics 1992 – Plus Ltd

E92PLUS.CO.UK   E92PLUS.CO.UK

FACILITA Software Development Ltd

FACILITA.CO.UK   FACILITA.CO.UK

Fretwell Downing Data Systems

FDGROUP.CO.UK   FDGROUP.CO.UK

SWAN.FDGROUP.CO.UK   SWAN.FDGROUP.CO.UK

Finite Element Analysis Limited

FEAUK.CO.UK   FEA-LTD.CO.UK

FEGS Limited

FEGS.CO.UK   FEGS.CO.UK

FFAD

FFAD.CO.UK   FFAD.CO.UK

Financial Times

FTLONDON.CO.UK   FINANCIAL-TIMES.CO.UK

Dextel Findata AB

FINDATA.CO.UK   FINDATA.CO.UK

Firefox Communications Ltd

FIREFOX.CO.UK   FIREFOX.CO.UK

First National Bank of Chicago

FNBC.CO.UK   FIRST-CHICAGO.CO.UK

Firstgrade Computers Ltd

FIRSTGRADE.CO.UK   FIRSTGRADE.CO.UK

Fisons Pharmaceuticals

FISONSPHARM.CO.UK   FISONSPHARM.CO.UK

Fisons Instruments Surface Systems

FISONSSURF.CO.UK   FISONSSURF.CO.UK

Flagship Technologies UK

FLAGSHIP.CO.UK   FLAGSHIP.CO.UK

Fluent Europe Limited
FLUENT.CO.UK   FLUENT.CO.UK
Friends of the Earth Ltd
FOE.CO.UK   FOE.CO.UK
Foremost Training Ltd
FOREMOST.CO.UK   FOREMOST-TRAINING-LTD.CO.UK
Farncombe Technology Limited
FTL.CO.UK   FTL.CO.UK
Fujitsu Systems (Europe) Ltd
FUJITSU.CO.UK   FUJITSU.CO.UK
Fujistu Microelectronics Resear (Fujitsu Microelectronics Ltd)
FMLRND.CO.UK   FUJITSU-MICROELECTRONICS-RND.CO.UK
Fulcrum Communications Ltd
FULCRUM.CO.UK   FULCRUM-COMMUNICATIONS-LTD.CO.UK
Galviz Ltd
GALVIZ.CO.UK   GALVIZ-TELECOM.CO.UK
GEC Alsthom
GEC-ALSTHOM.CO.UK   GEC-ALSTHOM.CO.UK
GEC Marconi Avionics Limited
GEC-AV.CO.UK   GEC-AVIONICS.CO.UK
GEC Computers Ltd (GECnet)
D2.GEC-CL.CO.UK   D2.GEC-CL.CO.UK
D7.GEC-CL.CO.UK   D7.GEC-CL.CO.UK
Electrical Projects Ltd (GECnet)
GEC-EPL.CO.UK   GEC-EPL.CO.UK
Engineering Research Centre (GECnet)
GEC-ERC.CO.UK   GEC-ERC.CO.UK
Marconi Instruments Ltd (GECnet)
GEC-MI-AT.CO.UK   GEC-MI-AT.CO.UK
Marconi Research Centre (GECnet)
GEC-MRC.CO.UK   GEC-MRC.CO.UK
A.GEC-MRC.CO.UK   A.GEC-MRC.CO.UK
Hirst Research Centre (GECnet)
GEC-HRC.CO.UK   GEC-RL-HRC.CO.UK
Genasys (UK) Ltd
GENASYS.CO.UK   GENASYS.CO.UK
Meta Generics Ltd (Meta generics Ltd)
GENERICS.CO.UK   GENERICS.CO.UK
GENRAD Ltd
GENRAD.CO.UK   GENRAD-UK.CO.UK
Geo Strategies Ltd
GSL.CO.UK   GEO-STRATEGIES.CO.UK
Oilfield Systems Ltd
GEOSYS.CO.UK   GEOSYS.CO.UK

GeoVision Systems Ltd (GeoVision Systems Limited)
GEOVISION.CO.UK   GEOVISION.CO.UK
Glaxo Group Research Limited
GGR.CO.UK   GGR.CO.UK
UK0X08.GGR.CO.UK   UK0X08.GGR.CO.UK
Gill Jennings & Every
GJE.CO.UK   GJE.CO.UK
Glaxo Group Research
GLAXO.CO.UK   GLAXO.CO.UK
GEC–Marconi Communications Ltd (GEC–Marconi Communications Limited)
GMCL.CO.UK   GMCL.CO.UK
GEC Marconi Inflight Systems Ltd
GMIS.CO.UK   GMIS.CO.UK
Gnome Computers Ltd (Gnome Computers Ltd)
GNOME.CO.UK   GNOME-COMPUTERS.CO.UK
Goodwin Marcus Systems Ltd
GMSL.CO.UK   GOODWIN-MARCUS.CO.UK
Gould Electronics limited
GOULDUK.CO.UK   GOULD-COMPUTERS.CO.UK
GEC – Plessey Semiconductors Ltd (GEC–Plessy Semiconductors Ltd)
GPSL.CO.UK   GPSL.CO.UK
GPT Limited
GPT.CO.UK   GPT.CO.UK
BDGN57.GPT.CO.UK   BDGN57.GPT.CO.UK
BDSF28.GPT.CO.UK   BDSF28.GPT.CO.UK
Graseby Dynamics Ltd
GRADYN.CO.UK   GRADYN.CO.UK
–No short form–   DS5200.GRADYN.CO.UK
GRE (UK) Limited
GRE.CO.UK   GRE.CO.UK
Gresham Telecomputing PLC
GRESHAM.CO.UK   GRESHAM.CO.UK
Group ID Ltd (GID Ltd)
GID.CO.UK   GROUP-ID.CO.UK
PIO.GID.CO.UK   PIO.GROUP-ID.CO.UK
SIXNINE.GID.CO.UK   SIXNINE.GROUP-ID.CO.UK
The Guardian Newspaper
GUARDIAN.CO.UK   GUARDIAN.CO.UK
Habia Cable Limited
HABIA.CO.UK   HABIA.CO.UK
Harlequin Limited
HARLQN.CO.UK   HARLEQUIN.CO.UK
Health Care International (Scotland) Ltd
HCI.CO.UK   HEALTH-CARE-INTERNATIONAL.CO.UK

Hitachi Europe Ltd
HEL.CO.UK   HEL.CO.UK
Hewlett Packard Ltd
HP.CO.UK   HEWLETT-PACKARD.CO.UK
HPL.HP.CO.UK   HPL.HEWLETT-PACKARD.CO.UK
RC.HP.CO.UK   RC.HEWLETT-PACKARD.CO.UK
Hillside Systems
HILLSIDE.CO.UK   HILLSIDE.CO.UK
Hitachi Data Systems Limited
HDS.CO.UK   HITACHI-DATA-SYSTEMS.CO.UK
Hogg Insurance Brokers
HOGGIB.CO.UK   HOGG-INSURANCE-BROKERS.CO.UK
HOSKYNS Group plc
HOSKYNS.CO.UK   HOSKYNS-GROUP.CO.UK
Hydro-Electric plc
HYDRO.CO.UK   HYDRO-ELECTRIC.CO.UK
NEVIS.HYDRO.CO.UK   NEVIS.HYDRO-ELECTRIC.CO.UK
Ian Musson Ltd
IML.CO.UK   IAN-MUSSON.CO.UK
Ibex Limited
IBEX.CO.UK   IBEX.CO.UK
IBM (UK) Limited (IBM United Kingdom Ltd)
AIXSSC.IBM.CO.UK   AIXSSC.IBM.CO.UK
TS.IBM.CO.UK   TS.IBM.CO.UK
The IBM PC User Group
IBMPCUG.CO.UK   IBMPCUG.CO.UK
DOT.IBMPCUG.CO.UK   DOROTHY.IBMPCUG.CO.UK
KATE.IBMPCUG.CO.UK   KATE.IBMPCUG.CO.UK
NATS.IBMPCUG.CO.UK   NATALIE.IBMPCUG.CO.UK
RDTA.IBMPCUG.CO.UK   RADATA.IBMPCUG.CO.UK
TYA.IBMPCUG.CO.UK   TANYA.IBMPCUG.CO.UK
UUJ.IBMPCUG.CO.UK   UUJOHN.IBMPCUG.CO.UK
ICAD Engineering Automation Ltd
ICAD.CO.UK   ICAD.CO.UK
International Computers Limited
ICL.CO.UK   ICL.CO.UK
CAMELOT.ICL.CO.UK   CAMELOT.ICL.CO.UK
CISAS.ICL.CO.UK   CISAS.ICL.CO.UK
CTU.ICL.CO.UK   CTU.ICL.CO.UK
DSBC.ICL.CO.UK   DSBC.ICL.CO.UK
FIVEG.ICL.CO.UK   FIVEG.ICL.CO.UK
FSS.ICL.CO.UK   FSS.ICL.CO.UK
KID01PML.ICL.CO.UK   KID01PML.ICL.CO.UK
LCEP.ICL.CO.UK   LCEP.ICL.CO.UK

OASIS.ICL.CO.UK	OASIS.ICL.CO.UK
ODA.ICL.CO.UK	ODA.ICL.CO.UK
TOM.RB.ICL.CO.UK	TOM.RB.ICL.CO.UK
SSS.ICL.CO.UK	SSS.ICL.CO.UK
SST.ICL.CO.UK	SST.ICL.CO.UK
VPM.ICL.CO.UK	VPM.ICL.CO.UK
WG.ICL.CO.UK	WG.ICL.CO.UK
WIN.ICL.CO.UK	WIN.ICL.CO.UK
WINS.ICL.CO.UK	WINS.ICL.CO.UK
ZEN.ICL.CO.UK	ZEN.ICL.CO.UK

International Discount Telecommunications Corporation

ICM.CO.UK	ICM.CO.UK

ICS Computing Group Ltd

ICSBELF.CO.UK	ICSBELF.CO.UK

Interactive Development Environments (IDE UK) Ltd

IDEUK.CO.UK	IDEUK.CO.UK

IDIS Software Technologies Limited

IDISTECH.CO.UK	IDISTECH.CO.UK

NAG Ltd (The Numerical Alogorithms Group Ltd)

IEC.CO.UK	IEC.CO.UK

International Factors Ltd

IFL.CO.UK	IFL.CO.UK

Integrated Information Technology Europe Ltd

IIT-EUROPE.CO.UK	IIT-EUROPE.CO.UK

Imperial Software Technology 60 Alber (Imperial Software Technology Ltd)

IST.CO.UK	IMPERIAL-SOFTWARE-TECH.CO.UK
ISTAR.IST.CO.UK	ISTAR.IMPERIAL-SOFTWARE-TECH.CO.UK
UPPER.IST.CO.UK	UPPER.IMPERIAL-SOFTWARE-TECH.CO.UK

The Independent (Newspaper Publishing plc)

INDEP.CO.UK	INDEPENDENT.CO.UK

Individual Network (UK)

INET-UK.CO.UK	INDIVIDUAL-NETWORK-UK.CO.UK

Inference Europe Ltd

INFERENCE.CO.UK	INFERENCE.CO.UK

The Infocheck Group Limited

INFOCHECK.CO.UK	INFOCHECK.CO.UK

Infocom Public Access Unix (DGI INFOCOM)

INFOCOM.CO.UK	INFOCOM.CO.UK

Informed Computing

INFORM.CO.UK	INFORM.CO.UK

Ingres Ltd (INGRES Ltd)

INGRES.CO.UK	INGRES.CO.UK

Inmos Ltd

INMOS.CO.UK	INMOS.CO.UK
ISNET.INMOS.CO.UK	ISNET.INMOS.CO.UK
Insignia Solutions Ltd	
INSIGNIA.CO.UK	INSIGNIA-SOLUTIONS.CO.UK
The Instruction Set Ltd	
INSET.CO.UK	INSTRUCTION-SET.CO.UK
Integral Solutions Limited	
ISL.CO.UK	INTEG.CO.UK
Integralis Limited	
INTEGRALIS.CO.UK	INTEGRALIS.CO.UK
Intera Information Technologies Ltd	
INTERA.CO.UK	INTERA.CO.UK
–No short form–	CCGATE.INTERA.CO.UK
–No short form–	PC-GATEWAY.INTERA.CO.UK
International Thomson (International Thompson Publishing)	
ITPUK.CO.UK	INTERNATIONAL-THOMSON-PUBLISHING-LTD.CO.UK
Intelligent Office Company Ltd	
IOC.CO.UK	IOC.CO.UK
Ionica 3l Ltd	
IONICA.CO.UK	IONICA.CO.UK
IOP Publishing Ltd	
IOPPL.CO.UK	IOPPUBLISHING.CO.UK
Iota Software Ltd	
IOTA.CO.UK	IOTA.CO.UK
IPSYS Software PLC (IPSYS Software plc)	
IPSYS.CO.UK	IPSYS.CO.UK
I S Solutions	
ISSOLUTIONS.CO.UK	ISSOLUTIONS.CO.UK
International Thompson Publishing	
ITPEUR.CO.UK	ITP-EUROPE.CO.UK
Ives & Company Ltd	
IVESCO.CO.UK	IVESCO.CO.UK
IXI Limited	
X.CO.UK	IXI-LIMITED.CO.UK
K-Net Ltd	
K-NET.CO.UK	K-NET.CO.UK
K-Par Systems Ltd	
K-PAR.CO.UK	K-PAR.CO.UK
Kapiti Limited (Kapiti Ltd)	
KAPITI.CO.UK	KAPITI.CO.UK
Software Maintenance Specialists (Microdot Aerospace)	
KAYNAR.CO.UK	KAYNAR.CO.UK

Kerridge Computers
KCC.CO.UK   KCC.CO.UK
Kernel Technology Limited
KERNEL.CO.UK   KERNEL-TECHNOLOGY.CO.UK
Kewill Systems PLC
KEWILL.CO.UK   KEWILL.CO.UK
Kratos Analytical Limited
KRATOS.CO.UK   KRATOS.CO.UK
KUBOTA PACIFIC COMPUTER INC
KPC.CO.UK   KUBOTA-PACIFIC-COMPUTER.CO.UK
K2 Software Developments Ltd
K2.CO.UK   K2-SOFTWARE.CO.UK
Lanware
LANWARE.CO.UK   LANWARE.CO.UK
Largotim Holdings Ltd
LARGOTIM.CO.UK   LARGOTIM.CO.UK
Laser-Scan Limited (Laser Scan Limited)
LSL.CO.UK   LASER-SCAN.CO.UK
Lasermoon Ltd
LASERMOON.CO.UK   LASERMOON.CO.UK
Lawrence Graham
LAWGRAM.CO.UK   LAWRENCE-GRAHAM.CO.UK
LBMS plc
LBMS.CO.UK   LBMS.CO.UK
Leabrook Computing Ltd
LBRK.CO.UK   LEABROOK.CO.UK
Leading Technology Ltd
LTECH.CO.UK   LEADING-TECHNOLOGY.CO.UK
Leaf Distribution Ltd
LEAF.CO.UK   LEAF.CO.UK
Learned Information (Europe) Ltd
LEARNED.CO.UK   LEARNED.CO.UK
Leica Cambridge Limited
LEICA.CO.UK   LEICA.CO.UK
EDA.LEICA.CO.UK   EDA.LEICA.CO.UK
ENG.LEICA.CO.UK   ENG.LEICA.CO.UK
SEG.LEICA.CO.UK   SEG.LEICA.CO.UK
VAX.LEICA.CO.UK   VAX.LEICA.CO.UK
Leo Systems Ltd
LEO.CO.UK   LEO-SYSTEMS.CO.UK
Level 7 Limited
L-7.CO.UK   LEVEL-7.CO.UK
CONCISE.L-7.CO.UK   CONCISE.LEVEL-7.CO.UK

Level V Distribution Ltd (Sphinx LevelV)
LEVELV.CO.UK   LEVELV.CO.UK
Level 7 Software Ltd (Level 7 Software Limited)
L7SWLTD.CO.UK   LEVEL7SOFTWARE.CO.UK
Lex Retail Group
LEX.CO.UK   LEX-RETAIL.CO.UK
leykam
LEYKAM.CO.UK   LEYKAM.CO.UK
Liant Software Ltd
LIANT.CO.UK   LIANT-SOFTWARE-UK-LTD.CO.UK
Lightwork Design Ltd (Lightwork Design Ltd)
LIGHTWORK.CO.UK   LIGHTWORK.CO.UK
Logistics & Industrial Systems Ltd
LIS.CO.UK   LIS.CO.UK
Lloyds Register of Shipping (Lloyd's Register of Shipping)
AIE.LREG.CO.UK   AIE.LLOYDS-REGISTER.CO.UK
Locus Computing Corporation Ltd
LOCUS.CO.UK   LOCUS.CO.UK
Logical Choice Ltd
LOGCHOX.CO.UK   LOGCHOICE-OXFORD.CO.UK
Logica International Limited
LOGICA.CO.UK   LOGICA.CO.UK
Logica Cambridge Ltd
LOGCAM.CO.UK   LOGICA-CAMBRIDGE.CO.UK
Logical Networks plc
LOGNET.CO.UK   LOGICAL-NETWORKS.CO.UK
Londis (Holdings) Ltd
LONDIS.CO.UK   LONDIS-HOLDINGS-LTD.CO.UK
Longman Cartermill
LCD.CO.UK   LONGMAN-CARTERMILL.CO.UK
The London Partnership Ltd
LONPAR.CO.UK   LONPAR.CO.UK
Sequent Computer Systems
LONSQNT.CO.UK   LONSQNT.CO.UK
Loot Limited
LOOT.CO.UK   LOOT.CO.UK
Loughborough Sound Images Ltd
LSI-DSP.CO.UK   LOUGHBOROUGH-SOUND-IMAGES-LTD.CO.UK
LSO Logic Europe PLC (LSI Logic Europe PLC)
LSI-LOGIC.CO.UK   LSI-LOGIC.CO.UK
Lucas Automotive (Lucas Industries PLC)
LAU.CO.UK   LUCAS-AUTOMOTIVE.CO.UK
AEC.LAU.CO.UK   ADVANCED-ENGINEERING-CENTRE.LUCAS-
                                AUTOMOTIVE.CO.UK

CIREN.LAU.CO.UK	CIRENCESTER.LUCAS-AUTOMOTIVE.CO.UK
EG.LAU.CO.UK	EG.LUCAS-AUTOMOTIVE.CO.UK

Lucas Industries PLC

LICIREN.LI.CO.UK	LI-CIRENCESTER.LUCAS-INDUSTRIES.CO.UK
LISHIRL1.LI.CO.UK	LI-SHIRLEY-AEC.LUCAS-INDUSTRIES.CO.UK

OLD Lucas Automotive (Lucas Industries PLC)

EG.LUCASAUTO.CO.UK	EG.LUCASAUTO.CO.UK

Merril Lynch Europe Ltd

M-L.CO.UK	M-L.CO.UK

MAID Systems Limited

MAID.CO.UK	MAID.CO.UK

Mai Research Limited

MAIRES.CO.UK	MAIRES.CO.UK

Mantis Consultants Ltd

MANTIS.CO.UK	MANTIS-CONSULTANTS.CO.UK

MANTIX Systems Limited

MANTIX.CO.UK	MANTIX.CO.UK

Manufacturing Products and Services Ltd

MAPS.CO.UK	MAPS.CO.UK

March Systems Consultancy Ltd

MARCH.CO.UK	MARCH.CO.UK

Marconi Simulation

MSIM.CO.UK	MARCONI-SIMULATION.CO.UK

The MARI Group Limited

MARI.CO.UK	MARI.CO.UK

MATROX UK Ltd

MATROX.CO.UK	MATROX.CO.UK

G. Maunsell & Partners

MAUNSELL.CO.UK	MAUNSELL.CO.UK

Mercury Communications PRISM Services (Mercury Communications City Switch Management)

MCLPRISM.CO.UK	MCLPRISM.CO.UK

Minicomputer Commercial S/W Ltd

MCS.CO.UK	MCS.CO.UK

Mead Data Central International

MDCI.CO.UK	MDCI.CO.UK

MDIS (McDonnel Douglas) Limited (MDIS (McDonnell Douglas) Information Systems Limited)

MDIS.CO.UK	MDIS.CO.UK
GANDALF.MDIS.CO.UK	GANDALF.MDIS.CO.UK
GOLLUM.MDIS.CO.UK	GOLLUM.MDIS.CO.UK
GX1.MDIS.CO.UK	GX1.MDIS.CO.UK
GX2.MDIS.CO.UK	GX2.MDIS.CO.UK
MOTX1.MDIS.CO.UK	MOTX1.MDIS.CO.UK

MOTX2.MDIS.CO.UK	MOTX2.MDIS.CO.UK
MX1.MDIS.CO.UK	MX1.MDIS.CO.UK
MX2.MDIS.CO.UK	MX2.MDIS.CO.UK
SAM.MDIS.CO.UK	SAM.MDIS.CO.UK
ZEUS.MDIS.CO.UK	ZEUS.MDIS.CO.UK

Meiko Limited

MEIKO.CO.UK	MEIKO.CO.UK

Memex Information Engines Ltd

MEMEX.CO.UK	MEMEX.CO.UK

Mercury Interactive Ltd (Mercury Interactive UK Ltd)

MERC-INT.CO.UK	MERC-INT.CO.UK

Aura Business Systems Ltd

AMJONS.CO.UK	MEREDITH-JONES.CO.UK

METADIGM Ltd (Metadigm Ltd)

METADIGM.CO.UK	METADIGM.CO.UK

Meta_Generics (Meta Generics Ltd)

METAGEN.CO.UK	METAGEN.CO.UK

Metrologie UK Ltd

METRO.CO.UK	METROLOGIE.CO.UK

Micro Focus Limited

MFLTD.CO.UK	MICRO-FOCUS-LTD.CO.UK

Micrognosis

MICROGNOSIS.CO.UK	MICROGNOSIS.CO.UK
–No short form–	CORP.MICROGNOSIS.CO.UK
–No short form–	HKG.MICROGNOSIS.CO.UK
–No short form–	INTEG.MICROGNOSIS.CO.UK
–No short form–	LONDON.MICROGNOSIS.CO.UK

MicroMuse Limited (MicroMuse Ltd)

MICROMUSE.CO.UK	MICROMUSE.CO.UK

Micronetics Consulting SA

MNETX.CO.UK	MICRONETICS-UK.CO.UK

LTSS Limited

MICROVITEC.CO.UK	MICROVITEC.CO.UK

Microware Systems (UK) Ltd (Microware Systems (UK) Limited)

MICROWARE.CO.UK	MICROWARE.CO.UK

Microway Europe Ltd

MICROWAY.CO.UK	MICROWAY.CO.UK

Mitsubishi Electric UK Ltd

MEUK.CO.UK	MITSUBISHI.CO.UK

Monotype Typography (Monotype Corporation PLC)

MONO.CO.UK	MONOTYPE.CO.UK
ADG.MONO.CO.UK	ADG.MONOTYPE.CO.UK
CTDL.MONO.CO.UK	CTDL.MONOTYPE.CO.UK

SOFT.MONO.CO.UK	SOFT.MONOTYPE.CO.UK
TYPO.MONO.CO.UK	TYPO.MONOTYPE.CO.UK
Morse Computers Ltd	
MORSE.CO.UK	MORSE.CO.UK
Mosaic Microsystems Ltd	
MOSAIC.CO.UK	MOSAIC.CO.UK
Mott MacDonald	
MOTTMAC.CO.UK	MOTT-MACDONALD-GROUP.CO.UK
Maspar Computer Corporation	
MPREAD.CO.UK	MPREAD.CO.UK
Molecular Simulations	
MSICAM.CO.UK	MSICAM.CO.UK
Marconi Underwater Systems Ltd	
MST.CO.UK	MSTUK.CO.UK
Marine Technology Directorate Ltd	
MTD.CO.UK	MTD.CO.UK
MTI Technology Ltd	
MTI.CO.UK	MTI.CO.UK
JSB Computer Systems Ltd	
JSB.CO.UK	MULTIVIEW.CO.UK
Thomas Miller & Co	
MUTUAL.CO.UK	MUTUAL.CO.UK
The National Computing Centre (National Computing Centre)	
NCC.CO.UK	NATIONAL-COMPUTING-CENTRE.CO.UK
National Physical Laboratory	
CSU.NPL.CO.UK	CSU.NATIONAL-PHYSICAL-LAB.CO.UK
DSG.NPL.CO.UK	DSG.NATIONAL-PHYSICAL-LAB.CO.UK
GW.NPL.CO.UK	GW.NATIONAL-PHYSICAL-LAB.CO.UK
HCI.NPL.CO.UK	HCI.NATIONAL-PHYSICAL-LAB.CO.UK
INFO.NPL.CO.UK	INFO.NATIONAL-PHYSICAL-LAB.CO.UK
NEWTON.NPL.CO.UK	NEWTON.NATIONAL-PHYSICAL-LAB.CO.UK
NPL1.NPL.CO.UK	NPL1.NATIONAL-PHYSICAL-LAB.CO.UK
OSG.NPL.CO.UK	OSG.NATIONAL-PHYSICAL-LAB.CO.UK
PPG.NPL.CO.UK	PPG.NATIONAL-PHYSICAL-LAB.CO.UK
PSG.NPL.CO.UK	PSG.NATIONAL-PHYSICAL-LAB.CO.UK
SEG.NPL.CO.UK	SEG.NATIONAL-PHYSICAL-LAB.CO.UK
National Power plc	
NATPOWER.CO.UK	NATPOWER.CO.UK
–No short form–	RESEARCH.NATPOWER.CO.UK
Nationwide Building Society	
NBS.CO.UK	NBS.CO.UK
Nicholas Caine Associates	
NCA.CO.UK	NCA.CO.UK

Network Computing Devices (UK) Ltd
NCD.CO.UK   NCD.CO.UK
NCR Ltd
NCR.CO.UK   NCR.CO.UK
NCRUK.NCR.CO.UK   NCRUK.NCR.CO.UK
NCRCSS.CO.UK   NCRCSS.CO.UK
NDC Ltd
NDC.CO.UK   NDC.CO.UK
Network Designers Ltd
NDL.CO.UK   NDL.CO.UK
NEC Electronics UK Ltd
EUK.NEC.CO.UK   ELECTRONICS.NEC.CO.UK
Netcomm Limited (Netcomm Ltd)
NETCOMM.CO.UK   NETCOMM.CO.UK
Network Analysis Limited
NAN.CO.UK   NETWORK-ANALYSIS-LTD.CO.UK
Network Managers (UK) Ltd
NETMGRS.CO.UK   NETWORK-MANAGERS.CO.UK
NEXOR Services Limited
NEXOR.CO.UK   NEXOR.CO.UK
Nomura International plc
NOMURA.CO.UK   NOMURA.CO.UK
Novell UNIX System Laboratories Europe (AT&T Unix Europe Ltd)
NOVELL.CO.UK   NOVELL.CO.UK
National Remote Sensing Centre
NRSC.CO.UK   NRSC.CO.UK
Northern Telecom Europe Ltd (Northern Telecom Ltd)
NORTHERN.CO.UK   NT-EUROPE.CO.UK
The Numerical Algorithms Group Ltd (The Numerical Alogorithms Group Ltd)
NAG.CO.UK   NUM-ALG-GRP.CO.UK
VAX.NAG.CO.UK   VAX.NUM-ALG-GRP.CO.UK
North West Water Limited
NWWL.CO.UK   NWWL.CO.UK
NYNEXMC (NI)
NYNEXMC.CO.UK   NYNEXMC.CO.UK
Object Design (UK) Ltd
ODI.CO.UK   OBJECT-DESIGN.CO.UK
Office Workstations Limited
OWL-UK.CO.UK   OFFICE-WORKSTATIONS-LTD.CO.UK
Oxford Information Technology Ltd
OIT.CO.UK   OIT.CO.UK
Omnimedia Ltd
OMNI.CO.UK   OMNIMEDIA.CO.UK

OMV (UK) Limited
OMV.CO.UK   OMV.CO.UK
On-Line Entertainment Ltd
ON-LINE.CO.UK   ON-LINE.CO.UK
Open System Sevices Ltd (Open System Services Ltd)
OPEN-SYSTEM.CO.UK   OPEN-SYSTEM.CO.UK
Open Systems Marketing Ltd
OSM.CO.UK   OPEN-SYSTEMS-MARKETING.CO.UK
Open Vision Technologies Ltd
OPENV.CO.UK   OPENVISION.CO.UK
ORACLE.CO.UK   ORACLE.CO.UK
Origin Automation Technology
OTIBUK11.CO.UK   ORIGIN-AT.CO.UK
ORT Administration Ltd
ORT.CO.UK   ORT.CO.UK
Ove Arup Partnership
ARUP.CO.UK   OVE-ARUP-PARTNERSHIP.CO.UK
Oxford University Press
OUP.CO.UK   OXFORD-UNIPRESS.CO.UK
PAFEC CAE Limited (Pafec Cae Limited)
PAFEC.CO.UK   PAFEC.CO.UK
Palmer & Webb Systems Ltd
PAWS.CO.UK   PALMER-AND-WEBB.CO.UK
Paradigm Geophysical (UK) Ltd
PARADIGM.CO.UK   PARADIGM.CO.UK
Parliament Hill Computers
PHCOMP.CO.UK   PARLIAMENT-HILL-COMPUTERS.CO.UK
PARSYS Ltd (PARSYS Ltd)
PARSYS.CO.UK   PARSYS.CO.UK
Productivity Computer Solutions Ltd
PCS1.CO.UK   PCS1.CO.UK
Perkin-Elmer Ltd (PERKIN-ELMER)
PELTD.CO.UK   PELTD.CO.UK
Perfect Recall Ltd
RECALL.CO.UK   PERFECT-RECALL.CO.UK
Perihelion Software Limited
PERISL.CO.UK   PERIHELION.CO.UK
Persistent Storage Europe Ltd (Persistent Storage Ltd)
PERSTORE.CO.UK   PERSISTENT-STORAGE.CO.UK
Personal Workstations
PERWORK.CO.UK   PERSONAL-WORKSTATIONS.CO.UK
Peterborough Software Ltd (Peterborough Software UK Ltd)
PS.CO.UK   PETERBOROUGH-SOFTWARE.CO.UK

Pet Plan Insurance

PETPLAN.CO.UK   PETPLAN.CO.UK

Pfizer Central Research (Pfizer Ltd)

SND01.PCR.CO.UK   SND01.PFIZER-CENTRAL-RESEARCH.CO.UK
SND02.PCR.CO.UK   SND02.PFIZER-CENTRAL-RESEARCH.CO.UK
SVAX00.PCR.CO.UK   SVAX00.PFIZER-CENTRAL-RESEARCH.CO.UK

Philips Research Laboratories (Philips Research Laboratory)

APG.PHIL.CO.UK   APG.PHILIPS.CO.UK
IMS.PHIL.CO.UK   IMS.PHILIPS.CO.UK
PMSR.PHIL.CO.UK   PMSR.PHILIPS.CO.UK
PPI.PHIL.CO.UK   PPI.PHILIPS.CO.UK
PRL.PHIL.CO.UK   PRL.PHILIPS.CO.UK

Pilkington Technology Management Ltd (Pilkington Technology Centre)

PILKINGTON.CO.UK   PILKINGTON.CO.UK

Pioneer High Fidelity (GB) Limited

PIONEER.CO.UK   PIONEER.CO.UK
PDD.PIONEER.CO.UK   PDD.PIONEER.CO.UK

PIPEX (UniPalm Limited)

PIPEX.CO.UK   PIPEX.CO.UK

Refection Systems Ltd

PLASMON.CO.UK   PLASMON.CO.UK

Soft Solution

POPTEL.CO.UK   POPTEL.CO.UK

Post Office Research Centre

UKPOENG.CO.UK   POST-OFFICE-RESEARCH.CO.UK

Power Technology

POWERTECH.CO.UK   POWERTECH.CO.UK

Praxis Systems plc

PRAXIS.CO.UK   PRAXIS.CO.UK

Programming Research Ltd

PRL0.CO.UK   PRL0.CO.UK

Prolingua Limited

PRLNG.CO.UK   PROLINGUA.CO.UK

PROTEK (Leading Technology Ltd)

PROTEK.CO.UK   PROTEK.CO.UK

Proteus Molecular Design Ltd

PROTEUS.CO.UK   PROTEUS.CO.UK

The Petroleum Science and Technology Institute (Petroleum Science and Technology Institute)

PSTI.CO.UK   PSTI.CO.UK
PIPER.PSTI.CO.UK   PIPER.PSTI.CO.UK

Psychometric Research & Development

PRD.CO.UK   PSYCHOMETRIC-RESEARCH-AND-DEVELOP
                                 MENT-LTD.CO.UK

Psygnosis Ltd

PSYGNOSIS.CO.UK	PSYGNOSIS.CO.UK
CH.PSYGNOSIS.CO.UK	CHESTER.PSYGNOSIS.CO.UK
LO.PSYGNOSIS.CO.UK	LONDON.PSYGNOSIS.CO.UK
LP.PSYGNOSIS.CO.UK	LPOOLB.PSYGNOSIS.CO.UK
ST.PSYGNOSIS.CO.UK	STROUD.PSYGNOSIS.CO.UK

Productivity Through Software Ltd

PTS.CO.UK	PTS.CO.UK

Pulse Train Technology Ltd

PULSETR.CO.UK	PULSE-TRAIN-TECHNOLOGY.CO.UK

Pyramid Technology Ltd (Pyramid Technology Ltd)

PYRA.CO.UK	PYRAMID-TECHNOLOGY.CO.UK

Quarterdeck Office Systems UK Ltd

QDECK.CO.UK	QDECK.CO.UK

Quantime Ltd

QUANTIME.CO.UK	QUANTIME.CO.UK

Dorotech Limited (successor to Racal ITD Ltd) (Racal ITD Ltd)

RITD.CO.UK	RACAL-ITD.CO.UK

Racal Survey Ltd

RACALSVY.CO.UK	RACAL-SURVEY.CO.UK

Radan Computational Limited

RADAN.CO.UK	RADAN.CO.UK

Radan Business Systems Ltd

RADANBS.CO.UK	RADANBS.CO.UK

Ram Mobile Data Limited

RAM.CO.UK	RAM.CO.UK

Raxco-UIS Limited

RAXCO.CO.UK	RAXCO.CO.UK

Richards Computer Products Ltd

RCP.CO.UK	RCP.CO.UK

Real Time Products Ltd

RTP.CO.UK	REAL-TIME-PRODUCTS.CO.UK

Racal Redac Systems Ltd

REDACT.CO.UK	REDACT.CO.UK

Redwood Design Automation

REDWOOD.CO.UK	REDWOOD.CO.UK

Reed Business Publishing

RBP.CO.UK	REED-BUSINESS-PUBLISHING-LTD.CO.UK

Research Engineers Europe Ltd

REEL.CO.UK	REEL.CO.UK

Reflex Manufacturing Systems Ltd (Relfex Manufacturing Systems Limited)

REFLEX.CO.UK	REFLEX-MANUFACTURING-SYSTEMS.CO.UK

Robobar Limited

ROBOBAR.CO.UK	ROBOBAR.CO.UK

ROKE Manor Research Ltd
ROKE.CO.UK   ROKE-MANOR.CO.UK
Order Processing Technologies Ltd (Order Processing Technologies (UK) Ltd)
ROLLCIM.CO.UK   ROLLCIM.CO.UK
Root Computers Ltd
ROOT.CO.UK   ROOT.CO.UK
Rosemount Limited
ROSEMNT.CO.UK   ROSEMOUNT.CO.UK
Real Time Consultants plc
RTC.CO.UK   RTC.CO.UK
RTZ Mining and Exploration Ltd
ME.RTZ.CO.UK   MINING-AND-EXPLORATION.RTZ.CO.UK
Southern Electric plc
S-ELECTRIC.CO.UK   S-ELECTRIC.CO.UK
Sadolin Nobel UK Limited
SADOLIN.CO.UK   SADOLIN.CO.UK
SAGE Publications Ltd
SAGELTD.CO.UK   SAGE-PUBLICATIONS-LTD.CO.UK
SAIC (UK) Limited
SAICUK.CO.UK   SAICUK.CO.UK
Salford Software Services
SSS.CO.UK   SALFORD-SOFTWARE-SERVICES.CO.UK
A.SSS.CO.UK   A.SALFORD-SOFTWARE-SERVICES.CO.UK
B.SSS.CO.UK   B.SALFORD-SOFTWARE-SERVICES.CO.UK
D.SSS.CO.UK   D.SALFORD-SOFTWARE-SERVICES.CO.UK
D-TEST.SSS.CO.UK   D-TEST.SALFORD-SOFTWARE SERVICES.
                                    CO.UK
E.SSS.CO.UK   E.SALFORD-SOFTWARE-SERVICES.CO.UK
NRSB.SSS.CO.UK   NRSB.SALFORD-SOFTWARE-SERVICES.CO.UK

Salomon Brothers International Ltd
SBIL.CO.UK   SALOMON-BROTHERS.CO.UK
SAST (Special Analysis & Simulation Technology Ltd)
SAST.CO.UK   SAST.CO.UK
Satelcom UK
SATELCOM.CO.UK   SATELCOM.CO.UK
Saville and Holdsworth Ltd
SHLV2.CO.UK   SAVILLE-AND-HOLDSWORTH-LTD.CO.UK
Swiss Bank Corporation
SBC.CO.UK   SBC.CO.UK
Scicomsys Consultants
SCICOMSYS.CO.UK   SCICOMSYS.CO.UK

EDS Scicon (EDS-SCICON PLC)

SCICON.CO.UK   SCICON.CO.UK

Scientific and Engineering Software Co. UK

SES.CO.UK   SCIENTIFIC-AND-ENGINEERING-
                                      SOFTWARE.CO.UK

BALDRICK.SES.CO.UK   BALDRICK.SCIENTIFIC-AND-ENGINEERING-
                                      SOFTWARE.CO.UK

BLACK.SES.CO.UK   BLACKADDER.SCIENTIFIC-AND-ENGINEERING-
                                      SOFTWARE.CO.UK

DARLING.SES.CO.UK   DARLING.SCIENTIFIC-AND-ENGINEERING-
                                      SOFTWARE.CO.UK

FLASH.SES.CO.UK   FLASHHEART.SCIENTIFIC-AND-ENGINEERING-
                                      SOFTWARE.CO.UK

MELCHETT.SES.CO.UK   MELCHETT.SCIENTIFIC-AND-ENGINEERING-
                                      SOFTWARE.CO.UK

Scientific Generics

SCIGEN.CO.UK   SCIENTIFIC-GENERICS.CO.UK

Scotprint Ltd

SCOTPRINT.CO.UK   SCOTPRINT.CO.UK

SD-Scicon, Pembroke House (SD-Scicon PLC)

SDSPH.SDSCI.CO.UK   CAMBERLEY.SD-SCICON.CO.UK

SDSWAV.SDSCI.CO.UK   WAVENDON.SD-SCICON.CO.UK

Scottish Express International

SEI.CO.UK   SEI.CO.UK

BAeSEMA Ltd

SEMAGL.CO.UK   SEMAGL.CO.UK

SST.SEMAGL.CO.UK   SST.SEMAGL.CO.UK

SEMA Information Consulting (Sema Group plc)

SEMALC.CO.UK   SEMALC.CO.UK

Sequent Computer Systems

SEQUENT.CO.UK   SEQUENT.CO.UK

Serco Limited (Systems)

SERCO.CO.UK   SERCO.CO.UK

7E Communications Ltd

SEVENE.CO.UK   SEVENE.CO.UK

Systems Guidance Limited

SGL.CO.UK   SGL.CO.UK

Shape Data

SHAPE.CO.UK   SHAPE-DATA.CO.UK

Sharp Laboratories of Europe Ltd

SHARP.CO.UK   SHARP.CO.UK

Sherpa Corporation

SHERPA.CO.UK   SHERPA-CORPORATION.CO.UK

Sherwood Computer Services Plc
SHERWOOD.CO.UK   SHERWOOD.CO.UK
Siemens Nixdorf Information Systems Ltd
SIEBKL.CO.UK   SIEBKL.CO.UK
Siemens PLC Congleton
SIECON.CO.UK   SIECON.CO.UK
SIEMENS Ltd, System Development Group (SIEMENS LTD)
SIESOFT.CO.UK   SIESOFT.CO.UK
Simmons Magee Computers plc
SIMMAG.CO.UK   SIMMONS-MAGEE.CO.UK
Sintrom PLC
SINTROM.CO.UK   SINTROM.CO.UK
SLS Information Systems Ltd
DVLBOX.SLS.CO.UK   DVLBOX.SLS.CO.UK
DVLVAX.SLS.CO.UK   DVLVAX.SLS.CO.UK
IPGATE.SLS.CO.UK   IPGATE.SLS.CO.UK
SUPVAX.SLS.CO.UK   SUPVAX.SLS.CO.UK
XSERV1.SLS.CO.UK   XSERV1.SLS.CO.UK
Smallworld Systems
SMALLWORLD.CO.UK   SMALLWORLD.CO.UK
Smith System Engineering Ltd
SMITHSYS.CO.UK   SMITHSYS.CO.UK
Siemens Nixdorf Information Systems Ltd
SNI.CO.UK   SNI.CO.UK
Snowy Owl Systems Ltd
SOS.CO.UK   SNOWYOWL.CO.UK
Softcase Consulting
SOFTCASE.CO.UK   SOFTCASE.CO.UK
SOFTIMAGE UK Limited (SOFTIMAGE (UK) Limited)
SOFTIMAGE.CO.UK   SOFTIMAGE.CO.UK
Software Craftsmen Limited
SOFTC.CO.UK   SOFTWARE-CRAFTSMEN.CO.UK
Solbourne Computer UK Ltd
SOLBOURNE.CO.UK   SOLBOURNE-COMPUTER.CO.UK
Sony UK Ltd (Sony UK Ltd)
SONY.CO.UK   SONY.CO.UK
ATLEPCD.SONY.CO.UK   ATLEPCD.SONY.CO.UK
PCD.SONY.CO.UK   PCD.SONY.CO.UK
Specialix Systems Limited
SLXSYS.CO.UK   SPECIALIX.CO.UK
Spectrum Communications Ltd
SCHIL.CO.UK   SPECTRUM-COMMUNICATIONS-
                               LIMITED.CO.UK

Speedware plc
SPEEDWARE.CO.UK   SPEEDWARE.CO.UK

Sphinx Ltd
SPHINX.CO.UK   SPHINX.CO.UK

Spider Systems Ltd
SPIDER.CO.UK   SPIDER.CO.UK

Springer-Verlag London Ltd
SVL.CO.UK   SPRINGER-VERLAG-LONDON.CO.UK

Simon Petroleum Technology Ltd Geophysical Services
SPTGEO.CO.UK   SPTGEO.CO.UK

SQL Software Ltd
SQL.CO.UK   SQL-SOFTWARE LTD.CO.UK

SRI International (Cambridge Computer Science Research Centre)
SRI.CO.UK   SRI-INTERNATIONAL.CO.UK
CAM.SRI.CO.UK   CAM.SRI-INTERNATIONAL.CO.UK
CROYDON.SRI.CO.UK   CROYDON.SRI-INTERNATIONAL.CO.UK

Scientific Software-Intercomp (UK) Ltd (Scientific Software – Intercomp (UK) Ltd)
SSILON.CO.UK   SSILON.CO.UK

Stade Computers Limited
STADE.CO.UK   STADE-COMPUTERS-LIMITED.CO.UK

STC Submarine Systems Ltd
STCSSL.CO.UK   STCSSL.CO.UK

Stewart Hughes Ltd
SHL.CO.UK   STEWART-HUGHES.CO.UK

Strand Software Technologies Ltd (Strand Software Technologies Ltd)
STRAND.CO.UK   STRAND-SOFTWARE.CO.UK

Sun Microsystems Ltd
SUN.CO.UK   SUN-MICROSYSTEMS.CO.UK
SUNSOLVE.SUN.CO.UK   SUNSOLVE.SUN-MICROSYSTEMS.CO.UK

Symbionics Limited (Symbionics Ltd)
SYMBIONICS.CO.UK   SYMBIONICS.CO.UK

Symbolics Ltd
SYMBOLICS.CO.UK   SYMBOLICS.CO.UK

Alper Systems Limited
SYSDECO.CO.UK   SYSDECO.CO.UK

SysDrill Ltd
SYSDRILL.CO.UK   SYSDRILL.CO.UK

System Simulation Limited
SSL.CO.UK   SYSTEM-SIMULATION.CO.UK

System Strategies (Systems Strategies Limited)
SSIUK.CO.UK   SYSTEMS-STRATEGIES.CO.UK

Tadpole Technology plc
TADTEC.CO.UK   TADPOLE-TECHNOLOGY-PLC.CO.UK

Tagg Oram Partnership
TAGGORAM.CO.UK   TAGG-ORAM-PARTNERSHIP.CO.UK
Tardis Connect (Tardis Direct Ltd)
TARDIS.CO.UK   TARDIS-CONNECT.CO.UK
Taylor and Francis
TANDF.CO.UK   TAYLOR-AND-FRANCIS.CO.UK
Technology Business Computers Limited
TBC.CO.UK   TBC.CO.UK
TECC Ltd (The Electronic Conferencing Company Ltd)
TECC.CO.UK   TECC.CO.UK
LUGGAGE.TECC.CO.UK   LUGGAGE.TECC.CO.UK
Technology Applications Group
TAG.CO.UK   TECHNOLOGY-APPLICATIONS-GROUP.CO.UK
Technology plc
TECHPLC.CO.UK   TECHPLC.CO.UK
Tenet Systems Ltd
TENET.CO.UK   TENET.CO.UK
Tessella Support Services plc
TSS.CO.UK   TESSELLA.CO.UK
Text 100 Ltd
TEXT100.CO.UK   TEXT100.CO.UK
The Technology Partnership Ltd
TECHPRT.CO.UK   THE-TECHNOLOGY-PARTNERSHIP-LTD.CO.UK
Thorn EMI Central Research Labs
TECRL.CO.UK   THORN-EMI-CRL.CO.UK
3I plc (3I Group plc)
THREE-I.CO.UK   THREE-I.CO.UK
3L Ltd
THREEL.CO.UK   THREEL.CO.UK
P-D.THREEL.CO.UK   DELTA.THREEL.CO.UK
P-Y.THREEL.CO.UK   YANKEE.THREEL.CO.UK
P-Z.THREEL.CO.UK   ZULU.THREEL.CO.UK
Tigress Limited
TIGRESS.CO.UK   TIGRESS.CO.UK
TMB Computer Services Plc
TMB.CO.UK   TMB.CO.UK
TMSE Limited
TMSE.CO.UK   TMSE.CO.UK
TopExpress Limited
TOPEXP.CO.UK   TOPEXPRESS.CO.UK
Top-Log UK Ltd
TOPLOGUK.CO.UK   TOPLOG-UK-LTD.CO.UK
Toshiba Cambridge Research Centre Limited

TCRC.TOSHIBA.CO.UK	TCRC.TOSHIBA.CO.UK
–No short form–	MACMAIL.TCRC.TOSHIBA.CO.UK
TPD Publishing Ltd	
TPD.CO.UK	TPD-PUBLISHING-LTD.CO.UK
Transformation Software Ltd	
TSWL.CO.UK	TRANSFORMATION-SOFTWARE.CO.UK
Transtech Parallel Systems Ltd	
TRANST.CO.UK	TRANSTECH.CO.UK
Trevan Designs Ltd	
TRVN.CO.UK	TREVAN.CO.UK
Transport Research Laboratory	
TRL..CO.UK	TRL.CO.UK
Telecom Securicor Cellular Radio Ltd	
CELLNET.CO.UK	TSCR-CELLNET-LTD.CO.UK
Thermatool Limited	
TTOOL.CO.UK	TTOOL.CO.UK
Thames Water International Services Limited	
TWIRBH.CO.UK	TWIRBH.CO.UK
User Interface Technologies (ElectricMail Ltd)	
UIT.CO.UK	UIT.CO.UK
iT, The Information Technology Business of the Post Office	
UKPOIT.CO.UK	UKPOIT.CO.UK
Unilever Research Colworth Laboratory (Unilever Research Colworth House)	
URLCH.CO.UK	UNILEVER-RESEARCH-CH.CO.UK
Unilever Research, Port Sunlight (Unilever Research – Port Sunlight)	
URPSL.CO.UK	UNILEVER-RESEARCH-PS.CO.UK
UniPalm Limited	
UNIPALM.CO.UK	UNIPALM.CO.UK
UNIPLEX Limited	
UPLX.CO.UK	UNIPLEX.CO.UK
UNISYS Europe–Africa Ltd	
UNIEAD.CO.UK	UNISYS-EAD.CO.UK
Unisys Ltd (UK)	
UNISYSUK.CO.UK	UNISYSUK.CO.UK
AT&T Unix Europe Ltd	
UEL.CO.UK	UNIX-SYSTEM-LABS.CO.UK
Valstar Systems Ltd	
VALSTAR.CO.UK	VALSTAR-SYSTEMS-LTD.CO.UK
Vantage Analysis Systems	
VANTAGE.CO.UK	VANTAGE.CO.UK
VEGA Group PLC	
VEGAUK.CO.UK	VEGAUK.CO.UK
Visionware Ltd	
VISION.CO.UK	VISIONWARE.CO.UK

VLSI Technology Ltd
VLSI.CO.UK   VLSI.CO.UK
VLSI Vision Ltd
VVL.CO.UK   VLSI-VISION.CO.UK
VMARK Software Ltd
VMARK.CO.UK   VMARK.CO.UK
Visual Numerics International Ltd
VNIUK.CO.UK   VNIUK.CO.UK
Walker International
WALKERUK.CO.UK   WALKERUK.CO.UK
Wang (UK) Ltd
WANG.CO.UK   WANG.CO.UK
Watson Services Ltd
WATSONS.CO.UK   WATSONS.CO.UK
Wavedriver Ltd
WAVEDRIVER.CO.UK   WAVEDRIVER-LTD.CO.UK
The Wellcome Research Laboratories
WELLCOME.CO.UK   WELLCOME.CO.UK
White Cross Systems
WCS.CO.UK   WHITE-CROSS-SYSTEMS.CO.UK
John Wiley & Sons Ltd
WILEY.CO.UK   WILEY.CO.UK
Wolfram Research Europe Ltd
WREL.CO.UK   WOLFRAM-RESEARCH-EUROPE-LTD.CO.UK
World Conservation Moni (World Conservation Monitoring Centre)
WCMC.CO.UK   WORLD-CONSERVATION-MONITORING-CEN
                                    TRE.CO.UK
World Press Centre (Update News Limited) (Update News Limited)
WPC.CO.UK   WPC.CO.UK
WS Atkins (Services) Ltd
WSATKINS.CO.UK   WSATKINS.CO.UK
Xanadu Systems Ltd
XAN1.CO.UK   XAN1.CO.UK
Xi Software Ltd
XISL.CO.UK   XI-SOFTWARE.CO.UK
X-ON Software
XON.CO.UK   XON.CO.UK
X/OPEN Company Ltd
XOPEN.CO.UK   XOPEN.CO.UK
XTECH (UniPalm Limited)
XTECH.CO.UK   XTECH.CO.UK
X-Tel Services Limited
XTEL.CO.UK   XTEL.CO.UK

Xylogics International Limited
XYLINT.CO.UK   XYLOGICS-INTERNATIONAL.CO.UK
Xyplex (XYPLEX)
XYPLEX.CO.UK   XYPLEX.CO.UK
Y-NET National Operations Unit – UK (Level 7 Limited)
Y-NET.CO.UK   Y-NET.CO.UK
SP1.Y-NET.CO.UK   SP1.Y-NET.CO.UK
YACC
YACC.CO.UK   YACC.CO.UK
Yamanouchi Research Institute (UK) (Yamanouchi UK Ltd)
YAM-RES.CO.UK   YAMANOUCHI-RESEARCH.CO.UK
Zeneca Pharmaceuticals
ZENECA-PH.CO.UK   ZENECA-PHARM.CO.UK
Forestry Commission Research Division
P1.AH.FOREST-RD.UK   PRIME1.ALICE-HOLT.FOREST-RD.UK
AWE.GOV.UK   AWE.GOV.UK
CLEVELAND.GOV.UK   CLEVELAND.GOV.UK
DSS.GOV.UK   DSS.GOV.UK
ENG-H.GOV.UK   ENG-H.GOV.UK
ESTONIA.GOV.UK   ESTONIA.GOV.UK
RPU.HMG-HO.GOV.UK   RPU.HMG-HO.GOV.UK
MAFF.GOV.UK   MAFF.GOV.UK
MANCHESTER.GOV.UK   MANCHESTER.GOV.UK
NIHE.GOV.UK   NIHE.GOV.UK
HWAY.SCC.GOV.UK   HIGHWAYS.SUFFOLKCC.GOV.UK
CAMCNTY.GOVT.UK   CAMBRIDGESHIRE-COUNTY-
                                    COUNCIL.GOVT.UK
METO.GOVT.UK   MET-OFFICE.GOVT.UK
E-MAIL.METO.GOVT.UK   E-MAIL.MET-OFFICE.GOVT.UK
ORDSVY.GOVT.UK   ORDNANCE-SURVEY.GOVT.UK
Imperial Cancer Research Fund
ACL.ICNET.UK   ACL.LIF.ICNET.UK
ALPHA.ICNET.UK   ALPHA.LIF.ICNET.UK
BIU.ICNET.UK   BISON.LIF.ICNET.UK
BONNIE.ICNET.UK   BONNIE.LIF.ICNET.UK
CLH.ICNET.UK   MAHLER.CLH.ICNET.UK
CLYDE.ICNET.UK   CLYDE.LIF.ICNET.UK
DNASEQ.ICNET.UK   DNASEQ.LIF.ICNET.UK
GEA.ICNET.UK   GEA.LIF.ICNET.UK
ICRF.ICNET.UK   ICRF.ICNET.UK
LEEDS.ICNET.UK   BOREAS.LEEDS.ICNET.UK
NEBULA.ICNET.UK   NEBULA.LIF.ICNET.UK
OMEGA.ICNET.UK   OMEGA.LIF.ICNET.UK
VENUS.ICNET.UK   VENUS.LIF.ICNET.UK

JET Joint Undertaking

JET.UK	JOINT-EUROPEAN-TORUS.UK
TRANSP.JET.UK	TRANSP.JOINT-EUROPEAN-TORUS.UK

Army Personnel Research Establishment

APRE.MOD.UK	APRE.MOD.UK

Admiralty Research Establishment

ARE-PN.MOD.UK	ARE-PN.MOD.UK

Royal Signals and Radar Establishment, Malvern

HERMES.MOD.UK	HERMES.MOD.UK

Royal AeroSpace Establishment – Space Department

RAESP.MOD.UK	RAESP-FARN.MOD.UK
SNCOM.RAESP.MOD.UK	SNCOM1.RAESP-FARN.MOD.UK

Mail Relay for MOD Network (Royal Signals and Radar Establishment)

RELAY.MOD.UK	RELAY.MOD.UK

Royal Signals and Radar Establishment

RSRE.MOD.UK	RSRE.MOD.UK
CCINT1.RSRE.MOD.UK	CCINT1.RSRE.MOD.UK

National Engineering Laboratory

NEL.UK	NATIONAL-ENGINEERING-LABORATORY.UK

National Library of Scotland

ADMIN.NLS.UK	ADMIN.NATIONAL-LIBRARY-SCOTLAND.UK
BBCNC.ORG.UK	BBCNC.ORG.UK
BCSOC.ORG.UK	BCSOC.ORG.UK
BMA.ORG.UK	BRITISH-MEDICAL-ASSOCIATION.ORG.UK
DANTE.ORG.UK	DANTE.ORG.UK
GREENNET.ORG.UK	GREENNET.ORG.UK
IEE.ORG.UK	IEE.ORG.UK
KEHF.ORG.UK	KEHF.ORG.UK
MCI.ORG.UK	MCI.ORG.UK
NCET.ORG.UK	NCET.ORG.UK
RAFIHMT.ORG.UK	RAF-MEDICAL-INSTITUTE.ORG.UK
RBGKEW.ORG.UK	RBGKEW.ORG.UK
KEWA.RBGKEW.ORG.UK	KEWA.RBGKEW.ORG.UK
SHE.ORG.UK	SHARE-E.ORG.UK
WCMC.ORG.UK	WCMC.ORG.UK
AEA.ORGN.UK	AEA.ORGN.UK
ECMWF.ORGN.UK	EUROPEAN-WEATHER-CENTRE.ORGN.UK
UNCS.ECMWF.ORGN.UK	UNICOS.EUROPEAN-WEATHER-CENTRE.ORGN.UK
VAX.ECMWF.ORGN.UK	VAX.EUROPEAN-WEATHER-CENTRE.ORGN.UK
VE1.ECMWF.ORGN.UK	VE1.EUROPEAN-WEATHER-CENTRE.ORGN.UK
VEGW.ECMWF.ORGN.UK	VE1-GW.EUROPEAN-WEATHER-CENTRE.ORGN.UK
LNHL.ORGN.UK	LINENHALL.ORGN.UK

ULTH.ORGN.UK   ULTH.ORGN.UK
X.BLDD.SCOT-OFF.UK   X.BUILDING-DIRECTORATE.SCOT-OFF.UK

International Internet providers

Commercial Internet Exchange (CIX)

Commercial Internet providers' computer networking services enable organizations of every size to access and use computers located virtually anywhere on the globe. Whether by dial-up or dedicated lines, organizations can gain immediate use of electronic mail, news and information services, and Internet access.

Commercial Internet providers offer the advantage of handling all types of traffic (as long as it does not violate applicable laws) — without requiring their users to route commercial traffic differently from non-commercial traffic (research and education). While one division of a company may have access to the Internet, other divisions of the company may not and must route their traffic to another network. When using CIX member networks, all company traffic goes over the same network without fear of violating NSFNET or Internet acceptable use policies. Network managers need maintain only one external network, which connects to a CIX member.

The Commercial Internet eXchange Association is a non-profit, 501(c)6, trade association of Public Data Internetwork service providers promoting and encouraging development of the public data communications internetworking services industry in both national and international markets.

The CIX provides a neutral forum to exchange ideas, information, and experimental projects among suppliers of internetworking services. The CIX broadens the base of national and international co-operation and co-ordination among member networks. Together, the membership may develop consensus positions on legislative and policy issues of mutual interest.

CIX enhances the growth and potential of this industry by encouraging technical research and development for the mutual benefit of suppliers and customers of data communications internetworking services.

The CIX assists its member networks in the establishment of, and adherence to, operational, technical, and administrative policies and standards necessary to ensure fair, open, and competitive operations and communication among member networks. CIX policies are formulated by a member-elected board of directors.

Membership in the Commercial Internet eXchange is open to organizations which offer TCP/IP or OSI public data internetworking services to the general public in one or more geographic regions.

Organizations or individuals seeking Internet connections are urged to contact CIX members directly for further information. Qualified public data Internet service providers interested in exchanging commercial traffic with other providers on a peer basis are most welcome and encouraged to become CIX Association members.

CIX Association
3110 Fairview Park Drive, Suite 590
Falls Church, VA 22042 USA

Bill Washburn,
Executive Director
E-mail: washburn@cix.org
Voice: +1 303 482 2150
Fax: +1 303 482 2884

Lou Scanlan
Member Information and Services
E-mail: helpdesk@cix.org
Voice: +1 703 8 CIX-CIX (824 9249)

CIX members

June 24, 1994

AlphaNet	Wisconsin
AlterNet	National US
ANS CO+RE Systems, Inc.	National US
Apex Global Info Systems	Michigan
Ashton Communications	Mexico and Southwest US
Aurora.Net	Canada
a2i Communications	San Francisco Bay Area
BARRNet	Northern California
Berbee Information Networks	Wisconsin
CentNet	Boston Area
CERFnet	West Coast US
Commonwealth Telephone Company	Pennsylvania
ConnectedNet	Washington State
Cyberstore Systems	Canada
DataBank	Kansas
DataNet	Finland (Nordic Carriers)
DCI	Taiwan
Demon Internet	United Kingdom
EMi Communications	New York Area
EUnet	Europe
Fujitsu	Japan
Global Enterprise Services/JvNCnet	National US
HoloNet	San Francisco Bay Area
Hong Kong SuperNet	Hong Kong
HookupNet	Canada

IIJ	Japan
InfoRISC	Costa Rica
InfoTek	South Africa
INS Info Services	Iowa/Midwest
InterCon	Japan
Internetworks, Inc.	Northwest US
Korea Telecom	Korea
LYNX	Bermuda
Maine.net	Maine
MCSNet	Chicago Area
MV Communications	New Hampshire
NEARNET	New England
NETCOM	National US
Nordic Carriers	Scandinavia
NorthWestNet	Northwest US
Pilot Network Services	San Francisco Bay Area
Pipex	United Kingdom
Portal Communications	San Francisco Bay Area
PSINet	National US and Japan
SESQUINET	Texas
Singapore Telecom	Singapore
SouthCoastComputing	Texas
Sovam Teleport	Russia
SpinNet (AT&T Jens)	Japan
SprintLink	National US
SURAnet	Southeast US
Synergy Communications	Nebraska
THEnet	Texas
TICSA	South Africa
TIPnet	Sweden (Nordic Carriers)
USIT	Tennessee
WestNet	Rocky Mountain US
Wis.com	Wisconsin
Wyoming.com	Wyoming

Additional networks are joining each month.

JANET acceptable use

These are the verbatim JANET acceptable use guidelines.

JANET acceptable guidelines

Prepared by The Joint Network Team

Issue: 3
Date: August 25, 1993

1. Purpose of JANET

JANET and its associated value-added services are provided and maintained to support the data communications requirements of the UK education and research community, a concept defined in section 2. Members of this community are entitled to make use of the services provided by JANET, subject to the conditions placed on usage as described in this document and the JANET Connection Requirements document, and subject to current charging.

Note: This document is aimed at managers responsible for the provision of communication services in organizations that are part of the JANET co-mmunity, and relates to acceptable use of JANET services. It is the responsibility of organizations connected to JANET to ensure that members of their user community use JANET services in an acceptable manner; it is therefore recommended that each organization establishes its own statement of acceptable use within the context of the services provided to its users, and which is compatible with the conditions expressed in this document. It may refer to this document.

2. User Community

The User Community that is permitted to connect to JANET and to make use of its services is the education and research community in the UK, plus other organizations whose connection to JANET would benefit the activities of the education and research community. Annex A contains a list of organizations and institutions that are permitted to connect. These organisations fall into the following broad categories:

- Organizations involved in education or research activities which are funded directly or indirectly by the DFE, OST, SOED, WOED or DENI.
- Other UK government-funded research organizations.
- Other organizations involved in collaborative research activities with the education and research community in the UK.
- Other organizations involved in collaborative research activities with members of other national academic communities.
- Other organizations whose connection to the network is of demonstrable benefit to the UK higher education and research community.

3. Prohibited Use

The use of the network for purposes other than to support legitimate education and research activities is prohibited. In particular, use of the network, or attempts to use the network, for the following purposes is prohibited:

- Use of the network for activities or purposes which are not of benefit to the educational and research activities of the UK higher education and research community; e.g. commercial advertising and promotions.
- Provision of access to JANET for third parties without prior agreement of the Joint Information Systems Committee (JISC).
- Charging for the access to and use of JANET services without the prior agreement of the JISC; e.g. charging third parties for the provision of electronic mail access.
- Unauthorized access to facilities or services accessible via JANET.
- Deliberate waste of staff effort or networked resources, including machine time.
- Deliberate corruption or destruction of other users' data.
- Deliberate violation of the privacy of other user.
- Deliberate disruption of the work of other users.
- Any other deliberate misuse of the network or networked resources, such as the introduction of 'viruses'.
  Note: Attention is drawn to the the Computer Misuse Act, 1990.
- Any use of the network which is illegal in law.

4. Prevention of Prohibited Use

Users of the network and all personnel responsible for managing resources accessible via the network are responsible for taking all reasonable steps to ensure that prohibited use of the network does not occur. In particular:

- Users are responsible for maintaining the confidentiality of any passwords required for access to networked resources, and for changing them on a regular basis.
- Controllers of networked resources are responsible for providing reasonable-mechanisms for ensuring privacy and confidentiality, monitoring patterns of behaviour, tracing suspicious calls and detecting unauthorized access. Where unrestricted access is provided to particular networked resources, all reasonable steps must be taken to ensure that users accessing such resources are not thereby provided with unauthorized access to other resources.
  Note: Detailed recommendations with respect to network security issues are currently under development.

5. Consequences of Prohibited Use

Where necessary in order to safeguard the interests of the JANET community, violation of these conditions may result in the withdrawal of the right of individuals and/or their parent institutions to make further use of JANET services.

In extreme cases, where violation of these conditions is in breach of existing legislation or results in loss or damage to JANET resources or the resources of third parties accessible via JANET, users of JANET and its associated services are advised that the matter may be referred for legal action.

Note: It is preferable for misuse of the network to be prevented by a combination of responsible attitudes on the part of users to the use of JANET resources and appropriate disciplinary measures taken by connected organizations. Resort to legal redress or withdrawal of connection rights will generally occur only where internal disciplinary procedures have failed or are likely to fail.

6. Access to JANET

Communication with members of the JANET community can be achieved in the following ways:

- Via gateways provided at the periphery of JANET, which permit communication between JANET and other networks (e.g. PSS, the Internet, etc.).
- Via a connection to the JANET network.

Communication via any JANET gateway is subject to any conditions which may have been established between JANET and the community to which the gateways provide access.

Annex A

Connection to the JANET network is restricted to organizations that fall within the categories defined below, who are permitted connection to JANET subject to the connection requirements defined in the JANET Connection Requirements Document and current charging:

(1) Organizations involved in education or research activities which are funded directly or indirectly by the DfE, OST, SOED, WOED or DENI.

(2) Other government research establishments or agencies.

(3) Voluntary colleges requiring access to the network to promote collaborative research programmes.

(4) Libraries and related organizations.

- The British Library, the National Library of Scotland, the National Library of Wales and the Science Museum Library;
- The Standing Conference on National and University Libraries (SCONUL), the Birmingham Libraries Cooperative Mechanization Project (BLCMP [Libraries Services] Ltd) and the South West Academic Libraries Cooperative Automation Project (SWALCAP Library Services).

(5) Organizations involved in the support of the education and research programme.

(6) Learned Societies.

(7) Industrial and commercial organizations.

- Organizations involved in UK or international collaborative research programmes with the education and research community or other collaborative research activities, where connection to the network would significantly enhance those activities.
- Organizations providing an IT support service for universities and colleges, for the purposes of providing support to members of the community.
- Suppliers of computer equipment and software that is in use within the JANET community, for the purposes of providing support to members of the community.
- Publishing houses involved in the publication of major research-related journals, for the purposes of progressing material submitted for publication from academic institutions.

(8)   Charitable organizations involved in collaborative research with the education and research community.

(9)   Other institutions or organizations whose connection to the network would benefit the activities of the UK higher education and research community, on the agreement of the Secretary of State for Education.

Index

A *Directory of Electronic Mail* 10–11
Academic Internet 5
Acceptable User Policies (AUPs) 16
access, types of 24–7
AddMail 35
Adoba, B. D. 32
advertising, linked 10
Alternex 16
Americans Communicating Electronically Gopher
    17
Amiga,
    Amiga Mosaic 36–7
    information 37–9
Amsterdam, Digital City project 14–15
anonymous FTP,
    making connections 91–2
    sites 62
    WAIS 122
    see also FTP
anonymous mail, sending via e-mail 69
Apollo Advertising 139
Apple Macintosh,
    AddMail 35
    Fetch (FTP) 34
    Hytelnet 34
    InterSLIP 33
    LeeMail 35
    Mac Eudora 35
    MacPPP 34
    MacTCP 28, 32–3
    MacWeb 36
    NCSA Mosaic for Mac 35–6
    NCSA Telnet 34
    Sumex archive 36
    Turbogopher 34–5
Applelink 40, 55
Archie 6
Association for Progressive Communication
    (APC) 15

BBC, Networking Club 42, 53
booklist compiled by K. Savetz 208–46
BT 6, 10, 55
bulletin boards 4, 24, 25

CELLO 30
Cityscape 40, 42, 47, 139, 143
CIX *see* Commercial Internet Exchange
Clarinet newsgroups 90

Clearinghouse Internet Resource Guides 60–1
client, definition 24
client/server relationshp 24
Clinton, President 2, 6, 8
CNIDR, free WAIS 121, 123
CNS 54
college e-mail addresses FAQ 69

commercial activity 10
commercial domains in UK 248–83
Commercial Internet 139–51
    commercial contacts 140–51
Commercial Internet Exchange (CIX) 4, 25, 40,
    284–6
    members 285–6
    see also Compulink
Commercial Internet provision 11
commercial services 3, 6
CommUnity 20
Compulink 6, 8, 52, 40–1
Compulink, *see also* Commercial Internet
    Exchange (CIX)
CompuServe (CIS) 25, 41, 43, 52
Computer Communicators' Association *see*
    CommUnity
Computer Professionals for Social
    Responsibility (CPSR) 21
conferencing plus 40–1
conferencing services, Institute for Global
    Communications (IGC) 15
conferencing systems 6
    see also Commercial Internet Exchange
    (CIX)
ConflictNet 15
connection to Internet in UK 39–40
Cosine project for the European Research and
    Development community 66
credit card detail transmission 17
criminal activity 16

December's Guide to Internet Resources 60, 62
Demon 4, 11, 27, 39–40, 41–2, 46, 139,
Demon newsgroups 88–9
Dial–up Internet access 25
Digital City project (Amsterdam) 14–15
Direct Connection 46
Direct Line 46
distance education 9, 10
Dungeon Network 56

e-mail 4, 9, 43, 64–70
  bulletin boards 25
  college e-mail addresses FAQ 69
  CompuServe (CIS) 41
  description 64–5
  finding addresses 65, 67
  FTP 97
  general mail resources 67–70
  sending anonymous mail 69
  sending faxes – Faxnet 67
  store and forward system 65
  UK and European resources 65–7
  White and Yellow Pages 65
  see also mailbase; mailing lists
e-mail FTP 69
e-mail Gopher 70
e-mail guide 62
e-mail WWW 70
E–World 56
EcoNet 15
EdEx (Education Exchange) 42–3, 54
educational sector 6, 9, 10, 42–3
  see also EdEx; JANET
Electronic Freedom Foundation 20
Electronic Frontier Foundation (EFF) 20–1
electronic journals 9
Embassy BBS 52
Engst, A. *The Internet Starter Kit for Macintosh* 33
EUNet 8, 10, 27, 40, 47, 89–90,
EUNet Traveller 58
ExNet 25, 47

Fallows, J. 7
Faxnet 67
Fetch (FTP) 34
File Transfer Protocol *see* FTP
finger 65
Freenets 14, 101–3
Frequently Asked Question (FAQ) lists 12–13, 60
FTP 6
  by e-mail 97
  description 91
  sites informations sources 96–7
  sites in UK 92–6
  see also anonymous FTP
FTP FAQ 96
Full Internet access 25, 27

Galviz 6
GBNet *see* UKNet
GlasNet 16
Gopher 5, 6, 13, 25, 65, 104–49
  bookmarks 105
  description 104–5
  e-mail 43, 70
  Gopher Jewels 118–19
    list 118–19
  information sources 119

mailbase 72
  registration 106
  servers, *see* Veronica
  UK Gopher list 106–15
  UK point of entry 105
  useful sites 116–17
  useful UK gophers 115–16
  using 105
Gore, A. Vice President 2, 6, 8
government information on Internet,
  UK 18–20
  USA 17–18
GreenNet 6, 10, 15, 47

hacking 16, 17
Hackney Host ??
HENSA (Higher Education National Software
    Archive) 98
Hgopher 28, 29
Hughes, K., *Entering the World–Wide Web: A Guide to
    Cyberspace* 62
hypertext transport protocol (http) server 27
Hytelnet 103–4
  demo 104
  description 103
  guide to 104
  Readme 104
  software sources 104
  Telnet access 103–4

IETF/RARE Catalogue of Network Training
    Materials 159–209
individuals and small companies, Internet
    provision 41–2
Infocom Interactive 48
information, general 60–4
information linking systems 6
Information Superhighway 2, 8, 17, 124
Institute for Global Communications (IGC) 15–16
Inter–Network Mail Guide 68
International Internet providers 282–4
Internet Advertising/Marketing Agencies Directory
    140
Internet Bulletin Board Systems 101
Internet Relay Chat 5
InterNIC ftp 96
InterNIC Gopher 62
InterNIC via e-mail 67–8
InterSLIP 33
IP software 27–38
IRC (Internet Relay Chat), 135–9
  description 135
  mailing list 139
  newsgroups 138
  other sites 136–8
  technical information 139
  Telnet IRC 138
  UK servers 135–6

Ireland On–Line 57
ITTI (Information Technology Training Initiative),
      Network Training Materials Project 63

JANET 5–6, 10, 40, 51, 84,
JANET,
   acceptable use 287–90
   access 289–90
   JIPS 42
   prohibited use 288–9
   purpose 287
   user community 288–90
JANET news, Telnet 99
JIPS 42
Joint Academic Network _see_ JANET

Kehoe, B.P., *Zen and the Art* of *the Internet* 13, 64
Kirklees Host 57
Kriz, H.M. 32

Labornet 15
LeeMail 35
List of Lists 84
List of UK Internet Access providers in the UK 10
Listserv 72, 73, 83–4

Mac Eudora 35
MacPPP 34
MacTCP 28, 32–3
MacWeb 36
mailbase 71
   Gopher 72
   help 72
   joining lists 73
   lists,
      examples in UK 73–83
      obtaining 73
   Listserv 72
      for UNIX 73
   on–line service 72
   see also e-mail; mailing lists
Mailbase User Reference Card 151–7
mailing lists 70–84
   description and operation 70–1
   information sources,
      List of Lists 84
      Listserv info 83–4
      NetTools 83
      Publicly accessible mailing lists
      (PAML) 84
   list 63
   see also e-mail; mailbase
Manchester Host 51
Merit Internet Cruise 63
Microland Internet 56
Motiv Systems Ltd 54
multimedia network tools 13
   see also Gopher; World Wide Web

National Public Telecomputing Network 101
NCSA Mosaic,
   for Mac 35–6
   for Microsoft Windows 30
NCSA Telnet 34
NetTools 83
network search agents 6
Network Training Materials Project 63
   see also Training Materials
Networked Information Services Project (NISP),
      mailbase 71
newsgroups *see* Usenet News
Nicarao 16
NISP (Networked Information Services Project),
      Network Training Materials Project 63
NISS (National Information Services and Systems)
      97–8
Novalink 53

obscene e-mail 16
Oikarinen, J., IRC 135
On–Line 48
on–line publishing 12–14

Paradise 66–7
pay–to–view services 10
PC Eudora 29
PC User Group Connect 48
PC User Group Winnet 49
PeaceNet 15
Perry Rovers' Anonymous Sites Listing 96
Pipex 6, 8, 10, 27, 40, 42, 49, 89,
Point to Point Protocol (PPP) 25
policing Internet 16
POPTEL 6
pornography 16–17
providers,
   selecting 43
   UK list 43–58
   UK list, data interpretation 43–5
Psilink 53
Publicly Accessible Mailing Lists (PAML) 84

reasons for using Internet 3–5
Request for Comments (RFC) list 12

Savetz, K., Internet FAQ 12–13
School of Information and Library studies (SILS),
      Clearinghouse Internet Resource Guides
      60–1
schools Internet scheme 6
SCO 10
Serial Line Internet Protocol (SLIP) 25, 27
server, definition 24
Shaw, D.L. (MP) 18–19
shell accounts 25
Soft Solution – Poptel 57
software using Internet Protocols *see* IP software

Sound & Vision 49
Specialix 50
Spuddy 6
   Xanadu system 13, 14, 15, 50
Sterling, B. 13
stock–market quotes on WEB 9
Strathclyde Host 51
Sumex archive 36
SunSITE Northern Europe 98
SuperJANET 19

TCP/IP driver 27
TCP/IP stack 27, 28
   see also Amiga Mosaic; MacTCP; Trumpet
      Winsock
Telnet 5, 6, 30–1, 41, 97–103
   description 97
   information sources 103
   UK sites 97–100
   WAIS 122
Telnet IRC 138
terminal access 24
The Lynx Magazine 13–14
Training Materials Gopher 63–4
Transport Control Protocol/Internet
 Protocol *see* TCP/IP
TRMPTEL 31
Trumpet for Windows 29
Trumpet Winsock 27, 28–9, 30
Turbogopher 34–5

UK,
   government information on Internet 18–20
   net developments 7–11
   networks, extent of 10–11
UKNet 11
University of Michigan, Clearinghouse Internet
      Resource Guides 60–1
university sites *see* JANET
USA, government information on Internet 17– 18
Usenet 4
   user list 68
Usenet News 84–90
   categories 85
   Clarinet newsgroups 90

Demon newsgroups 88–9
description 84
EUNet newsgroups 89–90
information sources 90
miscellaneous newsgroups 87–8
obtaining list of newsgroups 85
Pipex newsgroups 89
UK newsgroups 85–6
UUCP 25

Veronica 120–1
   description 120
   information 121
   locations 120

WAIS (Wide Area Information Service) 5, 65, 121–4
   description 121
   free WAIS 121, 123
   information sources 122–3
   software 123–4
   Thinking Machines 121
   via Telnet 122
   white sheet 122
Waldegrave, W. (MP) 19
White House Press Release Service 17–18
Whois 6, 68
   UK Whois servers 65–6
WinQVT/Net 30
Winsock 28–32
   installing 28–9
   mailing lists 31–2
   Trumpet Winsock 27, 28–9, 30
   usenet groups 31
World Wide Web (WWW) 5, 6, 13, 65, 124–35
   browsers 7, 10
   e-mail 43, 70
   help 135
   information sources 133–5
   reasons for growth 124
   servers 10, 22
   UK guide 21–2
   UK sites 124–33
WS_FTP and WS_PING 30

Yanoff's List 60, 64

One Free Month on the Internet!

With CityScape's IP-gold - " Getting out there made easy"

Just fill in the form below and post it to CityScape and you will receive a copy of their **IP-GOLD** Internet package plus one free month on the Internet. If you do not wish to continue your CityScape Internet subscription simply return the pack within the month. Should you decide to keep the software an initial charge of £95.00 will be made for the first quarter and £45.00 for each quarter after that. *CityScape IP-GOLD - "Getting out there made easy".*

CityScape IP-GOLD offers

Powerful, Friendly and Simple to Use Software for Windows or MacIntosh
- Full featured Email software
- World Wide Web browser
- Usenet News client
- TCP/IP connection package

A full Internet connection with no online charges
- Full software support
- Full connection support
- Free software upgrades
- Full documentation

Minimum Requirements
- Hayes compatible V32 modem or better
  PC:
- Windows 3.1 or above
- 4M of memory
  Macintosh:
- System 7 or above
- 4M of memory

Just fill in the postcard overleaf . . . .